Antipater's Dynasty

Antipater's Dynasty

John D Grainger

Pen & Sword
MILITARY

First published in Great Britain in 2019 by
Pen & Sword Military
An imprint of
Pen & Sword Books Ltd
Yorkshire – Philadelphia

Copyright © John D Grainger 2019

ISBN 978 1 52673 088 6

Printed and bound in the UK by TJ International Ltd,
Padstow, Cornwall.

Pen & Sword Books Limited incorporates the imprints of Atlas,
Archaeology, Aviation, Discovery, Family History, Fiction, History,
Maritime, Military, Military Classics, Politics, Select, Transport,
True Crime, Air World, Frontline Publishing, Leo Cooper, Remember
When, Seaforth Publishing, The Praetorian Press, Wharncliffe
Local History, Wharncliffe Transport, Wharncliffe True Crime
and White Owl.

For a complete list of Pen & Sword titles please contact

PEN & SWORD BOOKS LIMITED
47 Church Street, Barnsley, South Yorkshire, S70 2AS, England
E-mail: enquiries@pen-and-sword.co.uk
Website: www.pen-and-sword.co.uk

Or

PEN AND SWORD BOOKS
1950 Lawrence Rd, Havertown, PA 19083, USA
E-mail: Uspen-and-sword@casematepublishers.com
Website: www.penandswordbooks.com

Contents

Introduction

In the aftermath of Alexander's destruction of the Akhaimenid (Persian) Empire during his campaigns of 334–323, four families emerged to found dynasties who ruled sections of that empire. The best-known, because of the proliferation of sources available for studying it, is the dynasty founded by and descended from Ptolemy son of Lagos, which governed Egypt from 323 to 30 BC. The greatest of the dynasties, however, was that descended from Seleukos, a friend, colleague, and enemy of Ptolemy, which ruled varying territories of Asia from the Aegean Sea to the borders of India from 311 to 83 BC. The family of Antigonos I began the process of assuming royal titles and, after an erratic early career, came to rule Macedon from 277 to 168 BC, as the Antigonid dynasty. The least known and shortest lived of the four was the dynasty descended from Antipater, whose members ruled Macedon as regent and king from 334 to 294 BC. But the family also had a strong effect on all the other dynasties, and the daughters of the first of the family, Antipater, married into the other dynasties, with apparently a major effect on their histories, and above all on the treatment of royal wives.

This is a study of that dynasty, one which had been curiously neglected, for the other three have all had several full-length studies and biographies made of them, and this appears to be the first study of this dynasty.

List of Genealogical Tables

Table I: The Family of Antipater.

A. Sons.

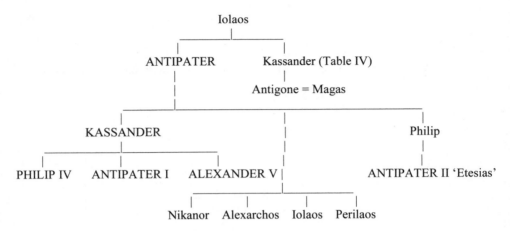

B. Daughters.

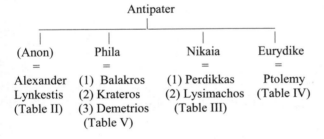

(Anon)	Phila	Nikaia	Eurydike
=	=	=	=
Alexander	(1) Balakros	(1) Perdikkas	Ptolemy
Lynkestis	(2) Krateros	(2) Lysimachos	(Table IV)
(Table II)	(3) Demetrios	(Table III)	
	(Table V)		

CAPITALS: Rulers of Macedon (see also Table VI)

Order of birth is uncertain.

Table II: The Family of Antipater's Eldest Daughter.

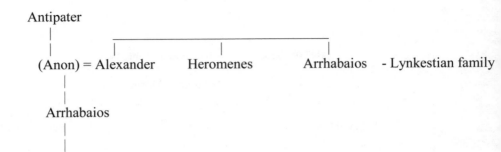

Table III: The Family of Nikaia.

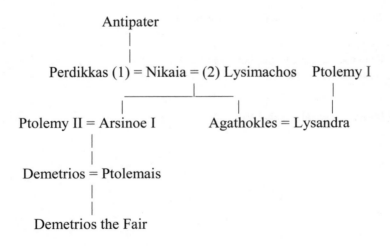

Table IV: The Families of Eurydike and Berenike.

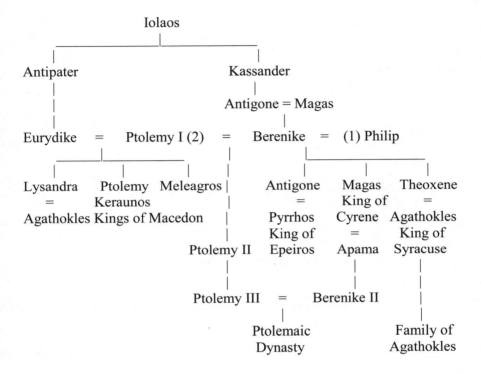

Table V: The Families of Phila.

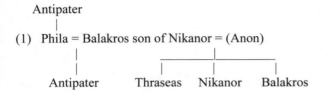

Antipater
|
(1)   Phila = Balakros son of Nikanor = (Anon)

| Antipater | Thraseas | Nikanor | Balakros |

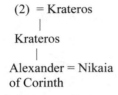

(2) = Krateros
|
Krateros
|
Alexander = Nikaia
of Corinth

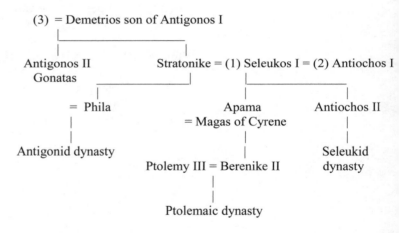

(3) = Demetrios son of Antigonos I

Antigonos II   Stratonike = (1) Seleukos I = (2) Antiochos I
Gonatas

= Phila   Apama   Antiochos II
| = Magas of Cyrene |

Antigonid dynasty   Seleukid
                    Ptolemy III = Berenike II   dynasty
                              |
                    Ptolemaic dynasty

Table VI: The Macedonian Kings, 359 – 239.

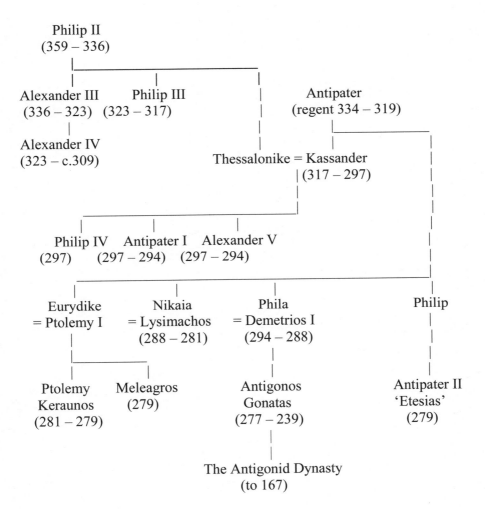

Philip II
(359 – 336)

Alexander III   Philip III
(336 – 323) (323 – 317)

Alexander IV
(323 – c.309)

Antipater
(regent 334 – 319)

Thessalonike = Kassander
     | (317 – 297)

Philip IV Antipater I Alexander V
(297)   (297 – 294) (297 – 294)

Eurydike   Nikaia   Phila   Philip
= Ptolemy I = Lysimachos = Demetrios I
          (288 – 281) (294 – 288)

Ptolemy   Meleagros   Antigonos   Antipater II
Keraunos   (279)   Gonatas   'Etesias'
(281 – 279)   (277 – 239)   (279)

The Antigonid Dynasty
(to 167)

Part I

Antipater

Chapter 1

Rise to Power

Antipater was a Macedonian gentleman, nobleman, and soldier. This we may assume since he emerges in all these roles during the reign of King Philip II (359–336). He was a contemporary, and possibly a rival, of Parmenion, and both of them became Philip's strong supporters, at least once he had demonstrated his capabilities. They figure prominently, even decisively, in the events of Philip's reign (and then in that of his son Alexander). But Antipater was the senior in age of all these men and, except for the king, the most notable in attainments – and he survived all of them.

They lived in a difficult but exhilarating period in Macedon. All three men were born in the early fourth century – the suggested year of Antipater's (and Parmenion's) birth is 399 or 397, and of Philip about 380 – and so they all grew to adulthood in a time when the Macedonian kingship was unstable and often in dispute, and when the royal government, and indeed the very existence of the kingdom, was threatened with destruction. It was in part the decision of these men to coalesce in support of Philip when he seized the kingship that was one of the foundations of the new king's strength. And the necessity for ensuring the king's power, and therefore the integrity of the kingdom, became the foundation of Antipater's conduct and work.

Antipater, the oldest of this group, was born in or just after the reign of King Archelaos (413–399 BC), who was one of the more effective, not to say ambitious, of the Macedonian kings of the Temenid (or Argead) line. He operated to reduce dissension within the nobility, and to this end he developed a new capital city at Pella, built on an imperial scale. But the king died, assassinated, in 399, and much of his political work was dissipated in the confused decade which followed.[1]

Antipater therefore grew up in a country which was, to say the least, disturbed, subject to royal assassinations and to invasions from all sides. His father, Iolaos (or Iollas), was no doubt a prominent lord, and has been tentatively identified with a man of that name who commanded a unit of

Macedonian horse in 432; but we know nothing more of him.[2] He, and therefore Antipater, is said to have lived in Palioura, though where that was is not known. The only two suggestions put it in the Athos Peninsula or near Cape Palinura, the southern tip of another of the Chalcidian peninsulas, but when Antipater was born neither of these was Macedonian territory. Palioura also only loosely fits these suggested names. We must conclude that we do not know where Antipater grew up, though he did so in a household of some wealth and importance, and somewhere in Macedon.[3]

We are only slightly better informed about his birth year. This is obtained by calculating back from his death in 319 BC, when he is said to have been 80 years old, and this gives his year of birth as 399 or 398 BC. But other sources claim an age of 78 or perhaps 79, so we have to accept a range of 399 to 397.[4] ('Eighty' looks very like a rough guess; many people in the ancient world did not know the year of their birth; when claimed ages are tabulated, the occurrence of multiples of ten and five outnumber all the rest put together.)

Antipater's family has been assumed to have been related in some way to the ruling dynasty, but this probably applied to many other families of similar prominence, and anyway it is impossible to prove in the absence of serious prosopographical resources. Marriages of kings with women of other noble Macedonian families was normal, as was royal polygamy and concubinage; both of these practices no doubt were intended in part to link the aristocracy closely to the royal family. Philip II's nine wives – he was extravagant in this as in other matters – were chosen for diplomatic reasons. His occupation of the throne was never secure, and he deliberately failed to link himself in marriage with any Macedonian family for fear of stoking jealousies. That he was right to do so is shown by the trouble which resulted from his eventual marriage to a Macedonian girl. His son Alexander was even more wary. But this avoidance would not apply to the aristocracy generally. Suffice it to say that the family of Iolaos was certainly prominent, rich (in Macedonian terms), and came from the unknown Palioura, where it no doubt controlled an estate and its peasant labour. Because of all these things the family was necessarily part of the governing system of the kingdom.

The earliest explicit mention of Antipater in public affairs was in 346, by which time he was already over 50 years old, when his participation in an embassy may be assumed. By contrast, his contemporary Parmenion appears as an active commander in 356, and there are strong indications that Antipater was active even before that.[5] He wrote an account of the Illyrian Wars of Perdikkas III, who was an active and busy king of Macedon between 365 and 359 BC and was killed in those wars.[6] It may thus be presumed that Antipater at the very least saw and recorded what was happening in those wars, but it is much more likely that he actually took part in them, and as a commander of troops. This would make him a reasonably well-known figure in Macedon by that time, when in his thirties.

There is little room in Macedonian history in the reign of Philip, at least until the last years, for anyone but Philip the king, and later Alexander the prince. Both Parmenion and Antipater, when they first appear in the sources, have high positions and responsibilities, arguing therefore that they had long been active in Philip's government, and probably even before Philip became king.

It would be normal for the son of a prominent Macedonian to be employed in a variety of public tasks. He was trained to war, which in the condition of Macedon in Antipater's first few decades of life was a necessity. But this training consisted largely of learning to use weapons, particularly the spear; hunting provided the essential training in bravery, accuracy, and cooperation. Actual warfare consisted too often largely of armed mobs fighting each other, though both Kings Archelaos and Perdikkas III had made attempts to instil greater discipline and organization into the Macedonian army – the subject was, therefore, already on the agenda.

Antipater was, however, also well educated for his time and place, and this was probably a precondition for high appointments. His history of the Illyrian War was presumably composed in the 360s, and much later he compiled and issued a collection of his letters. (These last would be particularly interesting and useful to modern historians.) He was a friend of Aristotle, one of whose works was addressed to him, and who made him an executor of his will.[7] Familiarity with the plays of Euripides, and probably of other Attic dramatists, was common among the Macedonian elite, as was a knowledge of the latest things in philosophy.[8] He was certainly capable also of speaking in public to the Athenian Assembly, which implies a training in rhetoric and an ability to speak clear Greek. His own local language at home and on his estates will have been the dialect of Macedonian Greek which the Athenians professed not to understand and tended to classify as a separate language. (This allowed them to describe the Macedonians as barbarians, of course.) It seems probable that Antipater was capable of switching from one dialect to the other without difficulty.

A number of anecdotes and odd references to Antipater during Philip's reign indicate his continued prominence. He persuaded the king to appoint a friend of his as a judge.[9] He was noted for his frugality,[10] but also for his disapproval of the king's dissolute lifestyle, so that Philip is said to have once hidden a game board away when Antipater arrived, no doubt to evade his disapproval.[11] And yet, despite their evidently antagonistic lifestyles, it is clear that the king trusted Antipater. When Philip drank too much he was confident that Antipater would have remained sober, and therefore that even if Philip was rendered incapable through drink – a condition fairly frequently achieved – he could be sure that Antipater would be able to cope.[12] One wonders if Antipater understood that it was to some extent his own sobriety which permitted Philip to drink so much.

This last point also implies that Antipater had developed into a near-equal in the royal administration, high enough to be able to substitute for the king when the latter was incapable or absent. This trust probably only developed over a considerable length of time and may well have been based on early friendship. It has been suggested that Antipater was entrusted with the command in the kingdom as early as 357 when Philip campaigned against Amphipolis, though whether this actually happened, and how much authority he could wield is not known. It may be thought unlikely that a new king, whose throne was still insecure, would surrender, even temporarily, very much power to anyone else.[13]

Antipater certainly had a high prominence by 346. In that year he was campaigning in Thrace in advance of Philip's attack on King Kersebleptes. He spent some time over the capture of a place called Apros, which softened up the opposition so that when Philip arrived he defeated Kersebleptes in a month. Then the king spent some time mopping-up.[14]

While he did that Antipater was sent, along with Parmenion and Eurylochos, as an envoy to Athens to negotiate the treaty which became known, in Athens, as the Peace of Philokrates.[15] Such prominence implies that Antipater had a capability in both military affairs and diplomatic missions. He was probably left in command in Macedon during 342 when Philip was absent in Thrace and Parmenion was busy in Greece, where a

new Greek war was brewing.[16] One of his duties, while the king was away
in Thrace, was to preside in his stead at the Pythian Festival at Delphi in
342.[17] At the same time Parmenion was busy in Euboia – a combination
of simultaneous visits to high-powered Macedonians which could only be
seen as threatening by Macedon's Greek opponents. He also had to control
a restless adolescent Alexander, who at 16 years of age (in 340) was anxious
to prove himself as a military commander. In the end Antipater sent him
– presumably with Philip's permission – on a subsidiary Thracian raid.[18]
Antipater himself may have had to join the Thracian campaign at the difficult
siege of Perinthos; he is also recorded in a chronologically detached notice,
as fighting a group called the Tetrachoritai, somewhere in Thrace (though
this may have occurred much later).[19]

One may therefore assume that Antipater's abilities had become clear to
Philip long before his use of him so prominently in the 340s, and probably
even before Philip seized the kingship, and that he was a prominent supporter
of the royal family during the preceding reigns. The later position he took
in royal crises provides some support for the suggestion that he was both
important and prominent much earlier.

Antipater, at least in his maturity, had a gift for friendship with men who
might have been counted as his enemies. Aristotle was one. He had probably
known the philosopher's father, who had been Philip's doctor in the 350s, but
Aristotle was from Stageira in Chalkidike, a city destroyed during Philip's
brutal conquest of the area. It took Aristotle over a decade to be persuaded
to return to Macedon, and he spent much of that time in Athens, which
was a constant Macedonian enemy. Aristotle probably remained at a distance
from Philip even after returning to Macedon, though he seems to have been
a moderately effective tutor to Alexander, while he clearly became friendly
with Antipater.

When he went to Athens on his diplomatic missions, Antipater also
developed a friendship with a couple of prominent Athenian politicians,
Demades and Phokion. One wonders just how sincere such a relationship
was, however, on both sides. None of the three men forsook their homelands,
though both Demades and Phokion were rendered objects of suspicion in
Athens for their friendship with such a prominent Macedonian. Demades
was detected later to have been intriguing against Macedon, and suffered for
it, his apparent friendship with Antipater notwithstanding.

Antipater was married by 356, by which time his eldest son Kassandros was probably born. This is, as with Antipater's own birth date, calculated backwards from a particular dated event. It is said that in 321 he had to sit at meals rather than recline because he had not yet, at the age of 35, killed a lion in the Macedonian fashion, with a spear and without a net, only after which a Macedonian son could recline in the presence of his father at a meal.[20] Counting back from that notice (in 321) brings us to 356. But, as with his father's birth date, this is a flimsy basis for such calculations, and may be out by some years before or after. It could mean, particularly since Kassandros was the eldest son, but not necessarily the eldest of his children, that Antipater may not have married till he was about 40.

Kassandros may have been the first of Antipater's eleven (or twelve) children.[21] It is quite possible to argue that Antipater had delayed marrying because of the disturbances of the times, but, as the eldest son of his father, it would have been his duty – as he pointed out to Alexander the king later – to produce a son to inherit.[22] It is possible that he had been married already and that the earlier marriage had proved barren. It is also, of course, possible that Kassandros had older siblings who had died.

Yet another possibility is that Kassandros was not Antipater's eldest child, though he certainly appears to have been his eldest male child.[23] Antipater had six more sons and four daughters. One of the daughters, whose name is not known, married Alexander of Lynkestis before Alexander went on his great campaign, and so before 334.[24] If she was married at 16 or so, the usual age of marriage for girls in ancient Greece, she had been born in the 350s, and possibly even before 356. The next girl, Phila, was married to a Macedonian called Balakros son of Nikanor, also before Alexander's expedition set out, in which he took part.[25] When she married a third time, after Balakros' death, and that of her second husband Krateros, to Demetrios son of Antigonos, she was about 30 years old, which put her birth at about 350 or before.[26] There is not much room for Kassandros' birth, therefore, after 356. This, of course, hardly solves another problem, that of Antipater's wife or wives, whose number and name or names are unknown.

All Antipater's children were probably born, if the first was born by 356, by the time Alexander set out on his expedition in 334. Supposing he had only one wife, the birth of eleven children (and possibly more) cannot have been accomplished in much less than twenty years. He also had at least one grandchild by that time, a son of Balakros and Phila, who was named Antipater after his grandfather.[27] There is no indication of any children of Alexander Lynkestis and the anonymous daughter, though it is possible that one or more were produced.

The kingdom Antipater grew up in suffered two major internal collapses, one during his childhood between 400 and 390 following the assassination of King Archelaos, and another in the 360s after the death of Amyntas III in 369. A third collapse occurred in 359, with the death in battle of Perdikkas III, and was only halted by the frantic activity of Philip II in 359–358. In addition to these internal crises, and in fact simultaneously with them, the kingdom suffered invasions. These could come from the south out of Greece, from the north-west out of Illyria and Epeiros, from the north out of Paionia, from the north-east from Thrace, or from the sea in the south-east – which was usually Greek once more. The kingdom was, in other words, surrounded by enemies, and in 359 all were active.

The main internal problem was the instability of the royal house. In the ten years after King Archelaos' murder in 399, ten kings were enthroned, or seized the throne, or were expelled. Only from 390 was a king, Amyntas III, seated firmly enough to see off competitors and retain his position, which he did for two decades. Unusually, he died of 'natural causes' in that year, but this was the signal for another dynastic crisis, including at least one prolonged usurpation.[28] The third collapse, after Perdikkas III's defeat and death, meant that Perdikkas' infant son Amyntas IV became king. His uncle, Philip, was installed as guardian (that is, regent). This was clearly a provisional arrangement, since Philip was no more than 24 or so years old at the time; he was then installed as king the year after, once he had proved his capability.

In none of these events does Antipater figure in our sources, but the intermittent and lethal turmoil was what he witnessed as he grew up. His contemporary Parmenion, who was from a provincial dynasty in western Macedon, and who was therefore probably a cut above Antipater socially, is recorded as commanding an army in battle in 356.[29] On the other hand, by the 340s the two men were clearly equal in capability in Philip's eyes, though he did tend to employ them separately, as did Alexander later: Parmenion commanding armies, Antipater administering the kingdom, though it may reasonably be presumed that they were both employed by King Philip as diplomats and as commanders more or less interchangeably, and in both roles they would act without direct royal supervision. The three men were clearly well able to work together on the greater project of building a secure and powerful Macedon. Antipater and Parmenion, however, were no doubt to a degree antagonistic and rivals for the king's favour, which would explain the king's tendency to employ them on separate tasks.

For sixty years, therefore, Antipater lived in and served a kingdom which was alarmingly unstable, under a series of kings who varied from the unfit and the usurping to the adequate and the superb. His younger contemporaries who went off to war in Asia with Alexander, most of whom were in their twenties and thirties – like Alexander himself – did not have the same unpleasant political memories, except from their parents, and so at second-hand. At most they had lived through the collapse of the 360s, and even then the memory will have been largely effaced by the achievements of King Philip. By 336, when Alexander became king, nobody under 30 will have had any direct memory of those hard times.

Antipater, on the other hand, had a much longer political memory encompassing the earlier collapse in the 390s in his childhood, the recovery under Amyntas III, which was in his twenties and thirties, but then the relapse in the 360s. And these crises were occasioned by the deaths of kings. To him the experience of Macedon under Philip II – success in war, increasing wealth, territorial expansion – was not necessarily a permanent condition, for the kingdom might once again collapse into invasion and internecine conflict; and the main safeguard was merely a single life, that of the king, and it had to be a capable king, for a weak king, or a child, would be a disaster. He had worked with Perdikkas III and with Philip II in building up Macedon to a power which was probably safe at least from invasion.

When he was given a similar responsibility to that of the king, therefore, his political aim was conditioned by his earlier experiences. He wanted to hold Macedon together, and in peace. In part this must be the king's task, and the death of Alexander without a viable heir in 323 was the second such crisis he had personally experienced. Without a king, the kingdom required a staunch population and a loyal aristocracy; it probably would have neither; above all, it required a powerful ruler.

In view of the prominence given in modern accounts to Alexander's adventure into the Persian Empire, which is often treated as an inevitable consequence of Philip II's success in Macedonia, it is worth spending a few words on detailing just what Philip and his men had achieved, for it was to be Antipater's work during Alexander's reign to attempt to maintain the position Philip had reached, but on much slimmer resources. But even before Alexander's expedition had set off Philip's murder meant that Antipater was faced with the likely destruction of his work.

When Philip took over the rule of Macedon in 359 as guardian of his nephew Amyntas and regent of the kingdom, it was facing collapse and invasion. Perdikkas III, Philip's elder brother, had been killed in battle with the Illyrian invaders, and more than 4,000 of his Macedonian soldiers died with him. The Illyrians were camped inside Macedon. From the north the Paionians had begun to carry out raids across the border along the Axios Valley. There were also three men who claimed the kingship, operating from both outside and inside the kingdom. One, Pausanias, was supported by a Thracian king; he was clearly able to put forward a plausible claim but did not last long once Philip had bribed his Thracian sponsor. Another, Argaios, had the support of Athens, with which city Perdikkas had been conducting a desultory war; Argaios had tried unsuccessfully to claim the throne years before, but was no more acceptable in 359–358, particularly when he arrived with an army provided by Athens; Philip was able to defeat this invasion with ease. A third claimant was Archelaos, Philip's own half-brother, who was already inside the kingdom; he was soon killed, but he had two more brothers, who still posed a threat to Philip ten years later. All these men had almost as good claims to the throne or to the regency as had Philip, and since they were all older than Philip and were all members of the royal dynasty, perhaps their claims could be seen as even better. Certainly one of them would gain the kingship if Philip died or failed. But Philip had been on the spot when the news arrived of Perdikkas' death, and this, as in several later Macedonian royal crises, was the crucial element. He had gained the position of power, which in Macedon was effective command of the army, and this relegated his competitors to the condition of pretenders, threats, and troublemakers, particularly those supported by outsiders.

The existence of these men, and their active claiming of the kingship, was profoundly destabilizing. Not until they were properly vanquished, killed or driven out, or discredited – or all of these – would Philip be safe, and Macedon with him. He began with a masterly display of duplicity, diplomacy, and military ability. He saw off almost all these threats in his first year, bribing, defeating, murdering – all these methods were acceptable in the crisis. At the end of that year he was acclaimed king, with the infant Amyntas pushed aside, yet he was still the spare king if Philip failed.[30]

Having survived, Philip then set out on the same work that Archelaos and Amyntas III and Perdikkas III had all attempted, but, for one reason or another, had been unable to complete. It had by then long been clear that what Macedon needed was an effective and loyal army, together with a developed economy which would support that army. This was to be Philip's work.

In the next twenty years Macedon's army was revolutionized and enlarged, and the kingdom's boundaries were expanded. Territories lost to invaders were recovered, and those enemies were then conquered. Trade was increased, and metal production encouraged, so that the royal treasury was filled and its contents could be used to finance the expansion, in part by hiring Greek mercenary soldiers, and so sparing the Macedonians some of the hard campaigning. Lands in all directions – Thrace, a swathe of the territory to the north, the mountain cantons to the west, Thessaly, were incorporated into the kingdom. The Greek cities along the Aegean coast from the Hellespont to the Gulf of Volos were incorporated also, though many in the Chalkidike were destroyed in the process of conquest. And finally, a coalition of many Greek powers brought together by Athens was defeated and brought to terms.

In these events Antipater was deeply involved. After his period as governor in Macedon while the king was campaigning in Thrace, he returned to his subordinate position under the authority of the king. The Greek crisis was resolved at the battle of Khaironeia, in which it may be assumed that Antipater fought, even at the age of over 60 years. He and Alexander then took Demades, who was captured in the battle, to Athens to present Philip's peace terms – which were simply an end to the fighting – and which the Athenians accepted at Demades' urging, with some vocal relief. They voted a statue of Antipater in recognition of his apparent friendship.[31]

Given that he had been used more than once as a diplomat it seems likely that Antipater may also have been involved in setting up the alliance of the Greek states with Macedon which is generally called the League of Corinth, though he is not mentioned in that connection; so maybe it was all Philip's own work – it was certainly his inspiration – with Antipater perhaps sent back to govern Macedon while Philip worked on the Greeks at Corinth. Afterwards, in 337, Philip's two main supporters were again given different tasks. Parmenion was sent to Asia with an advance force to begin the conquest of all or part of the Persian Empire, whatever it was that Philip aimed to do, while Antipater was retained in Macedon. As a result he was no doubt present at the celebrations which followed the wedding of Philip's daughter Kleopatra to her uncle Alexander of Epeiros, though once again his presence is not actually remarked. He was also therefore present when Philip was murdered.

Chapter 2

Alexander's Lieutenant

The marriage celebration at which King Philip was murdered was part of one of a series of measures he had taken to prepare for his intended invasion of Asia. His plan for the actual invasion is not known, though it cannot have been all that different from that which Alexander executed later. He had sent preliminary forces into Asia under Parmenion and Attalos (the uncle of his new wife Kleopatra), and they had won over several of the Aegean coastal cities and some of the islands with little difficulty, assisted by revolutions directed at getting rid of the rulers – referred to as 'tyrants' – who operated in the Persian interest. Ephesos on the mainland was secured in this way, as was Eresos on the island of Lesbos.[1] Some of the islands close to the Asian coast – Tenedos, Lesbos, and Chios, notably – were also won over.[2] Most of the violence seems to have been internal to the cities, as a result of the civic revolutions. The campaign lasted only a few months before news of Philip's murder brought it to a halt. This was more or less the campaign route followed by Alexander two years later.

What the next stage was to have been is quite uncertain. Philip would presumably have taken the main army across the Hellespont to join Parmenion and Attalos and then to campaign through Asia Minor, as Alexander did. What role Alexander would have in Philip's campaign is as unknown as the rest of Philip's plan. One suggestion – put forward rather too firmly, given that there is no evidence whatsoever – was that Alexander would supervise Greece while Philip was in Asia, and that Antipater would govern in Macedon.[3] But the division of responsibility this implied would be dangerous, even if, as seems to have been the case at that time, Alexander and Antipater were actually quite friendly. Such a plan would presume that they would cooperate, which was a rather different matter.

Alexander had already displayed a precocious and instinctive military ability, and it would obviously be shortsighted of Philip to leave such a talented leader in Greece when there was to be serious fighting in Asia. Nor would Philip be able to rely on Alexander staying in Greece, or wherever he was placed; he had already displayed an impulsiveness which would surely lead him to go off on individual activities. Philip had long been accustomed to recruiting talent wherever he could find it and was hardly likely to overlook that in his own son – he had given him a major command at the Khaironeia fight. The conclusion must be that he intended to take Alexander with him, and to use him as a subordinate general officer in the campaign, just as he would Parmenion.

Antipater was not directly involved, so it seems, in the military preparations for Philip's expedition, and it is probable that he was intended to stay in Macedon in the same role that he had already fulfilled while Philip campaigned in Thrace; this was the role which, in the event, he undertook for Alexander: governor of Macedon and overseer of Greece, a pair of tasks which clearly had to be run in tandem (and which is a major impediment to the suggestion that they both remain in Europe). This was, after all, a position he had held more than once in the past, to Philip's satisfaction. Antipater, in contrast to Alexander, was a wholly reliable man, and not given to any sort of impulsive behaviour, perhaps not very inquisitive. Philip had also appointed a supervisor for conquered Thrace, Antipater's son-in-law, Alexander Lynkestis.[4]

Alexander and his father had a difficult relationship, as is only to be expected, bearing in mind their powerful personal qualities. They were also different, in part the result of their differing earlier lives. Alexander was clearly army-mad, and though he also proved to have the political instincts which went with the job of being king, he was no match with his father in this respect.[5] Philip was a consummate political operator, as was demonstrated in the several measures he took in the last year of his life, in preparation for his great expedition, by deploying his own charm and his available family's persons to powerful political effect. His marriage to Kleopatra the niece of Attalos produced a daughter, whose sex defused for the moment any fear that Alexander might have had that he was being pushed out of the succession.[6] (There may also have been a son, Karanos, but a newborn child, even if male, was scarcely a threat to Alexander.) Alexander had fled with his mother Olympias to her homeland in Epeiros the year before, after a quarrel with his father, and with these two in Epeiros there was a clear danger that Olympias' brother Alexander, the king in Epeiros, would be roused to invade

Macedon, either in pursuit of revenge for his sister, or for more personal political motives.[7]

Philip scotched that thought by offering the Epeirote King Alexander his own daughter Kleopatra (she was Olympias' daughter too) as his wife.[8] When the offer was accepted, the threat from Epeiros vanished, and Alexander the prince could then be persuaded to return to Macedon; Olympias may have been left in Epeiros, but it is more likely she returned to Macedon along with Alexander; she did not attend her daughter's wedding, however. The reconciliation of father and son was successful, at least for the time being, though how long it would have lasted is not clear.[9]

Another of Philip's daughters, Kynnane, the daughter of Audata, one of his Illyrian wives, had already been given to his cousin Amyntas, the son of King Perdikkas III, who had briefly been king back in 359 as an infant.[10] This was a recognition of Amyntas' position and ancestry, and that he was within the line of succession, if both Philip and Alexander died. This marriage is best seen, therefore, as another of Philip's preparations for the great expedition, leaving in Macedon an adult representative of the royal house – and a man whom he clearly trusted and may have used in a diplomatic capacity already – who could be made king in the event of a disaster in Asia.[11]

These two women, Kleopatra and Kynnane, were formidable characters; their husbands would therefore very likely be kept under some control. Alexander of Epeiros in fact turned away from any idea of invading Macedon, if he had had one, while his brother-in-law was on campaign in Asia; he made a vigorous attempt at securing an empire in Italy instead.

In all this diplomatic activity Antipater is invisible, but, so long as it is accepted that he was intended to be Philip's deputy in Macedon while the king was away, it may therefore be assumed also that he was involved in all these manoeuvres, at least as a member of Philip's council of advisers. He was thus privy to Philip's plans and intentions and knew that he had to watch the activities of Olympias, Alexander of Epeiros, and Amyntas. The latter two were now married to Philip's daughters, who were as forthright and characterful as Olympias. Kleopatra as Alexander's wife fully counteracted Olympias' influence on her Epeirote brother; Kynnane had been trained to arms, perhaps by her Illyrian mother, who was a tough warrior, and had fought in Philip's Illyrian Wars.[12] She would be as capable of controlling her husband as Kleopatra was Alexander.

When Philip was murdered, therefore, there were, as he had no doubt intended, at least three adult males who had strong hereditary claims to the kingship if he should not return: Amyntas Perdikka, and his own sons, Alexander, and Alexander's elder brother Arrhidaios. This last was usually counted out, due to his mental incapacity. Amyntas' claim was as strong as that of Alexander and may have made tentative moves to seize the post, but, as with the seizure of the kingship by Philip in 359, it was the man on the spot who gained the prize.

It is noted in three of the sources for Alexander's reign that Alexander Lynkestis was the first, or one of the first, to bring Alexander forward to be acclaimed as king after Philip's murder.[13] Alexander Lynkestis was, of course, Antipater's son-in-law, married to the daughter whose name is not known; he was also, from 336, and possibly before, governor of Thrace, Macedon's immediate neighbour to the east. This is the basis, possibly, of claims that Antipater was present at Alexander's presentation-cum-proclamation, though no source actually says this.[14] But the appearance of the Lynkestian Alexander would be quite sufficient to indicate Antipater's silent role in support of Alexander the new king. He may also have appreciated that giving Lynkestis such a role would save his life, given that the new king blamed the Lynkestis family for Philip's death from the start.

Philip may have been willing to embark on a distant and difficult and dangerous expedition while leaving an adult claimant to the kingship alive and in Macedon, but Alexander was not, even if Amyntas was under the control of Kynnane. At the same time, Alexander had not been laggard in acting as king from the moment his father was murdered. One of his initial acts, perhaps even before his acclamation by the troops, was to plan his father's funeral, an action that was always the task of the next king, and which therefore amounted to a claim to the kingship. He also, according to Justin's summary of Trogus' history, planned to execute the murderers at the funeral as a sort of sacrifice to his father's memory.[15]

The actual murderer, Pausanias, was known. He had performed his action before a large audience – in the theatre – and had run away. He tripped and was then killed by several members of Philip's bodyguard (of which Pausanias himself had been a member). The man who is credited with wielding the fatal *sarissa* was Perdikkas, who came from the same region of Macedon, Orestis, as the murderer.[16] So if Alexander planned more killings of murderers, he had very quickly acquired information that the murder was not just the sordid result of a homosexual affair, which was the official version, but that it was a wider conspiracy of which Pausanias was only the agent. Of course, it is possible that Trogus had it wrong, that Alexander was mistaken, that the official story of the assassination was cooked up to explain things away, or to implicate Alexander's victims. Also it may be that Alexander was so distraught at what happened he simply blamed those he did not like. But Alexander was certainly convinced of the guilt of the men he identified as the murderers.[17]

Or perhaps he was merely an uncertain young man, afraid – his father had just been killed in front of him – and was much less confident of his own position than Philip had been. He saw threats everywhere, and it is certain that some of them were both real and imminent. Internationally the death of Philip cancelled any treaties and agreements made in his name. So the Greek cities which had been dragooned into the League of Corinth almost at once withdrew and prepared to fight, and the Balkan tribes to the north, as was usual at the death of a Macedonian king, prepared to invade. Meanwhile the internal dynamics of the Macedonian political system, if it can be called that, rumbled with the ambitions of the rich and powerful. For all these men and groups the removal of Alexander was now a major aim, the essential preliminary to realizing their own aims. He was right to be fearful.

The internal Macedonian situation was sufficiently threatening in Alexander's eyes that he felt justified in striking first. Amyntas Perdikka may have put forward a claim to the kingship, possibly encouraged by his domineering wife; he was killed.[18] His claim was strong enough – and perhaps he had sufficient support to make it credible – that Alexander could not possibly leave him in Macedon while he went away, once any sort of claim had been put forward, and it was necessary, due to the foreign threats, that he should go on campaign almost at once.[19]

It was first necessary to investigate the killing of Philip and so to detect any conspiracy. The first to be killed was the 'diviner', the man who had read the omens on the morning of the killing and pronounced all was well. He was, in effect, the sacrifice at Philip's funeral.[20] More importantly, Alexander identified two families in Macedon as likely or active enemies. One was the Lynkestis family to which Alexander Lynkestis belonged. His two brothers, Arrhidaios and Heromenes, were executed, like the diviner, at the funeral of

Philip as participants in the murder conspiracy.[21] The choice of the execution place makes it abundantly clear that Alexander the new king was convinced of their guilt. How far this was based on good evidence is not known, but one cannot rule out that it might have been one of Alexander's impulses. That he was convinced so quickly might also suggest that Alexander had advance knowledge of his father's killing.

There is more to this than Alexander's suspicious mind, however. The three Lynkestian brothers were descended from a king of the Lynkestai of the mid-fifth century and were connected to the Temenid royal family by marriage.[22] It was a tenuous link, but if the Temenids killed each other off, the Lynkestians might be able to mount a claim. After the killing of Amyntas Perdikka only the halfwit Arrhidaios stood between Alexander and the Lynkestians – though, to be sure, there were others with approximate claims as well.

Alexander Lynkestis was spared, possibly because he was the son-in-law of Antipater, but also because he had been one of the first to acclaim Alexander as king, which rather ruled him out as a conspirator. He was also governor of Thrace, and this may have separated him – as did his marriage – from the rest of the family's involvement in the killing. He was, however, spared only for a time. In this connection it cannot have escaped Alexander's military eye that the Lynkos area was strategically vital in the coming wars, for it lay on the border of Macedon with Illyria to the north, and with Epeiros to the west. The three brothers were members of the local Lynkestian royal family, so eliminating all of them at once could well set off local troubles there; Alexander Lynkestis' survival may thus be one of King Alexander's more careful political calculations. This consideration could also be reversed, of course: if the Lynkestians at court should bring about a rising at home, the way was open for an Illyrian invasion into the rest of Macedon, and removing two of them could prevent that problem, at least for the moment. And in fact it was just south of Lynkestis that Alexander eventually defeated the Illyrian invasion in the battle of Pelion.

The family to which Philip's final wife, Kleopatra, had belonged were also seen as a threat. Her uncle and guardian, Attalos, was with Parmenion in Asia, in joint command of the advance force that had been campaigning there for the past year. He was also Parmenion's son-in-law, and reputedly popular with the soldiers. Alexander sent a man called Hekataios, who was tyrant of Kardia, and was a man he trusted, to the camp in Asia to see Attalos and to persuade him to return to Macedon; if he refused, he was to kill him. No doubt a refusal to return would be taken as an indication of his guilt. But Attalos was a well-connected man, and as Parmenion's son-in-law as well he may have felt he was safe amid Parmenion's army. Even so, having apparently failed to persuade him to return to Macedon, Hekataios resorted to murder.[23] Attalos was accused of having corresponded with Demosthenes in Athens with a view to concerted action against Alexander. He is said to have already confessed this to Alexander, but such an act was clearly treasonable, and knowledge of it may well have persuaded Parmenion that the killing was really necessary.[24]

For Parmenion must have known what was happening, what Hekataios' mission was, and what Attalos' likely fate was, whether Attalos decided to go to Macedon, or resist in the camp. He could have supported Attalos, which would presumably have meant eliminating Hekataios, but this would also have set him and his army in opposition to the new king (assuming the army supported the generals); the result would have been a civil war. Conditions in the kingdom must have been very tense, with wide expectations of trouble from one internal faction or another; the killing of a royal agent followed by overt disobedience from two of the senior generals in command of a large part of the Macedonian army could well be the trigger for outbreaks, even if they were not in support of Attalos and Parmenion.

A further casualty, though not one to be laid at Alexander's door, was due to Olympias. She drove Kleopatra, her fellow widow, to suicide and killed her daughter.[25] This appears to have been her own initiative and Alexander was reported to be angry as a result, but by this time he had also killed many of her relatives, and Olympias' actions were surely in tune with Alexander's wider intentions.

Kleopatra is said to have given birth to a baby boy a few days before Philip's death. This has been identified with an obscure, indeed an unknown, son of Philip called Karanos, but his existence has also been widely doubted. It has been very difficult to decide if Kleopatra could have produced two babies during her relatively short marriage with Philip.[26] The fact that Alexander did not purge the child or her mother implies that he was, in his murder policy, targeting Attalos particularly. And this in turn implies that he may have identified Attalos as one of those involved in the conspiracy which he believed to have taken place to kill Philip – and that the aim was to seize the kingship. At the same time none of this is alleged, and the relationship of Attalos to Kleopatra, plus the connection with Demosthenes (which Attalos had already confessed to in a message to Alexander) could be enough to spark Alexander's already sharp sensitivity to opposition. Another victim of the same social rank was Eurylochos, who had been Antipater's and Parmenion's colleague in the peace negotiations in 346; absolutely nothing is known to explain Alexander's reasons for having him killed.[27]

This purge was, overall, very similar to that which Philip had conducted on his own accession in 359–358, in that it was in part directed at removing possible royal rivals (including the Lynkestians in this), as well as his revenge for his father's death. Philip, however, had had the greater excuse for his murder spree in that the competing pretenders were actually in arms against him at the time, and in at least two cases they were in alliance with active enemies of the kingdom. (Philip had also actively pursued his own half-brothers for the next ten years, before killing them; no doubt the existence of a feud was a danger even to a king and would be some justification for Alexander's action.)

The whole killing business, however, did set up personal difficulties for many men. The death of Amyntas did not drive Kynnane into opposition, though she made it clear to Alexander that she did not wish to marry again.[28] One of Amyntas' friends, Amyntas son of Antiochos, fled from the army in Asia, with other exiles, and joined the Persian cause, at first at Ephesos; his flight may have followed the killing of Attalos rather than that of Amyntas, or perhaps it was the cumulation of killings which drove him away.[29] Parmenion chose a different course, that of loyalty to the king and the kingdom over loyalty to his son-in-law. (This in turn might suggest that he also was convinced of Attalos' guilt.)

This brings us back to Antipater. He knew all the people involved in these events. He was faced with the same dilemma as many other men when Alexander began his purge. Many of the victims were his friends, or at least his associates. Yet his whole life, and all the work he had done since at least the reign of Perdikkas III, had been devoted to loyalty to the successive kings, and to the development and defence and aggrandizement of Macedon. He and Parmenion faced the same dilemma: support the king, even if some of the cases of his murdering activities were unjust, or support

their friends, in which case they might find themselves in Alexander's line
of fire and fighting against him. This would obviously encourage the outside
enemies of Macedon. Both generals could see, perhaps more clearly than
anyone, the consequences of defying the king – rebellion, civil war, invasion,
destruction. And if they won, and Alexander died – he would have to be
killed – where would they be then? Later the Persian King Dareios III
offered to make Alexander Lynkestis the king of Macedon,[30] which implies
that his claim as a relative of the Temenid dynasty was well known.[31] So here
was a further temptation for Antipater: with Alexander Lynkestis king, he
himself and his family would become part of the royal family. And there was
probably no one else with a tenable claim since Amyntas was killed, with
Arrhidaios excluded. Alexander had cleared the board of pretenders just as
his father had a generation earlier. The killings did not drive these men away,
at least not yet, but they will have begun to strain their loyalty to the king,
and his loyalty to them.

Philip was killed in July 336, and the subsequent settlement of Macedon
took perhaps a couple of months. By the autumn Alexander was assured
that no rebellion against him could take place and was ready to deal with
the foreign problems which had meanwhile arisen. The Greek states were
first, because they were seen as being militarily the most dangerous. It was
also an opportunity to see that Antipater was as able to govern Macedon in
Alexander's name as he had been in Philip's. Parmenion remained with the
advance force in Asia, being all the more needed there after the unsettling
experience of the killing of Attalos.

Alexander also wanted to test his own powers of command, and to
accustom the army to his style and methods. There was no fighting, at
first, in Greece. His 'Macedonian advisers' urged him to ignore events in
Greece, and to attend to the more direct threats to the kingdom, which
were manifested among the northern tribes from Illyria and Paionia and
Thrace.[32] Among these advisers must have been Antipater, and since all
the men apparently offered the same counsel, no doubt he proffered such
advice in private as well as in council. This would fit with what is known
of Antipater and his preceding life, for although he was relatively familiar
with Greece, he was above all a Macedonian; his concentration was always
on what benefited Macedon. At the same time, he knew when to stop
'advising', and when Alexander chose to march south he is not noted as

objecting. Antipater's opposition could be easily evaded by leaving him an adequate defence force.

Antipater was thus left in Macedon in command of a force with which to defend the kingdom, just as Parmenion retained a sufficient force to hold on to the minimal position already gained in Asia. We do not know the size of Antipater's force at this moment, but it was surely about the same size as that which Alexander left with him when he went on the Asian expedition – 12,000 infantry and 1,500 cavalry.[33] Parmenion's army was rather smaller, originally 11,000 men.[34] So Alexander cannot have had more than half the Macedonian army with him in the campaigns of 336–335.

In the Greek campaign to suppress incipient opposition, Alexander's speed of march magnified the shock of his force, and those Greek states which had been contemplating action swiftly succumbed. Aitolia, Thebes, Athens, Ambrakia were all taken aback and the preliminary measures they were taking which had been designed to extricate them from the position imposed on them by Philip, were now abandoned. Alexander demonstrated his dominance of Delphi's Amphiktyonic League, was elected President of the Thessalian League, and convened a meeting at Corinth of the league of Greek cities that his father had founded and accepted the position of hegemon (commander) of the league forces for the campaign in Asia. It had all been very easy, brought about by swift movement rather than directly applied force, and by a willingness to ignore the earlier opposition.[35]

He then followed this with an equally speedy campaign into Thrace and the Danube Valley, compelling a series of tribes either to submit to his army, or to send submissive messages designed to fend off a possible attack. The involvement of Alexander Lynkestis in this is surely probable, since he was governor of Thrace, but he is nowhere mentioned. Then the king turned to deal with the most important of these northern peoples, the Illyrians; it may be that he was able to use Antipater's troops in this fight. A display of consummate generalship sufficed to produce a victory, assisted by King Langaros of the Agrianians (who was Kynnane's proposed husband as a result of this alliance).

The campaign involved Lynkos, Alexander Lynkestis' homeland, which was probably damaged by the Illyrian invasion – Alexander's successful defensive battle took place south of that country. The Agrianians lived in Western Thrace, by the upper Strymon Valley; the alliance formed with

Alexander the king was perhaps negotiated by the Lynkestian Alexander as governor. These links are speculative, but a connection clearly must be expected between the two Alexanders, Thrace, and Lynkos, and this may well have been one more reason for the 'sparing' of Alexander when his brothers were executed.

While the king was involved in these and other campaigns in the north opposition was gathering once more in Greece. It would seem that a speedy campaign without a display of violence was not enough to convince many of the Greeks that Alexander should be obeyed. Antipater from Macedon detected what was happening, in particular that the Arkadians from the Peloponnese were either sending a force, or perhaps more likely, an embassy, to Corinth to coordinate with others of like mind. Getting this intelligence so quickly implies an efficient network of communications, and a series of agents in the major Greek cities. He sent off his own embassy to dissuade the plotters.[36]

The Greek 'revolt' which came soon after is dominated by the siege of Thebes and in accounts of Alexander's life, by his great march south from the Pelion battlefield to Thebes.[37] The usual assumption is that the Theban revolt came as a surprise, but it seems clear that Antipater knew what was going on sometime before Thebes blew up, and it is obvious that he will have kept Alexander informed. Antipater was probably based at Pella, and so he could reach Alexander in Lynkos fairly easily – the distance is less than 100km. The previous Greek campaign, involving no fighting, had clearly failed in its purpose, and the Greeks equally clearly had little respect for Alexander's position as hegemon of the Corinthian League, so perhaps Alexander deliberately waited until he heard of actual fighting – the siege of the Macedonian troops in the Theban Kadmeia – before moving south. He was not actually surprised; his rapid march south, using highland pathways, was equally clearly not something he had to explore on the way, but was anticipated.

At Thebes, between the start of the siege and Alexander's arrival, there was a rumour circulating that Antipater was on his way.[38] The rumour had it that Alexander had been defeated in the north and was clearly linked to this. Antipater's involvement in attempting to dissuade the Arkadians (and others[39]) at Corinth was perhaps the basis for this rumour, or possibly he had begun to march south with his own forces, only to be told by Alexander that he would deal with the problem himself. This rumour is presumably the basis for the later story that Antipater actually took part in the siege and capture of the city, which does not seem to be correct.[40] Another version of the rumour had Alexander Lynkestis marching south from Thrace.[41]

What all this does suggest is that Antipater's role was not just to act as Macedon's defender. He was actively engaged in Greek affairs. He knew of the Arkadians' moves well before the Theban revolt, even before the Arkadians had reached Corinth. In turn the Greeks were fully aware of his involvement, which was the basis for the rumours of his approach that were spread at Thebes. (The rumour that Alexander Lynkestis was coming seems to have been a deliberate effort to maintain the viability of the rumour of the king's death.) That is, the Greeks expected that, if any military activity from Macedon resulted from their actions, it would be commanded by Antipater. It would seem that nothing was known of King Alexander's work in the Balkans, and certainly not of his victories; his arrival was thus a surprise.

It was the rumours of the king's defeat and/or death in the Balkan fighting that stimulated the Thebans to attempt to drive out the Macedonian garrison from their Acropolis, the Kadmeia. Several other cities were moving at the time, or were preparing to join the Thebans, including Athens. Alexander's swift march brought him to Thebes long before he was expected. He was quickly joined by the Boiotian cities who had long resented the local Theban supremacy. He tried to avoid a fight, and asked for, as a form of submission, the surrender of two Theban leaders; in reply, the Thebans asked him to surrender Philotas, the commander of the garrison in the Kadmeia, and Antipater, neither of whom were actually with him.[42]

Perhaps the Thebans thought that Antipater was there. Philotas was certainly in the Kadmeia, and his surrender would imply, if not the surrender of the Macedonian garrison, then an armistice; the surrender of Antipater would block any hostile moves by Alexander himself. The suggested exchange of the four men is usually dismissed as an impertinence by the Thebans, but it might also have been the preliminary to a negotiation leading to peace. Maybe Alexander was annoyed at what he saw as the Theban presumption of political equality; but maybe he was already determined on the city's destruction and dismissed any possible negotiations by deciding that his enemy was contumacious. The confrontation ended with the capture of the city and its destruction, by order of the Greek allies – though Alexander generally was blamed, quite rightly.[43] Shocked, Greece subsided into resentful submission. Alexander arranged for the restoration of Plataea and Orchomenos, Theban neighbours, which had been destroyed by Thebes.[44]

Opposition by the Greeks, for the present, was now not worth attempting. Alexander had placed strong garrisons at Corinth, Chalkis in Euboia, and at Ambrakia during his first visit as well as at Thebes.[45] These garrisons were no doubt maintained, or if driven out, were returned; maybe others were installed.

After this it could hardly be claimed that the defeated were reconciled to Macedonian supremacy and control; to escape, it was clearly better now to wait until a more suitable opportunity arrived. Athens, the broken reed of the opposition, descended into political backbiting and lawsuits, but devoted many resources to fortifications and warships over the next decade.

Back in Macedon, Alexander brought his council together, including Parmenion, who was brought back from Asia for the occasion, to discuss the arrangements for the Asian expedition.[46] Parmenion would go on the expedition with Alexander, and Antipater would stay at home. Of the two, it was clearly Antipater who would have the more difficult task, given Macedon's surrounding enemies.

The army had to be divided. This was not difficult to arrange. Parmenion had '10,000' infantry and '1,000' cavalry already in Asia – or rather, that was supposed to be the original strength of the advance force; it was probably a good deal less than that by now, even if the numbers are accurate.[47] Antipater would keep the same force in Macedon that he had presumably commanded during Alexander's recent campaigns, 12,000 infantry and 1,500 cavalry.[48] Alexander took the rest, the main army plus recent recruits such as the Agrianians provided by Langaros' successor, together with contingents from the Greek allies of the League of Corinth, and Greek mercenaries, to a total of 32,000 infantry and 5,100 cavalry. He also had a fleet of about 180 ships, manned probably almost exclusively by Greeks.[49] One of the commanders he took with him was Alexander Lynkestis.

How long the Lynkestian had been governor of Thrace is not altogether clear. Arrian says he was appointed to the post by Alexander soon after proving his loyalty by proclaiming the new king, that is, in 336.[50] When taken away to Asia, therefore, he had been governor for at least two years. It could have been longer, for he may have held that post under Philip. He will certainly have been involved in Alexander's Thracian campaign, and he must have held Thrace quiet while the king was engaged in Illyria and in Greece. The rumour of his approach during the Theban War implies that he had a substantial force at his command.

This was no doubt all very well while Alexander the king was close by, or present in Macedon, but the situation became more difficult when the king left on a campaign in Asia, which would probably last for years, or might bring his death. Antipater in Macedon with a quarter of the Macedonian army, and Alexander Lynkestis, Antipater's son-in-law, in Thrace, with potentially a large army of his own, was not a political situation King Alexander was going to tolerate. So he brought the Lynkestian to Asia with the expedition. He was a king's companion, one of the officers of the army, but had no official post until after the battle at the Granikos River.

On the king's arrival in Asia, Parmenion will have been able to describe the situation in western Asia Minor, and to make clear what opposition Alexander would probably face. Many of the Greek cities were likely to accept him, but the Persian governors were clearly going to fight, and there was an imperial Persian force under the command of Memnon, a capable Rhodian mercenary, who had been fighting the Macedonian advance force already, with some success.

In Macedon Antipater 'had been left in charge' by Alexander – an almost identical form of words is used by all the historians.[51] This meant governing in the king's name, administering the law, supervising Greek, Balkan, and Thracian affairs, and sending regular reinforcements to the main army as they became available. One of his primary tasks, therefore, would be recruiting more soldiers. The reinforcement numbers quoted for the first three years of the campaign are all roughly multiples of 3,000 infantry, plus small numbers of cavalry, which suggests that this was the annual crop of new troops reaching military age. This would not diminish Antipater's own forces, but another of his tasks would be recruiting and training other new forces in readiness for when Alexander required them.[52]

Of course, it was not clear to anyone, to Alexander, to his advisers, to the Greeks, to the Persians, or to anyone else, exactly what Alexander intended by this expedition. Conquest was certainly part of his plans, but how much of the Persian Empire he would be satisfied with was something still to be decided. There was probably little said about this at the meeting since it was such a nebulous matter, but it may be pointed out that if Alexander had stopped at the Taurus Mountains and been content with annexing Asia Minor, he would not have required many extra forces from Macedon – but 'the appetite grew by what it fed on', and he went on, and once in Syria there was no obvious line at which to stop.

Finally at that preliminary meeting, Antipater and Parmenion together urged Alexander to marry and beget a son before he set off.[53] Both men are named as suggesting this, and so it might imply that they were acting in concert, which, given the situation in the royal family, seems quite probable. The line of succession, now that Amyntas Perdikka was dead, was very awkward. Alexander's immediate heir was his dimwit brother Arrhidaios, and the next in line after him appears to have been Alexander Lynkestis, at least by one calculation. No doubt Antipater the more strongly urged Alexander to set about procreation in order to deflect any suspicion that he was looking for his son-in-law to become the next king – but if Alexander died in the next year or two, Arrhidaios would surely be bypassed, and the Lynkestian might be made king.

Alexander rejected the suggestion with a bit of nonsense about not being willing to wallow in domesticity while men fought or worked, as if that was the choice before him. Yet it would not have been difficult to satisfy the request of his senior generals – a reasonable suggestion on their part, which, had he complied with it, would certainly have helped Macedon survive later. (A son born in 335/334 would have been 12 when Alexander died, and would have been a Macedonian, and under Antipater's protection and tuition until he was 16, by which time he would be old enough to rule in the Macedonian system.) Polygamy being a royal habit, Alexander could have collected half a dozen wives and impregnated some or all of them within that time. Once it was clear that at least one of the wives was pregnant he could have gone on campaign with his generals satisfied that the succession was at least partly secured. What Alexander clearly did not want, though he did not say it, was to have any heir whatsoever, at least for the moment, and not least one who came under Antipater's control for his formative years. He had seen the problems caused by marrying a Macedonian girl in his father's last year, and he knew full well that the existence of an heir would very likely provoke plots and attempts at assassination, particularly given the relative unpopularity of the expedition he was setting out on. That was why he had cleared out the possible heirs before the expedition.[54] Whether he put this argument to Antipater, who would be left in Macedon, is not known; if he did, it would be a clear warning to the appointed governor not to involve himself. Parmenion had already received the lesson when he had had to choose between his son-in-law and his king – and this was exactly the situation Antipater would soon be faced with.

The dilemmas of these men become clearer still when the timing of the expedition is considered. The Theban War was concluded in the autumn of 335; the expedition set off for Asia in May 334 – there was therefore plenty of time for the king to marry and procreate. If he had married before the Theban War, he would have known whether a wife was pregnant by the time he set off. The timing makes it quite clear that Alexander was quite determined in the matter – and he refrained from fathering a 'legitimate' child until the last couple of years of his life.

The problem of an heir, and Alexander's unwillingness to think about it other than negatively, became even more obvious and difficult when, only six months into the campaign, Alexander Lynkestis was accused of treason and loaded with chains. The charge was quite probably false, arising from information from a captured Persian agent and relayed by Parmenion.

The agent, Sisines, was a Persian aristocrat, so his message carried some weight. He was intercepted by Parmenion at Gordion where he was attempting to reach Alexander Lynkestis, who had been appointed to command the Thessalian cavalry after the original commander Kalas had been made satrap of Hellespontine Phrygia. Parmenion got the story of Sisines' task out of him and then sent him on to Alexander, who was at Phaselis in Pamphylia on the south coast of Asia Minor.

Alexander accepted the truth of Sisines' story and sent Amphoteros, a brother of Krateros, to Parmenion with instructions to arrest Alexander Lynkestis. Amphoteros was compelled to travel from Phaselis to Gordion in disguise, wearing 'native dress', presumably because it was dangerous for a Macedonian to travel alone, or perhaps because he expected to be intercepted by a partisan of Alexander Lynkestis. He carried orders that Alexander Lynkestis be arrested on a charge of treason. The story Sisines related was that he was to offer the Lynkestian 1,000 talents if he would assassinate King Alexander, whose place he would then take.

The problem with the story is that it seems all too well linked with past events. This is exactly the charge that the king had brought against the other

Lynkestians. The different versions are also at variance over the timing. Alexander was in Phaselis in the winter of 334/333, but one version of the arrest puts it just before the battle of Issos, several months later. Then, having arrested the accused, he was loaded with chains and carried around with the army for the next three years or more – even after being condemned by a court composed of others of the king's companions. It looks very much as though the arrest was precautionary, the condemnation by a kangaroo court, and that the king had a bad conscience over the issue.

So far as we can see Alexander Lynkestis had been unexceptionally loyal. He had governed Thrace competently – the trouble his successor got into implies that – then had obediently joined the expedition and had taken command of the Thessalian cavalry. He had joined with his predecessor in that role, Kalas, in conquering part of his satrapy called 'Memnon's land', seemingly in the Troad. The two men had concluded this minor campaign competently (perhaps more so due to Alexander, since Kalas had not shone in earlier military episodes). In his career therefore, there was nothing to imply any disloyalty towards the king, and much, from the proclamation after Philip's murder till his imprisonment at Gordion, to show the reverse.

But he was close to the succession; he was competent; he was Antipater's son-in-law; he had command of a notably efficient cavalry unit. And could any man easily resist an offer of 1,000 talents and a kingdom? Alexander the king may have had a bad conscience over his prisoner's detention; it is just as likely that he was wholly uncertain over the man's guilt. Arresting him was a way of making sure he could do nothing; and killing him in the end may have been no more than another clearing of the decks – by the time the execution order was given, the king's conscience must have thoroughly coarsened.

The relationship of Alexander Lynkestis to Antipater is generally assumed to have had a bearing on the king's decision not to insist upon immediate execution. If so, the question arises why he should risk doing so later, when he was almost 3,000km away, and Antipater was by then at the head of a victorious army. It could be, alternatively, that as with the execution of Attalos, where it could be seen that it took place with Parmenion's acquiescence, Antipater was consulted and did not dissent.

Alexander marched into central Anatolia and then into Kilikia, and to the battlefield of Issos. Meanwhile Dareios' strategy involved a naval campaign by his fleet into the Aegean. Until the ships arrived Antipater had been largely a spectator of the campaign. The enemy fleet now posed an apparently serious threat to the Macedonian homeland, but it has to be said that it was largely ineffective in its presumed main purpose, which must have been to compel Alexander to leave off his Anatolian campaign and return to the west. Its commander, Memnon of Rhodes again, faced difficult choices. He was faced by a Greek–Macedonian fleet of roughly the same size, which had been gathered mainly from the Greek cities. If he attempted to recapture the places already taken by Alexander he could become locked into a series of city sieges, which would cause constant casualties and immobilize him. Many of the Greek cities of the Asian coast and islands had gone through democratic revolutions in accepting the Macedonian conquest and returning to Persian allegiance would probably mean returning to oligarchic or tyrant rule, not something the city democracies would easily accept. Memnon could strike at Alexander's communications, notably at the Hellespont, if the Macedonian fleet would let him. But it was now rather late for this to have any effect on the Asian campaign, when the army was free of any necessary connection back to the homeland. A strike directly at Macedon would be to face the army under Antipater and would be as futile as the idea of besieging his way to recovery in Asia.

The most attractive policy might well have seemed one of inducing the great cities of the Greek mainland to break from Macedonian rule, and contacts had certainly been made. Yet most of the cities had men marching with Alexander, or serving in the Macedonian fleet, and several were dominated by Macedonian garrisons. Until Memnon had given evidence that he could win fights no one was going to risk joining him. After all, Alexander was winning battles and conquering territory, Memnon had only been beaten so far.

He had some successes. Samos, an Athenian colony, allowed him to resupply.[55] He began to besiege Mytilene on Lesbos, having overrun the rest of the island. He was presumably also keen to display his willingness to fight and win. This would also give him a secure base from which to menace both the Asian coast and the Hellespont. Chios welcomed the Persian fleet, the ruling oligarchy appreciating that Alexander was inimical to oligarchies. If Samos were friendly, so would be Lemnos, Imbros, and Skyros, which were also Athenian. With Lesbos he would control much of the nearby Aegean as well. Several of the Kyklades Islands sent envoys to him, though none ever showed any real support – possibly they were mainly attempting to avoid being involved. But then he died, at Mytilene.[56]

He was succeeded in command by Pharnabazos, his nephew, who maintained the pressure on the city, which soon succumbed.[57] The democratic regime was replaced by a tyrant, Diogenes, who was backed up by a garrison, and fines were levied. None of this would persuade any other Greek city to join the Persian cause. Pharnabazos took the fleet south in search of orders. He met his cousin Tymondas, who brought confirmation of his command, but took away his mercenaries to serve in the main imperial army. With his colleague Autophradates, Pharnabazos returned to the Aegean and captured Tenedos, much to the annoyance of the population.[58]

The opposing Macedonian fleet displayed as little activity as the Persian, but then it did not really need to do much. Indeed, for the winter of 334–333 Alexander disbanded it, supposedly to save money, but he was not really short of money, and the fleet could hardly keep the sea in the winter months anyway.[59] He sent money to Antipater to finance the defence of Macedon, and more to reconstitute the fleet next year, with two new commanders, Hegelochos (a relative of the late Attalos) who set to work to fortify the Hellespont, and Amphoteros, who had carried the message about Alexander Lynkestis from Phaselis to Gordion. This was sufficient to bring out the fleet again in the spring, and to fortify places along the Hellespont.[60]

The two men Alexander had sent to Macedon with the money were a curious pair. Hegelochos, who took charge at the Hellespont, was a nephew of the dead Attalos, but he was also the brother of Philip II's last wife Kleopatra, recently murdered by Olympias. It is thus hardly surprising that Hegelochos stayed at the Hellespont rather than going on to Macedon. Amphoteros took command of the fleet, for which he would need to move about the Aegean collecting the ships. Between them these two men had brought 1,100 talents, of which 600 went to Antipater to finance the defence of Macedon and Greece. He will have visited Antipater, both to deliver the money and to coordinate their actions. He would be able to report on the arrest of Alexander Lynkestis (though the king had surely sent his own report by that time). He may also have reported to Olympias who is said to have complained earlier to the king about the Lynkestian.

Hegelochos at the Hellespont had to cooperate with Kalas, satrap of Hellespontine Phrygia, and with another Memnon, the new governor of

Thrace. Kalas, of course, was Alexander Lynkestis' colleague in the conquest of the Troad, and his predecessor as commander of the Thessalian horse. He may thus also have been affected by the disgrace and arrest of his successor, while Memnon, as the successor of Alexander in Thrace, might have feared a certain reaction among his subjects. There is no hint of argument or intrigue (unless by Olympias), but one must surely expect strong personal feelings at the least. Antipater's lack of reaction at his son-in-law's arrest is as notable as was that of Parmenion in the same situation a year before.

The implications of the various connections were surely fully appreciated by King Alexander, and it would not be out of character for him to be deliberately testing all these men – it was only a short time later, after all, that he deliberately tested his own doctor in a similar way, after information was passed on to him from Parmenion that the doctor was conspiring against him. The lack of reaction by all those involved suggests that they all knew exactly what the king was doing, and steeled themselves to maintain poker faces, and to watch their words.

Pharnabazos took over Tenedos for a time, until the population rebelled. He contacted King Agis of Sparta, sending a small squadron to Siphnos to do so, but that squadron was mainly captured by a rival squadron sent by Antipater under the command of Proteas from Chalkis of Euboia (where there was a Macedonian garrison).[61] Proteas succeeded in interrupting the Persian detachment at Siphnos and capturing eight out of its ten ships. The main city which it was necessary to recruit if any sort of serious naval opposition to Macedon was to be mounted – Athens – was neither contacted nor showed any interest. It had a squadron of twenty ships with Alexander, which may have deterred rebellions. And King Agis, for the moment, was not persuadable.

Antipater, in all this, was apparently scarcely disturbed. He was able to send a contingent of 3,650 recruits to Alexander at Gordion in the winter of 334–333 (at the same time as Alexander Lynkestis was being reported on and arrested), probably the products of the annual crop of young men graduating as ephebes.[62] This was enough to bring the main expedition force back to the size it had begun with, several thousands of men having been detached into garrisons in the conquered areas. The naval war already did not seem to be a serious threat.[63]

All was changed when the news came that Alexander had defeated Dareios in the great battle at Issos, on the border of Kilikia and Syria. This opened up all sorts of possibilities for Alexander. He could, as Parmenion recommended, take what he had gained and make peace – though how long such a peace would last was unclear – or he could march on to gain control of the Levant and Egypt, after which he would clearly need to fight Dareios again. In the Aegean the Persian fleet soon broke up, and ceased to be a threat, though it left an item of poison behind by sending funds to Agis as it disappeared. And one further result was the appointment of Balakros son of Nikanor as satrap of Kilikia. This was Antipater's other son-in-law, the husband of Phila. So just as he had lost one son-in-law to prison, another emerged in a position of significant authority, for Kilikia was the key position for maintaining communications between Macedon and Asia Minor and Alexander's forces. Thus it would seem that Alexander operated to bring Antipater's loyalties back into balance.[64]

Chapter 3

Macedonian Governor I – Thrace and Agis

The battle of Issos in 333 was decisive in that it opened up the whole Persian Empire for Alexander to exploit, if he wished; it also broke the Persian navy in the Aegean, for the several contingents, which were primarily from the Phoenician or Cypriot cities, broke away when their home cities were threatened by the Macedonian army.[1] And yet, Pharnabazos had encouraged King Agis, and had given him a substantial sum of money with which to recruit an army large enough to face the Macedonian army under Antipater.

The presence of the Persian fleet in the Aegean, however, may be assumed to have disrupted the regular trade of the area. In particular it must have interfered with the grain trade. Mainland Greece depended on the import of grain by sea to feed its population. The fighting in 334/333 largely concentrated in the north-east of the Aegean and this will certainly have disrupted the trade in grain through the Hellespont from the Black Sea to Greece; the fleet had also been able to range widely through most of the rest of the Aegean. It is known that Greece suffered a 'great grain crisis' in the decade after 330, for which several reasons have been adduced.[2] It is evident that this crisis predated 330, and the naval campaign was probably partly responsible. The problem did not necessarily become acute for some time, since the cities that depended on imported grain laid up a store for such an emergency. Athens, for example, had a permanent organization directed to the issue, and it was the first item on the council's agenda at every monthly meeting.[3]

Into this situation came Alexander's treasurer Harpalos, a childhood friend of the king's, who 'fled' from the army in Kilikia – 'before the battle of Issos' – and took 'refuge' at Megara, apparently carrying with him a quantity of money.[4] The pejorative description of the event was Arrian's, but his words may be reinterpreted. A little time before this, Kleandros son of Polemokrates had been sent by Alexander from Lydia – probably from

Phaselis at about the same time that he was considering what to do about the revelation of the problem of Alexander Lynkestis – with a quantity of money to hire mercenaries in the Peloponnese.[5] And it was not long after the victory at Issos that Hegelochos and Amphoteros brought 1,100 talents to fuel the naval war and to be used by 'Antipater and those defending the Greek cities'.[6]

This concentration by Alexander on Greek affairs before and after the great battle indicates that he expected trouble there. The contacts of Pharnabazos with King Agis were known, and it was apparent that Agis was dangerous, especially once he had received the Persian subsidy. The flight of the Greek mercenaries in Dareios' employ after the battle had sent some of them to Cyprus and on to Egypt, but others had headed west to Crete, and to the developing mercenary market at Cape Tainaron in the southern Peloponnese – Spartan territory.[7] These were men who had deliberately chosen to fight on the Persian side and whose subsequent travels indicated quite clearly that they retained a loyalty towards Persia and an enmity towards Macedon.

It was in this period of unrest, hunger, and confusion that Harpalos arrived to 'take refuge' at Megara. This episode is coloured in the sources (and in modern accounts) by the fact that, as Arrian comments, Harpalos had done this before and, notoriously, did it again.[8] The first flight was scarcely that, and can be ignored; the third flight ended in his death, and will need to be discussed later, for on the way he created great confusion in Athens. This second 'flight', however, was different. The arrival of the former royal treasurer with plenty of money at Megara was no doubt something of a sensation, but it can only be explained as a 'flight' – desertion from Alexander's forces and the theft of a considerable quantity of money – if he was punished for it. Yet Alexander welcomed his return to the royal camp in 331, and put him back in charge of the treasury, displacing the two men who had been jointly appointed in 333 when Harpalos left.

It is necessary to disregard the interpretation of this event, which is retrospectively affected by his much more notorious and complex later flight in 324, when he really was deserting from Alexander. Taking the story without the retrospective interpretation imposed by Arrian it looks instead as though Harpalos was sent to Megara, just as Hegelochos and Amphoteros were sent at this time to take charge of naval affairs, and Kleandros was sent to recruit mercenaries. That is, his movement to Megara was as an official sent by the king and was part of a concerted set of actions by Alexander to block any trouble in Greece. All these were measures taken to deal with the simmering problems of Greece at that particular time. Kleandros recruited 4,000 soldiers in the Peloponnese during 333–332, and brought them to Alexander at Sidon during the siege of Tyre in 332; this would represent a significant reduction in the political war-making capacity of the Peloponnesian cities, though we do not know where he recruited.[9] Amphoteros and Hegelochos dealt with the naval campaign, though it was the news of the Persian defeat at Issos that was the determining factor in reducing that threat. Harpalos, with a substantial cash treasure, seems to have involved himself in the grain trade.[10]

He travelled with Tauriskos, who is described by Arrian as 'an evil man' and has been credited with exerting his influence on Harpalos to fly. But the reinterpretation that makes Harpalos travel on official business means that Tauriskos cannot be Harpalos' evil genius. It was never very convincing, since Tauriskos went straight on to Italy to contact Alexander of Epeiros, who was campaigning there, and died there soon after his arrival. If Harpalos' move to Megara was not a flight, then Tauriskos' move to Italy was similarly an official journey, presumably to establish diplomatic contact between the two kings.

The grain crisis was not wholly caused by a shortage of grain produced in Greece, though there seems to have been a succession of bad harvests in the 320s, but by inability to transport the grain from the outside producers to Greece, resulting in a great increase in both the wholesale and retail prices. This problem could be remedied most easily by the application of money, especially now that the Persian fleet was out of the way. The price of grain in Athens increased by up to six times the 'normal' price during the crisis (though these are only figures picked out in Athenian speeches as examples; they were not necessarily always so high).[11] Such an increase would naturally attract grain merchants if they could be sure that their shipments would reach the Greek markets. But in the meantime, the price increase fuelled Greek discontent and unrest, and it would be easy to fix the blame on Alexander and the Macedonians – the armies would require large quantities of grain, and this will have contributed to the shortage.[12] Harpalos' money could be used to bring in grain and thus defuse the situation. The best record of the relief provided is in an inscription from Cyrene, one of the main breadbaskets of the Mediterranean at the time, which records large shipments to a wide variety of Greek cities.[13] The date is not clear though mention of Kleopatra, the wife of King Alexander of Epeiros, and Olympias, sister and mother of Alexander, implies that it took place at about 330. (The date of the inscription will be some time after the time of the shipments.) But this was not an indiscriminate supply of grain to whoever needed it; instead, the distribution of the grain was concentrated towards particular cities, all of which were friendly, or potentially friendly, towards Macedon. Athens was generously provided, for example, but so were a whole series of other cities along the eastern part – the Aegean side – of mainland Greece, and several of the islands. Those which were inimical to Macedonian power were omitted.[14]

None of this supply was free, of course, but it has been suggested that it was sold by the Cyrenians at below market price. This seems most unlikely behaviour by grain growers and grain merchants, however sympathetic to the plight of the recipients they might be, and the high prices quoted by the Athenian sources rather suggest otherwise, though the highest refer to the 320s, whereas Harpalos was in Megara from 333 to 331, something over a year. What may have happened, therefore, is that Harpalos used his treasure to buy the grain at market price at the source (which was somewhat inflated for the occasion), and then sold it on to the Greek cities at below his cost – that is, Alexander was subsidizing the grain supply to Greece in order to keep the Greeks quiet while he dealt with the Persian army.

In exile from Athens at Megara at this time with the entrepreneur Leokrates, who had expertise in the grain trade; his advice would be useful. (His exile was due to a threat of prosecution for having moved his family out of the city when the Macedonian army seemed to threaten it.) Cyrene was not the only possible source of grain, but a combination of factors besides the naval war had restricted supplies from elsewhere – Egypt was the scene of fighting in 332/331, and its surplus would probably go to feed the Macedonian army; Sicily and South Italy were also the scene of fighting as Alexander of Epeiros attempted his conquest; piracy in the Adriatic was serious enough to provoke Athens to send a military colony there a few years later; supplies in Asia were likely to be mopped up by the Macedonian forces. Cyrene was thus probably the principal source available at that particular time, though it was by no means usually the only one; its prominence in accounts and discussions of these events is largely due to the fact that it is the only place where a major documentary source on the subject is available.

The process of purchase and shipment began while the Persian fleet was still operating in the Aegean and was too strong to be fought, unless a detachment could be caught, as by Proteas from Chalkis at Siphnos. This brings us back to Antipater, for Proteas had been put in command of the ships at Chalkis by Antipater. Antipater himself is not otherwise mentioned in this series of events, apart from receiving a substantial tranche of Alexander's cash with which to assist those in Greece who were Macedon's friends – but this fits well with the activities of Harpalos and the precision he applied in subsidizing the grain prices. Antipater was, in all likelihood, preoccupied during part of the time that Harpalos was at Megara with the revolt of the Thracians, which is best dated to 332 (and will be discussed later).

Harpalos therefore had the main task of keeping Greece quiet. He was not a military man, being disabled in some way from serving in the army, which may be the reason he was originally appointed treasurer; when he was sent to Megara, no doubt his financial expertise was useful in the purchase process. His presence will have relieved Antipater of much concern over Greece and allowed him to deal with Thrace.

It is difficult to construct a chronology because of the fragmentary and discontinuous sources for all the events in Greece in these years, which has clearly allowed items to drop out of the record. But the presence of Antipater in Macedon, of Harpalos in Megara, of Kleandros in the Peloponnese, and Proteas at Chalkis, together with Macedonian garrisons at Corinth, Chalkis, Ambrakia, Thebes, and probably elsewhere, all add up to a formidable Macedonian presence in Greece in 333–331, and this can only have been designed to hold Greece under control.

The delicacy of the Greek situation is demonstrated by the fact that more or less as soon as Kleandros and Harpalos returned to Alexander (at Tyre in 332 and 331 respectively) and Amphoteros and Hegelochos somewhat earlier to Egypt, the 'rebellion' of King Agis of Sparta began. That is, Agis had been busy preparing for his Macedonian War while Harpalos was in Megara but was clearly unable to gather any overt Greek support until after Harpalos had ceased subsidizing Macedon's friends, and with Antipater exercising some general imperial control over the region. The more distant

Antipater was perceived as less of a threat, particularly once he became absorbed in the Thracian fighting.

The arrival in succession from Greece of all these men at Alexander's headquarters in Egypt and in Syria ensured that Alexander was well informed about events and circumstances in Greece. To this we may add the reports on events that Antipater sent, probably at irregular intervals whenever a courier was available, or when some other group or individuals – such as contingents of reinforcements – were sent out to the king. Anything particularly important or urgent would, of course, be sent at emergency speed; it may be presumed that news of Agis' War was the subject of one of these last.

The imprisonment of Alexander Lynkestis had not directly affected Antipater, as far as can be seen. This may have been because King Alexander needed him to defend his Macedonian base, though it is noticeable that the king also used other agents – Harpalos, Kleandros – in his policy of suppressing Greek discontent, rather than Antipater. This was, however, no more than a temporary measure, and both Antipater and Alexander may have been resigned to the probability of a Spartan War sooner or later. All his Greek agents, and probably Antipater as well, will have warned him that Greek trouble was coming. However, when it came, fighting began in a perhaps unexpected place.

Alexander Lynkestis had been made governor of Thrace at the beginning of Alexander's reign. When he was then appointed commander of the Thessalian horse after the Granikos fight, he was replaced in Thrace by a man called Memnon (no relation to the Persian commander). It is difficult to believe that the removal and detention of Alexander Lynkestis had no effect in Thrace, where he had governed until a few months before. This was a territory only recently conquered by Philip and was therefore restless – there were 'free Thracians' still unconquered in 336, according to Arrian.[15] It had also taken a long time to effect the conquest of Thrace, and it really required a steady and lengthy period of subordination if it was to remain under Macedonian control and in peace. Instead Memnon was the third governor in three years.[16] It is therefore hardly surprising that the news of the arrest of the former governor was followed by the outbreak of a rebellion, which appears to have begun in 332. Governor Memnon is said, in the only notice we have of the rebellion, to have been at the head of that rebellion, but he turns up later in India, in command of a substantial group of reinforcements being delivered to Alexander.[17] Former rebels were never trusted by the chronically suspicious king, and it seemed very doubtful that Memnon had been the leader of the Thracian rebellion. His career is less than exciting: failure as a governor, in command of a reinforcement force, then nothing. It is better to assume that Diodoros, whose notice of the rebellion consists of only two sentences, misunderstood his source, or has excessively concentrated it. Given that Memnon remained in some favour with Alexander, it is perhaps best to interpret Diodoros' words as suggesting that Memnon's policies had stirred up the rebellion, and that he then commanded an army aiming to suppress it. He was less than successful, and Antipater had to help out.

The rebellion was thus suppressed mainly by Antipater's efforts. The employment of Memnon later has led to the suggestion that, having led the rebellion, he was then reinstated in Thrace as a compromise with Antipater, but this would be going far beyond Antipater's authority: appointments at governor level were the prerogative of the king, and not of a neighbouring governor, no matter how respected and victorious. If Memnon was later re-employed, it must follow that he had not rebelled. A rebellion did take place, so it may be assumed that Memnon, having survived, was then removed. He was succeeded by an equally obscure man called Zopyrion, who held the post for the next six or seven years.[18]

The appointment of Zopyrion is not recorded as immediately following the dismissal of Memnon and Curtius' words in recording Memnon's arrival in India with the reinforcements – 'from Thrace' – might suggest that Memnon remained as governor there until the reinforcements were ready. But Zopyrion is known to have been busy in Thrace by 330, which means that Memnon had ceased to be governor by that time.[19] Coming with reinforcements from Thrace did not necessarily mean he came directly from Thrace, only that the troops came from there.

Alexander may have known that Memnon would not be a success as governor. It may well be therefore that his appointment was part of a political manoeuvre by the king designed to remove Alexander Lynkestis from Thrace, where he was the neighbour of his father-in-law. Evidence that Antipater was not wholly trusted by King Alexander mounts steadily during the years of the great campaigns; perhaps here we have an early example. (Another may be the disappearance of Amyntas son of Arrhabaios, Alexander Lynkestis' nephew, and the son of one of those executed in 336, who commanded cavalry units at the Granikos and Sagalassan fights, but is never heard of again.[20]) Moving Alexander Lynkestis away from Thrace and away from the proximity of Antipater, into a command which placed him much closer to the king not only separated him from a powerful supporter, but brought him within Alexander's reach.

The link between the Thracian rebellion and the Lynkestians' disgrace is somewhat distant, to be sure, though the Thracians were always ready to rebel against any outside domination, and the condemnation of a former governor would be a possible excuse. Equally tenuous is any Thracian connection with the later events in the Peloponnese, though Antipater was still fighting in Thrace when Agis' 'rebellion' began[21] – that is, the outbreak in the north happened well before that in the south; this is not to say, however, that Agis did not realize the advantage to him of Antipater's involvement in Thrace.

King Agis of Sparta had met the Persian naval commanders Pharnabazos and Autophradates at Siphnos. The Persians arrived with 100 triremes, a large enough force to deter any interception from Chalkis such as had interrupted the earlier Siphnian rendezvous. Agis arrived in one ship. He asked for money to pursue his aim of raising an army powerful enough to challenge the Macedonian domination. In the middle of the meeting the news arrived of the Persian defeat at Issos, which dates the Siphnos meeting to the end of 333. The Persians hurriedly withdrew, but they did give Agis thirty talents and ten triremes before leaving.

This was not much to start a war with, and it is unlikely to have been enough to recruit the large army which Agis eventually commanded, though most of the soldiers were Spartans or Peloponnesian allies, and these might not be paid, though supplies would need to be purchased. He gave the Persian money to his brother Agesilaos, who first arranged to pay the crews of the ships (but not soldiers), and then ranged through Crete, securing allies and recruits, some of whom were the former Persian mercenaries who had fled from the Issos battlefield. Agis himself followed Autophradates to Halikarnassos, which had been recaptured by the Persians, and then himself went to Crete.[22] (Did he get more money from Autophradates at Halikarnassos? Certainly Agis must have had more than thirty talents with which to recruit and supply the army he collected.) Activity in Crete meant recruiting mercenaries, but some of the cities also supported his anti-Macedonian policy – others were in receipt of food supplies from Cyrene, presumably orchestrated by Harpalos from Megara and so were pro-Macedonian.

Agis and Sparta did have a part way legitimate grievance. Philip II had, rather contemptuously, stripped the city of its borderlands on three sides, leaving Sparta controlling little more than the Eurotas Valley. This was done by Philip's own decision and, though it was ratified by the League of Corinth, that ratification was also an act of power by Philip. There was perhaps a degree of sympathy for Sparta over this, particularly as such a drastic weakening of the city upset the power balance within the Peloponnese, while leaving Sparta resentful, and seeking for revenge. Agis' aim, though nowhere actually stated, was probably to recover the lost territories at least, but also to reconstitute the old Spartan alliance, which had covered the whole Peloponnese.

Agis was going about his task fairly systematically, but he clearly had a major task in attempting to produce a new war, for he had both to recruit an army and to persuade members of the League of Corinth to join him. In the time of the Spartan preparation (i.e. 333–331) Antipater faced and defeated the rebellion in Thrace which had been provoked in some way by Memnon, and Harpalos reduced the discontent in Greece which would have helped a Spartan attack on the Macedonian position. Antipater had still not completely finished off the Thracian War when fighting began in the Peloponnese, and he had then to respond by gathering a substantial Macedonian army, probably all the forces he could collect, to fight the rebels.

Since it seems best to assume that Memnon had been responsible for 'stirring up' the Thracians in some way, perhaps merely by being obnoxious, and that they were therefore rebelling against his authority, Antipater was campaigning in the governor's support. To do this he will have needed the whole of his Macedonian forces, which had originally been 12,000 infantry and 1,500 cavalry. This force had not been seriously reduced by sending Macedonian reinforcements to Alexander, for those he sent off were probably the annual crop of new adults; Kleandros' group were Greek mercenaries. In 332, when Agis was visibly recruiting his own forces – Harpalos in Megara will have been aware of this – Antipater was doing the same, partly to put down the Thracians, and partly in anticipation of Agis' War.

He also had to fulfil Alexander's orders to deliver the annual crop of young soldiers. Amyntas son of Andromenes had been sent to Macedon from Gaza about the end of 332, with ten triremes, to collect these men, not just the Macedonians but also a force of Peloponnesian, Thracian, and Illyrian mercenaries. He gathered 6,000 of the Macedonians (which would seem to be two years' supply), presumably those of 332 and 331, 4,000 Peloponnesians, and 3,500 Thracians. In addition, there were just over 2,000 cavalry.[23] This is a large force, and that it included men from two regions that were about to be, or had been, in rebellion suggests they were ex-enemies dragooned into 'volunteering'. The whole process took at least a year, from Amyntas leaving Gaza to delivering the troops to Alexander, which explains the large number of Macedonians. The delivery took place in Sittakene in Babylonia, some time after the battle of Gaugamela, and so late in 331. If they were intended as reinforcements ordered in advance of the anticipated decisive battle with Dareios, they were too late – though this may be due to Antipater using the men first in his fighting against Agis; recruiting Thracians and Peloponnesians would hardly be possible until after the battle of Megalopolis and the final suppression of the Thracian War.

As it happens we know marginally more about Agis' activities than about those of Antipater, but in the end Antipater had gathered the larger army. One reason for the discrepancy was money. Pharnabazos had given Agis thirty talents. Alexander had already sent 1,100 talents to Macedon in the face of the Persian naval campaign; maybe Harpalos handed over still more. When it became clear to Alexander, after the arrival of Amyntas' reinforcements, that Agis' War was serious, he sent Antipater 3,000 more talents.[24]

It is not known how long it took for Antipater to put down the Thracian rebellion, but he did not neglect the events that were developing in the Peloponnese. There was at least one Macedonian force in the region that was large enough to be considered an army and was able to stand and fight against Agis' force. The commander was Korrhagos, who may have been the commander of the Corinth garrison. If so, he left enough men in the Akrokorinth to keep control of the city even after his defeat by Agis.[25] It was possibly he who acted for Alexander in installing the Olympic victor Chairon as tyrant of Pellene in Achaia,[26] though if this really took place while Alexander was in Syria or Egypt or further east, Korrhagos was probably acting as Antipater's agent rather than Alexander's; after all, the king tended to favour democracies rather than tyrannies or oligarchies, whereas Antipater later generally favoured oligarchies; or possibly Chairon was installed by Harpalos from his base at Megara. Harpalos in Megara and Korrhagos in Corinth were surely in contact with each other. The coup in which Chairon seized power was presumably arranged as part of the political manoeuvres designed to block Agis' schemes; he certainly kept Pellene out of Agis' alliance.

These events were developing in Greece and Thrace while Alexander campaigned slowly through Syria and into Egypt and back again; the final battle is roughly synchronized with Gaugamela in the autumn of 331, though the exactitude implied is not correct. By sending the 3,000 talents to Antipater from Susa later, Alexander certainly believed the fighting was still on. Gaugamela was fought on 1 October; after a visit to Babylon and two long marches, Susa was reached only in December 331. On the other hand, none of this provides any precise information about the dates of events in the Peloponnese. In Greece neither side was rushing matters. The elimination of Korrhagos' army left Agis able to campaign in the Peloponnese, though continuing Macedonian control of Corinth restricted him to that peninsula, as did the fact that large areas did not support him, notably Messene and Argos. Corinth also, of course, held open the gateway into the Peloponnese for Antipater. He had a large naval force as well, 100 triremes sent by Alexander under Amphoteros, plus whatever ships he already controlled, so that, if necessary, he could have invaded by sea. But until well on into 331 Antipater had plenty to do in the north.

This is, however, a series of events in which, as will already have become obvious, the chronology and the numbers are less than clear. Almost every detail is a matter of discussion, if not also for barbed academic comment. For chronology the problem is that the ancient sources depend on attempts to coordinate events in Greece with Alexander's movements in Asia, though as Alexander moved steadily eastwards during the Greek crisis the distance imposed increasing delays on his reactions. It is best to take the Greek events as a distinct set, and to ignore correlations with Alexander.[27]

The question of army numbers is less difficult, but in fact the size of the two armies is quite startling, always bearing in mind the inaccuracies of all figures in ancient sources. Both Agis and Antipater had to recruit armies based around their own relatively small core forces – 6,000 for Agis, 13,500 for Antipater – and the fact that the deciding battle was fought by a combined total of over 70,000 men is a testimony to the quantity of military manpower still available in Greece, even when almost as many were campaigning with Alexander, and still more in the Persian forces against him.[28]

Agis gathered several allies, all of them in the Peloponnese, and all probably joined him only after his defeat of Korrhagos' army, which showed that he could win battles. The departure of both Kleandros (and his recruits) and Harpalos (and his money) will have also helped. Even so his allies were few enough: Mantineia and Tegea, some of the Arkadian and Achaian cities, and Elis.[29] It is the participation of these states, all members of the League of Corinth, which allows the fighting to be termed a 'revolt' against Macedonian domination; for Sparta it was a Macedonian War, since Sparta was not a member of the League. Agis' major enemy, apart from the Macedonians, who held Corinth, was the city of Megalopolis in Arkadia. Megalopolis owed its very existence to Sparta's defeat at Leuktra forty years before, and its resistance provided the first test of the new Spartan power.

Megalopolis' people may well have had mixed feelings over this war; the city's foundation was due to a Theban victory over Sparta, and Sparta had been an enemy ever since; but Macedon had now brutally destroyed its founder sponsor, which can only have angered the Megalopolitans. A defter diplomat than Agis might have been able to bring Megalopolis onto his side by playing on Megalopolitan feelings, or at least he might have persuaded the city into neutrality; but deft diplomacy was not usually the Spartan way, and Agis really wanted to gain control of the city.

Agis' army eventually numbered over 30,000 men. His own Spartan force numbered about 6,000 – Spartan citizens and *perioeci* – and the Peloponnesian allies contributed perhaps 16,000 (including 2,000 cavalry from the Arkadian allies). To these must be added an uncertain number of mercenaries, possibly as many as 10,000, but perhaps fewer.[30]

In reply Antipater gathered an army of 40,000 soldiers. These included (presumably) most of his 13,500 Macedonians, together with a contingent of 5,000 Thracians and Illyrians, and the rest (23,000) were either mercenaries or Greek allies called up by the League of Corinth. How many came from the allies is not known, but assuming that half of the 23,000 were mercenaries and half were allies, Antipater may well have had fewer Greek allied troops in his army than Agis.[31] The two armies were thus curiously mirror images of each other: relatively small contingents of the main driving states – Sparta and Macedon – were accompanied by much larger, and probably much less enthusiastic, allies and mercenaries.

Agis had been compelled to begin by attacking Megalopolis, which defied him and then successfully resisted his attack. He then laid siege to it. Unless he could take the city, he could not move on elsewhere, since his homeland would then be threatened; if he could take the city, quite possibly more of the Peloponnese would fall into line with him, and he would at least be able to move on to attack Corinth. But the siege pinned down the Spartan forces, allowing both armies time to bring their allies' forces together – but the time advantage worked for Antipater, not for Agis.

Antipater is explicitly stated to have been very slow at collecting his forces, though if he had to finish off the Thracian War first and then gather more than 20,000 allies and mercenaries, this is not surprising.[32] Once he understood that Agis was committed to a siege of Megalopolis, and that Corinth was secure, he knew he could take his time. In Syria Alexander, on his march from Egypt to invade Babylonia and Iran, reacted to the news of the war by sending Antipater yet more money, and 100 ships, commanded by Amphoteros once again, from what was now his own navy; some of these ships and crews were now serving in the Aegean for the second time, having been there earlier under Persian command.[33] The ships were intended to assist Macedon's Peloponnesian allies, but their usefulness was probably somewhat limited; all the fighting took place on land.

The army under Antipater moved south, probably, like Agis' army, collecting extra allied contingents along the way. Some, perhaps many, League members stayed neutral; others owed too much to Macedon to afford to stay out. Athens stayed neutral: supporting an expansion of the Spartan power was not something any Athenian could ever accept, particularly since it was well known that Agis had accepted considerable Persian backing – Greece, and particularly Athens, had been through a well-remembered period of such joint hegemony before, and had no wish to repeat it, but assisting a Macedonian warlord was equally an obnoxious notion. Neither side had the interests of Athens at heart, and the allocation of 100,000 *medimnoi* of the Cyrenian grain was not enough to bribe the Athenian democracy into the Macedonian alliance.[34]

The actual course of the war is unknown but was perhaps fairly straightforward. The final battle took place near Megalopolis, though exactly where is not recorded. This means that Agis was still vainly attacking the city when Antipater's army arrived. Antipater had therefore marched from Macedon to Greece, probably having to negotiate the army's route, and when he reached the Peloponnese the contingents from the enemies of Sparta also joined him, perhaps forming the majority of his allied troops. Before the battle at least one of Agis' allies, Mantineia, pulled out, no doubt dismayed at the presence and size of the Macedonian army; it is possible that others did so as well.[35] The battle pitched a Macedonian-led force of 40,000 against a Spartan-led force of 30,000, and in view of the primitive techniques of Greek warfare, it was almost inevitable that the larger force won; one detail suggests that Agis had drawn up his army between two hills, thus partly negating the effect of the larger Macedonian army.[36]

The competence of Agis or Antipater in command of an army is not known, but two such forces normally faced each other at push of pike, and the greater weight of the larger force generally prevailed. The unsophisticated nature of warfare in Greece is suggested by the renown that Epameinondas of Thebes acquired by simply concentrating a heavier force on one wing of an army. Both Philip and Alexander had a rather better technique than that, though Philip's successes were in large part due to his use of the longer than 'normal' spear, the *sarissa*. Alexander's forces were generally outnumbered in his major battles, which put a premium on his ability to manoeuvre and adapt – the fact that he was so young when he began to command was no doubt an advantage in this. There is no sign that Antipater ever displayed the flexibility of Alexander's command style, but then with the larger army at Megalopolis he did not need to. He had learned his fighting and command skills even before Philip became king, and by gathering an overwhelming force he displayed a clear appreciation of the necessities.

The one item about the battle that might suggest a display of political rather than military cunning on Antipater's part is the casualty list. The Macedonian side suffered 3,500 killed; the Spartan 5,300 (from a smaller army), of which it seems most were in the Spartan contingent – and the dead included King Agis.[37] Either the Spartans were particularly active in the fighting, as the stories of Agis' despairing bravery might suggest, or, more likely, Antipater deliberately targeted the Spartan contingent as being the most important politically; the Spartan casualties suggest that their contingent was almost wiped out.

Whether he did concentrate in that way or not, the result of the battle was to eliminate Sparta as a political and military power for the next generation. When the Spartans asked for peace terms Antipater handed the peace process to the League, as was proper and legal. The league was also able to deal with the issue of the members who had participated in the 'rebellion' – the Tegeans, the Achaians, and the Eleians (and presumably the non-Megalopolitan Arkadians) – who were punished, fined, or both. Sparta was different. Long discussions produced a stalemate among the representatives in the League, perhaps because it proved impossible in the League's procedures to frame a treaty of peace with a non-member. It may also be that it was seen that dealing with Sparta would always be difficult, or that many did not wish to see Sparta's power quite so drastically reduced. Whatever the difficulties the League failed to reach a decision and it was eventually decided to hand the problem back to Antipater who, having secured control of fifty important Spartans as hostages, sent them and the problem on to Alexander; he was in eastern Iran before he had to decide anything.[38]

One of the sources for this peace-making episode, Curtius Rufus, comments that Antipater was worried that his own victory would be greeted by Alexander as a rebuke to the king; that is, he feared that Alexander might not be able to bear the thought of a subordinate who was as successful militarily as himself. It is embedded in a rather rhetorical passage, which may well be of Curtius' own composition, but it rings true nonetheless. Alexander's own victory at Gaugamela, which the sources tend to equate in time with the battle of Megalopolis, if not in importance, was big enough to deflect such feelings, at least for a time. Yet Alexander's reported comment on the Greek fighting as a 'conflict of mice' might be derogatory, but it also suggests a degree of relief that Antipater had won; if he had been defeated all Alexander's plans would have been deranged.

As it happened Antipater's report on recent events in the west – the war against Agis, the death of Alexander of Epeiros in Italy, the campaign of Zopyrion in Skythia – reached Alexander shortly after the death of King Dareios in eastern Media.[39] This was followed by the internal army crisis in which Philotas and his father Parmenion were executed, and to which, almost as an afterthought, Alexander added the execution, finally, of Alexander Lynkestis.[40] If Alexander had stayed his hand over the killing of the Lynkestian because of his relationship with Antipater, killing him now sent a clear message to Antipater that he was out of favour.

With the death of Parmenion, Antipater was the last of the men who had been Philip's equals and contemporaries. There were already stories circulating that he and Alexander were at odds, but the two men were separated by several thousands of kilometres of territory. Antipater's life was clearly saved, at least for the moment, by his victory, and by the death of his old colleague Parmenion. The murder of Parmenion left many Macedonians aghast; the murder of Antipater at the same time would quite possibly trigger a real conspiracy against the king, not just one he invented out of his paranoia. Then again Antipater himself was busy enough in Macedon, what with Greece to watch over, Zopyrion fighting in Thrace, political problems in Epeiros after King Alexander's death in Italy, and Philip's widow Olympias nagging him and reporting on him to her son. And Alexander turned out to have a very busy time before him as well, in Baktria and India. By the time any news from Macedon reached him in these areas he was quite unable to affect matters. Antipater's victory at Megalopolis thus prolonged his life: Alexander might well be jealous of a fellow Macedonian winning a victory, but he could not afford to be seen to be jealous.

Antipater understood well enough what Parmenion's death meant. If Parmenion could be killed, no one was safe.

Chapter 4

Macedonian Governor II – Surviving Alexander

A ntipater's family grew in the early years of Alexander's reign. His daughter who had married Alexander Lynkestis and whose name is not known, had at least one child, named Arrhabaios, perhaps after his brother who was killed by King Alexander at King Philip's funeral.[1] After the Lynkestian's arrest and imprisonment she very likely returned to her father, with the child, his grandchild. The child had been born in the early 330s, probably between 338 (the earliest possible date of the marriage) and 334, when Alexander went off to the war.

A second daughter, Phila, had also married before the expedition to Asia began, to Balakros, son of Nikanor, who in 333 was appointed satrap of Kilikia.[2] She is usually thought to be the eldest of Antipater's daughters, perhaps because she was eventually the most prominent, but it seems that she was in fact the second to be married, so it is likely that the anonymous wife of Alexander Lynkestis was actually the eldest. Phila may or may not have travelled to Kilikia to live with her husband during his tenure of the satrapy, which lasted from 333 to 324, but she certainly produced at least one child between her marriage and 324, when Balakros was killed in fighting in Pisidia.[3]

Balakros appears to have been born about 380, and so was a contemporary of King Philip and Antigonos – the latter of whom was his neighbour across the Taurus Mountains as the new satrap of Phrygia. These two joined with Kalas, the satrap of Hellespontine Phrygia, in campaigning against the recovering Persian power in Asia Minor in 333–331.[4] Balakros and Antigonos will have undoubtedly done the main work, since Kalas seems to have been less than militarily capable. They certainly succeeded in establishing control over the inland regions. Kalas at some point also secured control of Paphlagonia,[5] but the region that later became the kingdom of Pontos further to the east remained outside Macedonian control.[6] On the other hand, Kalas was defeated by a Bithynian chieftain called Bas in 328/327.[7] (Bas was the ancestor of the later Bithynian dynasty.)

Balakros, as a contemporary of King Philip, was at least thirty years older than Phila. He was the son of a man called Nikanor, and it seems also that Balakros was the father of another Nikanor, and perhaps of a man called Philip.[8] Both are all too common Macedonian names, but their identification as sons of Balakros rather pins both of them down. Philip was a commander of infantry at the Granikos fight, a commander in Alexander's Balkan campaign the year before, and again at Gaugamela.[9] Nikanor's career is impossible to disentangle from all the other Nikanors, but every possible identification involves him in active command somewhere or sometime during Alexander's campaign. These two men were therefore adult in the late 330s, which makes them sons of Balakros by an earlier wife than Phila, and so they were step-grandsons of Antipater. Phila was therefore Balakros' second wife, married just before he was to set off, with his sons, as part of Alexander's Asian adventure.[10]

It may be presumed that both Phila and her anonymous sister were married to Balakros and Alexander Lynkestis as a means of forging political alliances. Both marriages probably took place very late in Philip's reign, or in the brief period between the death of Philip and the beginning of Alexander's Asian campaigns. The eminence of the Lynkestian family at the time is obvious, and it may be assumed also that the family of Nikanor was also prominent, but only just less so than either Antipater or Alexander; after all, Balakros was selected as the governor of a major satrapy and held the post for nine years.

It does not seem as if any other of Antipater's children were married during Alexander's reign. He certainly had two more daughters available to marry off for political reasons in the period after Alexander's death. They may have been too young before 334 to be married, and after that date their possible husbands were away on campaign. Two of Antipater's sons, Philip and Iolaos, were living as pages at Alexander's court during the last years of the king's life.[11] This implies that they were not yet 18 years of age in 323, since it was at that age they would graduate to serve for a year or so as an infantryman before moving on to become companions.[12] They were (obviously) not yet married. They have been described as the youngest of Antipater's sons, but this may not be correct.

There were also four more sons – Nikanor, Pleistarchos, Alexarchos and Perilaos. These were all born after Kassander, who was 30 years old in 325. None of them is recorded as attending on King Alexander during any of the campaigns, and it is thus to be assumed that they remained with their father at his Macedonian court, as did the two unmarried daughters. But Kassander certainly was old enough at the start of the campaigns to be serving in the army (aged about 20 in 335), and in one source he is said to have commanded a unit of Thracians and Paeonians at the battle at the Granikos, though it is generally argued that this name is a mistake for an Asander.[13] He did not go on the great campaign with Alexander. He was probably a page at Philip's court, and this may have applied also to one or two of his brothers. Iolaos was old and mature enough in 322/321 (but probably still no more than 19) to act as an envoy for his father to Perdikkas in negotiating the marriage of his sister Nikaia,[14] and Philip was an accomplished military commander by 313[15] and even before – and so in his mid-twenties.

We do not hear anything like this about Pleistarchos, Perilaos, or Alexarchos. Pleistarchos is first recorded in 313, by which time he was clearly adult; he later took a major part in Kassander's wars.[16] Alexarchos and Perilaos are even less visible in the sources, which might suggest that they were even younger than Philip and Iolaos. All three would appear therefore to have been too young to attend Alexander's court even in his last year.

There was also another branch of Antipater's family. He had a brother, probably younger than he, called Kassandros (after whom his own son was no doubt named). Little is known of him, and his existence is only recorded in a *scholion* of a poem of Theokritos. This recorded that Berenike, one of the wives of Ptolemy I, was the daughter of Antigone, who was the daughter of Kassander the brother of Antipater.[17] Antigone had married a man called Magas, and their daughter Berenike married another Philip. If Kassander was Antipater's brother, Antigone and Magas were contemporaries of Kassander and the elderly Antipater and Berenike and Philip were contemporaries of Antipater's younger children; Berenike was perhaps a little older than Antipater's daughter Eurydike. Magas and Philip are generally referred to as 'obscure' and 'of low birth', but their obscurity is only in our own modern knowledge, not necessarily in their own time. It is highly likely that these women, niece and grand-niece of the formidable Antipater, would be married to men of standing, wealth, and importance in Macedon. It may thus be assumed that both men represented families with whom it was worth Antipater and Kassander joining politically. The fact that we do not know who they were is not relevant.

Berenike and Philip had two or three children, two named for her parents, and one, less certainly theirs, called Theoxene; it may also be that they had others – this is another 'obscure' area, for those who were recorded are only the ones who made a mark on the man who wrote the *scholion* on Theokritos' poem. These children had been born before 321, by which time Philip was probably dead. Berenike went to Egypt as a companion for her cousin Eurydike; it may be assumed that Berenike was married by 326 and probably before – she had three children at least by 321. Therefore she had been born in the late 340s. The marriages of this branch of the family might be considered further attempts at linking Antipater with other Macedonian families.

Neither Philip nor Magas appear to have taken part in the Asian campaigns. If Berenike was born in the 340s, her mother Antigone had probably married in that decade. Both men were thus of the right age to participate in the wars: like Antipater's sons, therefore, they had stayed in Macedon. It is worth noting that this was not used against any of these men in the polemics of the years after Alexander's death. The exchange of insults was vicious enough to include an accusation that Kassander and Iolaos had been involved in poisoning Alexander and so securing his death, yet none of those who stayed in Macedon were accused of avoiding the dangers of the Persian war.[18] Presumably it was well enough understood that staying in Macedon was not a safe or soft option – more men were killed in the battle of Megalopolis than in all Alexander's great battles put together. Antipater, after all, fought two strenuous wars during Alexander's lifetime and another shortly afterwards, and no doubt such men as Magas and Philip, and perhaps those of Antipater's own sons who were old enough, took an active part – every Macedonian man was trained to arms, after all.

Antipater's attempt at building a network of family alliances through the marriages of his daughters thus suffered a serious setback when his son-in-law Alexander Lynkestis was imprisoned and then executed; another serious blow came six years later in 324 with the death of Balakros. There is no record of further attempts at constructing such alliances while King Alexander was alive. Why this was so may have several explanations. The eligible husbands were mainly involved in the Asian wars, though it cannot be that Kassander and his cousins were the only such men who were left in Macedonia – the 13,500 Macedonian soldiers left with Antipater presumably had some commanders who were eligible as husbands for Antipater's daughters. Yet their names are unknown (Korrhagos the commander defeated in the Peloponnese is almost the only one), and most of the most prominent Macedonians of later years were in Asia. This would not stop them from marrying, of course, though less formal liaisons seem to have been much more likely and are well attested for all ranks from Alexander to the private soldiers. Alexander compelled the officers to marry Persian ladies in the great ceremony at Susa during his last year, though few of these marriages lasted. Negotiating a marriage alliance with a man in a campaigning army thousands of kilometres away would scarcely be easy.

One wonders, also, if the forging of political alliances among the Macedonian aristocracy was something that became especially difficult while King Alexander was still alive. The king had dealt harshly with at least two such alliances already – that linking his father with Attalos and Kleopatra, and that around Amyntas Perdikka, a set that also included the Lynkestians. He could not do much to dissuade a renewal of a network centred on Antipater, though by eliminating the Lynkestians he had made his attitude quite clear, and Antipater was sensitive enough to the general situation to avoid reawakening Alexander's fears, perhaps assisted by the youthfulness of his daughters, who may not have been of marriageable age until the late 320s. Alexander had also eliminated the group around Parmenion – who was also connected with Attalos – in the most dramatic way, as Antipater clearly noted.

It is not known why Antipater's male children all stayed in Macedon during the great campaigns; some were clearly too young to be sent to war, but Kassander was not, and perhaps one or two others may have been old enough to take part; two were only teenagers when Alexander returned from the east, and so would have been far too young at the start of the campaign. Age was clearly part of the explanation, but this does not cover all of the boys, nor does it apply to Magas and Philip – or even perhaps to Antipater's brother, though he may have been too old, or perhaps had already died. It must therefore be that Kassander at least was deliberately kept at home by his father, and maybe also a couple of the others. Their youth is a reasonable explanation, Kassander's supposed poor health is another, but it is worth considering that by not allowing his sons to campaign with Alexander, Antipater was saving them from becoming hostages; Alexander was certainly not above controlling men by such means. (The prolonged detention of Alexander Lynkestis may well be a case of this.) The two sons who became Alexander's pages were presumably sent to his headquarters towards the end of that campaign. If they were 18 in 323, they could even have joined him in the Indian campaign, though it is much more likely that they were sent to Babylon, or perhaps to Susa, to await his return.

This is all to a degree conjectural, of course, but it remains a fact that almost as soon as Alexander was dead, and Antipater had survived the outburst of Greek rage that followed (the 'Lamian War') he set about constructing a new network of alliances, deploying three of his daughters for that purpose, though apparently not his sons. This was a necessary part of the politics of the Macedonian aristocratic society, of which Antipater after Alexander's death was the head, a process that Alexander's campaign and his suspiciousness had put on hold for several years.

Suspicion of Antipater had clearly existed in Alexander's mind from the time he began his great adventure. Given the history of the previous years this is hardly surprising. The treason of his son-in-law Alexander Lynkestis was fuel for the flame, but any chance of toppling the Macedonian governor – if the king had wished to do so, which is perhaps unlikely for some time – disappeared with the problems of Thrace and the Spartan War, for removing Antipater in the midst of war was clearly unwise. The fire continued to be fed by the accusations and warnings of Olympias in her letters,[19] but by the time he might have been able to remove Antipater the latter's victory in the Spartan War rendered him well protected; he was clearly necessary by that time to maintain control of Thrace and Greece, and removing him would probably incite new rebellions; and then the sheer distance from Macedon of the king and his preoccupation first with the chase after Dareios, then with Baktria, then with India, made it impractical to move against Antipater, since the king was so far away he was then months out of touch with European events. Actually, there is no serious evidence that Alexander had any intention of moving against Antipater until the last year of his reign – unless it is the treatment of Alexander Lynkestis – and even then, his move was ambiguous. It is clear that Olympias' complaints were understood by Alexander to be complaints about her lack of power, but he would not yield to her in this. Antipater was as willing to complain of her attitude as she was about him; but in neither case did Alexander yield.[20] Having them complain about each other was a useful source of information, even if the allegations had to be discounted.

If Antipater's authority was originally intended to cover Macedon only, the problems of Thrace and Greece in effect expanded it to the Danube and Crete. From 331, if not before, Antipater was wielding the authority of a Macedonian king, in succession to the power of Philip and Alexander between 340 and 334. This may not have been Alexander's original intention, for Memnon in Thrace, Korrhagos and other Macedonian commanders in Greece, including Harpalos in Megara, and the naval commanders – Hegelochos and Amphoteros – were all his own appointees, and theoretically they were only removable or controllable by him as king, or as league hegemon. But this was not how it turned out. Whatever really happened in Thrace, Memnon, the king's appointment, had to be removed and replaced, and it was Antipater and his Macedonian forces who had dealt with the problem. Similarly in the Peloponnese Korrhagos, who was presumably the garrison commander in the Corinth citadel, was defeated by Agis and, again, the Macedonian (and League) position had to be rescued and revived by Antipater and his Macedonian army.

Alexander in effect recognized this by sending to Antipater the supplies of money with which he had increased the size of his army from 13,500 men to 40,000. To recruit, or levy, forces from the League allies, Antipater would need to be seen to have Alexander's backing and authority. And so from 331 onwards he had a quasi-royal position, despite the henpecking from Olympias.

But one result of the victory at Megalopolis was that Olympias saw that it was impossible for her to persuade her son to remove Antipater. As the most senior and most prominent Macedonian after Antipater actually in the kingdom she probably expected that if Antipater died or was killed she would be able to step in as his successor. In doing so she would merely be replicating the methods of seizing power by which both Philip and Alexander had received the rule of the kingdom – by being on the spot at the crucial moment. Whether Alexander would have acquiesced in such an internal *coup d'état* is of course unknowable, for Antipater survived. But for Olympias it was obviously a chance worth taking. So when he had survived and was victorious and had established his own power so that he was unremovable, and when it became clear that Alexander, heading ever further east into parts unknown even by hearsay, and losing any interest in events in Greece, Olympias moved to Epeiros. Her brother had died in Italy, and her daughter Kleopatra was the effective regent of this kingdom; Olympias went to help out and ended effectively in control. For Antipater this was an unexpected benefit of his victory; he had no more trouble from Olympias for the rest of Alexander's lifetime.

Both Diodoros and Pausanias claim that Olympias' move to Epeiros was in fear of Antipater.[21] But both notices are tacked on to accounts of later events, and it is unbelievable that Antipater was such a threat to her that she feared for her life. More convincing is an explanation that the death of her brother at Epeiros had opened the way for her to exercise real power there, rather than struggle for influence in Macedon.[22] But the effect was to move her out of Antipater's orbit, so that both of them were relieved of the other's presence.

From 330 onwards, therefore, Antipater was unopposed in Macedon and Greece. His military victories had seen off the internal critics, including Olympias, and had cowed his Greek enemies. But the one enemy, as he seemed to be becoming, was the distant, paranoid king. Antipater had to assume that if Alexander survived, and if he himself was still governor of Macedon when Alexander returned from distant parts, he would be removed, one way or another. It was likely, given the fates of Parmenion and Philotas, of Amyntas Perdikka, and of Alexander Lynkestis, and of all the others whom the king decided were his enemies, that he would be killed, probably after a show trial in which the verdict would be rendered by a gang of Alexander's own sycophantic courtiers, or by an assembly of soldiers harangued by the king.[23]

It therefore behoved Antipater to look to his defences. He had to gather supporters in both Macedon and Greece, and he had at the same time to make himself indispensable to Alexander. He could reasonably assume that the king would no longer wish to return to Macedon but would wish to go on more expeditions when he came back from wherever he had gone. If Antipater could maintain control in Greece and Macedon, preferably by a visible and pervasive control that only he was competent to understand and deal with, he might well be safe.

The removal of Olympias from Macedon left Antipater with a clear field to attach individual Macedonians and Macedonian families to him by links of patronage. These links were likely to be fragile, since all would know that the king's return might well upset all such arrangements, even if he operated at a distance, and it would not be difficult for Alexander to snap such links. But some at least would stay with Antipater, and Macedon had a long history of faction among the aristocracy.

We have more information about the control of Greece, all of which can be seen in two antagonistic ways. For example, there is the case of the Aitolians and the city of Oiniadai. The city was in a strategic position so far as the Aitolian League was concerned, at the mouth of the Kampelos River, which provided a convenient route into the league's territory. About 333 the Aitolians seized the city and drove out the population, either into exile or into slavery. They had therefore 'destroyed' the city as a community, though no doubt they kept control of the place itself as a part of their league. Alexander claimed to be angered by this and vowed to punish the Aitolians on behalf of the Oiniadaians.[24]

When the Spartan War began, therefore, the Aitolians took the Spartan part, though without undertaking any serious military activity. Antipater in his march south from Macedon ignored the Oiniadian issue – the main enemy was Sparta, and to be distracted into another fight in Aitolia would hand the victory to Agis. Nevertheless, the vow of the king seemed to be an instruction to Antipater to attend to the matter. This would require a war between Macedon and Aitolia, not a prospect to be undertaken lightly by either side. Antipater instead chose to be diplomatic, negotiated with the Aitolians, and appears to have established friendly relations with the League. Oiniadai remained Aitolian.[25]

This could be seen as recruiting a Greek power as his personal ally, by defusing a potentially very difficult political situation, or a deliberate disobedience of the king's wishes, in order that Antipater might assert his effective independence. It is not known how explicit Alexander had been on the matter, and what exactly he aimed to do, but Antipater surely knew that Alexander was angered by the Aitolian action and had vowed revenge on behalf of the victims. By befriending Alexander's stated enemies he was setting himself up for punishment. It is also possible, of course, that Antipater did not take Alexander's threat seriously, especially since it was uttered far off in Iran, and the king then went even further away.

Antipater was on friendly terms with at least three prominent Athenians; Phokion, Demades and Pytheas, all notable orators and politicians. Athens had held aloof from the Spartan War, nor had it provided more than minimal naval assistance in the Aegean naval crisis in 334 – 333, sending only twenty triremes to the allied fleet, and the crews could not be paid due to Alexander's cash shortage.[26] On the other hand, when the grain fleet had been blocked from getting through the Hellespont, 100 Athenian ships were suddenly available.[27] That is, Athens' policy was dictated purely by self-interest, as was only to be expected. A naval stand-off in the Aegean was by no means unwelcome, given that two of Athens' enemies were fighting each other, but opening the way for the grain ships was a vital interest for the city. The politicians no doubt had in mind the Athenians serving with Alexander as part of the League forces, and those captured by Alexander at the Granikos fight, who he released in the midst of the Spartan crisis, either as an inducement to Athens to join Antipater, or to remain neutral.[28] But it was clear that Athens would cooperate with Macedon only when it was seen as providing an advantage to the city. Antipater clearly understood this and had no complaints about Athens' neutrality; its open enmity was, however, something to avoid, and if it could be so avoided by diplomacy, all the better. Hence his apparent friendship with Demades, Phokion and Pytheas.

These three politicians were linked to Antipater in different ways. Demades was bribable and gulped down Antipater's bribes without stint; he was consistently pro-Macedonian. Phokion was wholly unbribable, but was loyal to Antipater as a friend, while openly advocating an accommodation with Macedon.[29] Pytheas was a friend of Antipater, and yet he advocated an anti-Macedonian policy; when the crisis came he was able to take refuge with Antipater, and no hard words said. But friendship was not wholly the point, though it clearly seems to have existed. Antipater's contacts with these Athenian politicians would allow him to exert influence in Athens, or at the least to be informed of what was happening in the city. It was a system that clearly worked well enough for several years and helped to promote Athenian neutrality.[30]

It would not necessarily have appealed to Alexander, who could count several instances suggesting clear Athenian hostility – the assistance given by Samos, an Athenian island, to the Persian fleet, the Athenian mercenaries fighting against him, the Athenian envoys sent to Dareios whom he had captured after the battle of Issos. In addition, Antipater may well have preferred that Alexander retain the Athenian soldiers and prisoners under his control as a means of holding down that Athenian hostility. It is not known what precisely Alexander expected by releasing the prisoners, but it was hardly a friendly gesture towards Antipater, who faced the consequences, which were likely to relieve Athens of the need for neutrality.

Contacts with Athenian politicians were tricky matters; in Athens contact with Macedon might be construed as treasonable; in Macedon friendship with Athenians might be considered similarly. As an example there was the case of Leokrates, the grain merchant who had been at Megara alongside, and possibly advising, Harpalos. He had exiled himself from Athens with his family in 338 when the Macedonian army seemed to be threatening, and he returned to Athens in 330, presumably believing that all was forgiven. He might also have reckoned that his activities in negotiating the movement of supplies of grain might have been regarded in Athens as helpful – he was involved in the export of Epeirote grain through Megara at one point. Instead he was prosecuted on his return by the politician Lykourgos, the most important man in Athens at the time, in effect accused of treason for having left the city. He was acquitted, but only because the jury tied. It may also be that one element in his prosecution was that he had Macedonian contacts, including no doubt Harpalos.[31] It is also an indication of the powerful anti-Macedonian sentiment in the city. Antipater's contacts could also be considered as attempting to suborn prominent Athenians, but from Alexander's point of view they might be seen as building a potential alliance between Antipater and the city, directed against the king.

Antipater's diplomatic effectiveness neutralized the two major powers of Greece for a time. Between them the Aitolians and Athens, in the absence of Thebes and Sparta, were the only serious military powers of any size in Greece south of Macedon; each was supervised by nearby Macedonian garrisons: at Ambrakia (not far from Oiniadai), which blocked any westward moves by the Aitolians, at Chalkis and at the Theban Kadmeia, which may be said to, if not threaten, then overlook, Athens. A garrison at Corinth blocked the land routes out of the Peloponnese, as Agis had found, and provided a point for overseeing the Peloponnesian states.

A further strand to the Macedonian rope of control constraining the Greek cities was Antipater's support for a series of tyrannies. Chairon at Pellene had been installed with Antipater's direct support; others ruled at Sikyon, and in Messene.[32] Sparta, of course, was now flat on its back after the defeat at Megalopolis. Megalopolis itself and Argos had been supporters of

Macedon in the Spartan War and were therefore stuck with that policy. The League's decisions on Elis, Tegea, and the Arkadians sufficiently weakened those states, partly by the fines imposed; more effective, perhaps, were the internal convulsions which always followed defeat, bringing to power groups who were either not hostile to Macedon or were prepared even to be friendly; so these states remained quiet.

But here again we find Antipater instituting his own policy in defiance of Alexander's stated wishes. Alexander had favoured democracies, yet Antipater supported, or installed, several tyrannies. No doubt he found it more convenient to deal with a single man than a potentially turbulent democracy, or even an awkward oligarchy, to which he was also partial. Tyrannies were more amenable than either of the alternatives, yet they were also even more unstable than democracies, at least in the long run, and Alexander's preference had been clear. Antipater in this, as over Oiniadai, was acting directly against Alexander's instructions.

The relative ease with which Agis had produced a major army, and the similar facility with which Antipater had recruited an even bigger force to oppose him, demonstrated that Greece was still a land of soldiers. Not long after the end of the Spartan War, Alexander dismissed the League troops he had taken on campaign with him, though they were allowed to re-enlist as mercenaries if they chose.[33] One would imagine that those who had collected a substantial booty would take it, and their pay, and return to Greece. Since some at least of these men would be anti-Macedonian, their arrival at their home cities would certainly fuel local hostility towards Macedon. At about the same time, Antipater recruited 6,000 mercenaries in Greece and sent them into Asia.[34] The sheer number of soldiers available in Greece was a clear threat to Macedonian power. Alexander when he invaded India had an army that was largely composed of mercenaries; these would, if they survived, also eventually return to Greece.

Resentment in Greece at Antipater's policies grew during the six years after the Spartan War. He might hope to keep Aitolia and Athens quiet by diplomacy, he might control the Peloponnese by supporting tyrannies and Macedonian supporters, he might keep strategic garrisons alert, but all this angered many of the Greeks, both in those cities and in others. Alexander encountered large numbers of mercenaries from Greece in the Persian forces, all the way from the Granikos to Baktria; some he killed, many he dismissed or even recruited; some were recruited by his satrapal governors, but many of them evaded his control in the end and returned to Greece. They were, by definition, inimical to Macedon. Many of them gathered at the well-organized mercenary market at Cape Tainaron.

Thrace became a problem again. Memnon's replacement as governor there, Zopyrion, may have been in office by 330.[35] His activity is wholly unknown except that in 325 he was involved in a war far to the north of his province, of which the only incident is the end, a siege of the city of Olbia.[36] Within Thrace, the heir of the former Odrysian Thracian kingdom, Seuthes, controlled an area of the northern inland. He had already attempted to renew contacts with Athens by sending his son Rheboulas as his envoy there in 330. This was soon after the trouble connected with Memnon, but, after the latter's elimination and the defeat of Agis, Athens could do no more than merely acknowledge Rheboulas' presence.[37]

Zopyrion may be invisible in the years between his appointment and his war (that is, *c.*330–325), but he was clearly busy. The war he fought was conducted, so it is claimed, by an army of '30,000' men, so this would be unlikely, given the demands of both Alexander and Antipater for Macedonian soldiers and mercenaries, to be in any way a 'Macedonian' army, nor is the quoted number really believable. Zopyrion had surely recruited Greeks where he could, particularly mercenaries, but mainly his own subject Thracians. In 322, his successor Lysimachos conducted a war against Seuthes with just 4,000 infantry and 2,000 cavalry; Seuthes fielded a force of 28,000. It may be supposed that Zopyrion had a larger force than Lysimachos, even if 30,000 seems extravagant. The resources and manpower of Thrace were substantial.

Zopyrion was beaten, though not until his campaign was well north of the Danube. One major result of his defeat was that Seuthes, who seems to have survived Alexander's and Antipater's wars by accepting Macedonian suzerainty, now renounced his subordination. Zopyrion had been fighting the Getai (who had been attacked by both Philip and Alexander in the previous generation); his force was destroyed, either by storms, according to Curtius, or by the enemy, according to Justin.[38] The collapse of the Macedonian position in Thrace followed; that this happened as a result of a single defeat illustrates the fragility of the whole Macedonian imperial system.

Antipater can only have watched this expedition with some anxiety. Zopyrion had been Alexander's appointee, so Antipater could not interfere with Zopyrion's war. If after his defeat Macedon was threatened he could then intervene, as when rescuing or fighting Memnon, but by the time the repercussions of defeat might have been apprehended, in 324, he had many other problems on his plate. And perhaps Seuthes was cunning enough not to become his open enemy – he fought Lysimachos only when attacked. Some official in Thrace must have taken up Zopyrion's job as governor and was perhaps able to hold the main position. At any rate Antipater did not become involved.

The balance in Greece and Macedon that had been achieved in the aftermath of Agis' War began to be upset as Alexander's return, from his Indian campaign, still alive, became known. He spent the winter of 325/324 in Karmania, where his depleted army recovered from the disaster of the desert crossing, and from there the news spread that he was on his way. A warning of his mood came when he ordered the execution of Kleandros and Sitalkes for oppression and maladministration in Media, together with '600' soldiers who had been their instruments of oppression. It is unlikely that it was coincidental that these were two of Parmenion's executioners; a third, Herakon, though 'acquitted' at first, was later accused by his subjects in Susiana and also executed. The fourth executed, Agathon, was included in those killed by one of the sources.[39] Alexander was thus punishing these men because of their continuing unpopularity for killing Parmenion, which had been done on his orders four years before. (Sitalkes was also a member of the Odrysian Thracian royal house, like Seuthes; no doubt this helped towards his condemnation, and perhaps towards Seuthes' hostility.) The accusation of oppression was a mere excuse. Justice and loyalty did not enter the question.

From Karmania Alexander marched westwards, having conducted a purge of satraps who had been abusing their positions. He arrived with particular ideas about the future of his empire, and with the knowledge that conditions in Greece were unstable. He had with him a large number of Greek soldiers, now mercenaries, who were due to be discharged, and their arrival in Greece would be disturbing. He was reminded, when he reached Susa, of another issue in Greece. A considerable number of Greek envoys were waiting for him there, and more at Babylon, with a variety of complaints, of which one common factor was Antipater. This was, however, not the only problem, for several of the envoys were exiles from their home cities or were speaking on behalf of exiles.[40]

It is probable that the complaints about Antipater enlarged his apprehensions about his power, but it was some time before he produced a method of dealing with him. For the exiles, however, he was able to look back and recall that he had already been annoyed about two places from which exiles had been driven: Samos, whose exiles were brought specifically to his attention by Gorgos, son of Theodotos, from Iasos; and the island had welcomed the Persian fleet back in 333 and provided supplies. Gorgos had already persuaded Alexander to grant an adjustment of territory at Iasos, and he was recorded as helping the Epidaurians in another dispute.[41] He was also a man who could speak directly to Alexander. Gorgos was clearly capable of persuading the king in relatively minor matters, and he and his brother Minnion brought the matter of the Samian exiles to him, for some of them were living at his home town of Iasos.[42] But Alexander went further than Gorgos' request to allow the Samian exiles to return to their island. He added those of Oiniadai to the package, and then enlarged the whole to an instruction that the Greek cities everywhere should readmit all their exiled citizens; this was the 'Exiles' Decree'.[43]

The issue was in part the problem of the large numbers of mercenaries who were now unemployed in Europe and Asia as a result of Alexander's own policies; they were a danger in that they could easily be recruited by an enemy, quite apart from their propensity to theft and riot; by ordering their home cities to receive them back Alexander may have thought he was solving the problem. This he announced first at an army assembly at Susa.[44] The news swiftly travelled to Greece, all the more speedily because, in the case of Samos and Oiniadai, the decree affected the two most powerful Greek states, Athens and Aitolia. When it was announced at the Olympic Games in August 324 20,000 exiles had turned up to hear it, and of course greeted the announcement with great enthusiasm. Indeed it may be that the wider 'Exiles' Decree' was developed as a way of avoiding direct strikes at Aitolia and Athens by launching a process that affected every other state. But it did challenge those two to accept Alexander's authority in the matter or defy him and meet the consequences. Other cities also had problems with the policy; a decree from Alexander – which he had no legal right to pronounce – was one thing, implementing it by decisions of city assemblies was quite another.

This was in fact a version of the method Alexander was using in the summer of 324. In an army assembly at Opis in Babylonia he had faced a 'mutiny' by his soldiers in which it is clear that his aim was to bring into his forces a newly trained band of 30,000 Iranian soldiers. This was not acceptable to the Macedonians, but Alexander first provoked them into the mutiny, and then dismissed them from his service. After a couple of days during which they came to the realization that he was actually serious, he brought forward the Persian troops as their replacements, at which the Macedonians gave in, begged his forgiveness, and when he gave it, he had achieved his aim. The process of the Exiles' Decree was very similar: Aitolia and Athens were provoked into a show of defiance; the rest of Greece is said to have generally supported the move, which sounds rather like a propaganda move, for it would likely cause real problems when implemented in detail.[45] Athens negotiated a partial surrender through Demosthenes, who was at the Games and negotiated with Nikanor of Stageira, who had brought the official decree, thereby accepting to some extent Alexander's authority in the matter.[46] There is, however, no sign that the Aitolians followed suit.

Antipater was evidently not consulted on any of this, though in the Exiles' Decree Alexander said he had written to Antipater to give him instruction to supervise the process. It is doubtful that he made any attempt to explain how this should be done, and it is unlikely that Antipater made any real attempt to do so. Antipater was conscious of Alexander's approach from out of the east, and he must have expected some measures to be announced – on the issue of Oiniadai in particular, and possibly on Samos too, and on that of his support for tyrannies; he had ignored Alexander's wishes on these for several years. He could no doubt fully appreciate the effects of the moves against both Greek powers, but the more general Exiles' Decree probably came as a surprise. He could also appreciate that the effort of integrating exiles with their domestic enemies would preoccupy most Greek cities for some time to come. But it was the two major states that would need the most careful attention.

By 324 two of Antipater's sons attended Alexander's court, one of them in a trusted position as his cup-bearer. As Alexander came west, also Antipater sent his son Kassander to meet him, possibly with a report on Greek and Macedonian affairs, perhaps, depending on the timing (which is inexact) with a warning about the implementation of the Exiles' Decree and the problems of Samos and Oiniadai. Antipater will have heard, probably about the same time as the first (unofficial) news arrived of the measures to restore the exiles, that Alexander had requested that the Greeks render him divine honours.[47] If the reaction of Antipater's son mirrored that of his father, Antipater will have been both dismissive and scornful of the request.[48] But it did not affect him or his position, since the request – which most Greek cities complied with, with whatever degree of reluctance – was not directed towards Macedon; Alexander retained enough sense to realize that the whole idea would offend the Macedonians. The reaction of Damis of Sparta – 'If Alexander wants to be a God, let him be a God' – and Demosthenes' scorn – 'let him be Poseidon or Ares if he wishes' – might well have been that of any Macedonian, but perhaps with a more pious overlay of disgust.[49]

Having been given the task of overseeing the implementation of the restoration of the exiles, Antipater found that in Athens the agreement between Demosthenes and Nikanor allowed for an appeal by the city to the king, thereby bypassing Antipater's stated task. On Aitolia Antipater could probably do nothing, given Aitolian obduracy, despite his earlier diplomatic contacts, and he must have been contemplating using force. Elsewhere he could do nothing but wait to see how in each city the issue was argued out. But then he was assailed by two new crises, which had a much more direct effect on Macedon and Antipater than either the divine honours question or that of the exiles. So far as can be judged he must have heard of them more or less simultaneously. One was that Harpalos, who had been Alexander's imperial treasurer since he returned to Asia from his mission in Megara seven years before, had arrived in Greece once more. But this time it was a true flight to escape Alexander's vengeance, and he had arrived with a small fleet of ships, an army of 6,000 mercenaries, a famous Athenian courtesan, and a very large quantity of Alexander's money, reported to be 5,000 talents' worth. He was blocked from entering Athens' harbour – it probably looked rather like an invasion – and sailed off to deposit his soldiers and ships at Cape Tainaron. He then returned to Athens in a single ship, but with part of the money. This time he was allowed to land. The money was deposited for safekeeping – to stop him using it to raise a revolution – on the Acropolis.

Harpalos had taken some considerable time on his journey. He had left his post at Babylon early in 324, when it became clear that Alexander was in a murderous mood over the misbehaviour of several of his satraps – exactly the offence Harpalos had committed. He had stopped in Kilikia for a time, where he apparently recruited his mercenaries, and arrived at Athens about the same time Nikanor was reaching Olympia with the Exiles' Decree. Two or three weeks may then be allowed for his journey to Cape Tainaron and his return to Athens. Antipater may have heard about his flight from Kilikia, where his daughter Phila was probably living – her husband Balakros was satrap there, though he may already have been killed in the war in the mountains. Antipater may not have felt any concern until Harpalos arrived in the Aegean. To him, as to the Greeks, the Harpalos issue and the exiles problem happened at much the same time.[50]

The reaction in Athens to Harpalos' new arrival was confusion. The presence of the money eventually persuaded the citizens to go to war, but not yet. For the moment it must have appeared that Alexander's empire was in great trouble, but how to deal with Harpalos became the subject of internal Athenian political disputes. The Macedonian reaction was threefold. From Asia Minor Philoxenos, who had some sort of wide authority there distinct from that of the satraps, demanded Harpalos' extradition, and the return of the money.[51] But Philoxenos was one of the men who had substituted for Harpalos during his mission to Megara, and had been ousted to his present job when Harpalos returned.[52] It may be assumed that he was acting in Alexander's name, but it is not altogether clear that he was acting with Alexander's authority, and his personal motive renders him suspect – he still resented his demotion all those years before.

From Macedonia, Antipater similarly demanded Harpalos' extradition, and the surrender of Alexander's money. Although this was Persian loot, it had certainly passed into Alexander's ownership, and it had certainly been stolen. In addition, Olympias from Epeiros made the same demand, though she cannot have been able to quote any authority other than herself – but no doubt the money would have been useful.[53] But with these separate and successive demands reaching them, the Athenians were able to delay any decision until word came directly from Alexander.

Harpalos eventually solved part of the problem by escaping from his open arrest in Athens, probably with Athenian help. He fled to the mercenaries' camp at Cape Tainaron again, then went to Crete, where he was murdered by one of his officers.[54] Athens got the money.

The second problem to be directed at Antipater was the news that a large force of disabled, old, and time-expired veterans was on its way from Babylonia to be demobilized in Macedon. They were commanded by Krateros and Polyperchon with three other subordinate commanders. Krateros was also given instructions that he was to replace Antipater as Alexander's governor in Macedon.[55] Whether this was publicized is very doubtful, though it was apparently not a secret; a message was also sent to Antipater that he should bring out the next set of recruits himself.[56] It was not difficult for him to put the two items together and understand that Krateros' ultimate mission was to take over his post, and he was to be, in effect, deported into Asia.

Krateros set out soon after the mutiny at Opis which had taken place in June 324, moving very slowly westwards. His convoy was slow because of the men it comprised, many of whom probably would only be able to travel slowly – Krateros himself was unwell, so much so that Alexander gave him Polyperchon as a second in command in case he did not live to complete the journey. The convoy was presumably also accompanied by a large number of baggage wagons. They will have travelled north along the Tigris, then west through Mesopotamia, crossing the Euphrates at Thapsakos, and on into Kilikia. The whole journey was a distance of at least 1,300km; travelling at 10km a day, with two days' rest in six, it will have taken them six months from Babylonia to Kilikia, where we know the convoy stopped. Beginning in June or perhaps July, they will have reached Kilikia in December or January, by which time the passes through the Taurus Mountains were closed. It is often assumed that Krateros moved slowly because he was reluctant to face Antipater with the news of his replacement, but his slow progress can be more easily explained by the distance involved and by the slow travel imposed by his convoy. And there is no indication that Alexander was concerned in the least at his slowness.[57]

At the same time there is no doubt that Krateros and his men seem to have become stuck in Kilikia. He did not move from that area for several months – the passes will have been open by March or April at the latest – until sometime after Alexander died (June 323), and did so only after Antipater had appealed to him for assistance when he was besieged in Lamia later in that year. Alexander's death will have rendered him uncertain about his instructions, and then new instructions arrived from Babylon. Some explanation for his delay in Kilikia before he heard of Alexander's death must be found, however, and several have been suggested, of varying plausibility. Kilikia itself was probably in some confusion. At some point in 324, before Krateros and his men arrived, the satrap Balakros was killed in fighting an insurgent group, the Larandians, in the Pisidian hills. No replacement satrap seems to have been appointed before Krateros arrived. Further, between Balakros' death and Krateros' arrival, Harpalos had spent some time in the province. Krateros could well have found it necessary to stop in Kilikia to help sort things out.[58]

Second, Alexander had ordered the construction of a large new navy in Syrian and Kilikian ports and shipyards, with the intention of campaigning in the western Mediterranean. These were to be ready for his use after his planned campaign around Arabia, and so probably in 322. When Krateros eventually moved on towards Greece, one of his subordinates, 'White' Kleitos, took command of a substantial fleet, which he sailed from Kilikia to the Hellespont. So one of the tasks being undertaken during the halt in Kilikia was to gather the fleet that Alexander had ordered. It could be that Krateros, perhaps on supplementary instructions from Alexander, had to take measures to speed up construction of the ships. This, it must be admitted, is one of the less likely reasons for his delay in Kilikia, but Krateros was one of the two or three most prominent men in Alexander's service, equivalent to Antipater (as his putative appointment to Macedon shows), and if anyone had responsibility for pushing forward Alexander's plans in the west, he did. Even less likely is the suggestion that Krateros was waiting for the new recruits ordered up by Alexander, who were to be commanded by Antipater, to arrive in Kilikia; this would have left Macedon without a governor for several months, and both Antipater and Krateros knew there was a crisis brewing.[59]

And finally there is one more possibility. It may be that Alexander had reconsidered his plan and had realized that removing Antipater before Krateros reached Macedon would cause trouble. In that case his obvious recourse was to delay everything. Here, the obvious source of his information will have been Kassander, who appears to have remained with the court until shortly after Alexander died. Krateros had already stopped his journey, for there is that gap of two months between April, when he could get through the passes, and June, when Alexander died. Of course, he could have been busy with all the tasks that have been suggested, but unless he had been given strict instructions to carry out those tasks, the best explanation for his delay in moving on is that he had been told by Alexander to wait. There is no evidence for this, but then there is no evidence for any of the other possible reasons.

There are, therefore, plenty of reasons to be discovered for Krateros' delay in Kilikia, some more convincing than others; only the first, the condition of Kilikia, has any real credibility to it. But there was one further reason (or perhaps a pair of reasons) that might be considered more convincing. Kilikia was probably in some confusion for more reasons than the aftermath of the death of the satrap Balakros. Harpalos in his flight from Alexander's wrath had stopped to recruit troops there. He was addicted to Athenian courtesans, and set up his current one, Glykera, in the satrapal palace at Tarsos while in the province; a statue of the lady was also set up at Rhosos on the border of Syria.[60] This implies a fairly lengthy stay, perhaps several months – he had left Babylon well before the arrival of Alexander there in May or June. No doubt the approach of Krateros was one of the reasons he moved on, to appear in Athens some time after the Olympic Games in August 324, to disrupt Athenian politics with his presence and his money.

Harpalos' stay in Kilikia was clearly disruptive. When Krateros arrived, therefore, quite apart from the closure of the passes, he had good reasons for a halt in his march. Even if he took no part in urging on the construction of the ships, he would need to see that Kilikia was restored to some sort of order and could take advantage of the winter to rest his party. He also found, in residence in the palace at Tarsos, Antipater's daughter Phila, the widow of Balakros. (Where she was during Glykera's residence is not known, but 'elsewhere' is a reasonable guess.) And there arrived at some point, while Krateros was present, Antipater's son Kassander.

Presumably Antipater understood that Krateros was intended to replace him, though he may not have been told officially. The instruction to conduct the recruits to Babylon was apparently sent out about the same time that Krateros began his march. It will have travelled much more quickly than the marching column, so the arrival of Kassander in Kilikia in the winter (January/February) of 323 is about the right timing for Antipater's reply to have reached Alexander. (Kassander reached Babylon some time before the king's death, in time to have a disagreement with him – so, say, by April 323 or earlier; he could have been the bearer of Antipater's reply.) Kassander naturally called in at Tarsos to visit his sister, and if he had not known it before, he will now have realized what Krateros' instructions were. Krateros had no reason to keep them secret, and it is not impossible that it was also well known among his troops. And, of course, Antipater and Kassander may well have understood it all along anyway.

Kassander will have undoubtedly explained to Krateros the problems Antipater was facing in Greece, with Harpalos, the Exiles' Decree, and the threat of trouble with Athens and Aitolia. One of the reasons for Kassander's journey had been to explain all this to Alexander, who by this time was undoubtedly well out of touch with Greek events and attitudes. This threatening situation constituted another good reason to delay in Kilikia and await new instructions from the king. Antipater's experience and authority in Macedon and Greece were such that replacing him in the midst of a crisis would only make matters worse, and Krateros was, if a competent military commander, wholly inexperienced in the problems and politics and diplomacy of Greece. Krateros quite probably sent back to Babylon for new instructions in view of the new situation.

For the last nine months of Alexander's reign, therefore, Antipater was effectively in a 'lame-duck' situation. As the word spread that he was to be replaced he would find his authority ebbing away. At the same time he would be able to see that the measures Alexander had recently taken had stirred up Greece in the same way that Memnon had stirred up the Thracians several years earlier. It is unlikely that any new instructions arrived from Alexander, and his replacement, Krateros, was moving either slowly towards him, or not at all. Hence Kassander's journey to Alexander, to report on the situation in Greece, to explain why the recruits were not coming, and to ask for new, up-to-date, instructions.

Chapter 5

The Lamian War

Alexander died on 10 June 323. At his court at Babylon at the time were three of Antipater's sons: Kassander, the eldest, who had arrived recently, and Philip and Iolaos, who were pages of the king, the latter being his cup-bearer and taster. This became one of the bases for the accusation that Alexander had been murdered by poisoning.

The story that Alexander was murdered was in part a result of the curious nature of his death, and of the general ignorance of causes of disease and death in the ancient world. Given that Alexander had lived an extremely hard life, drank too much, had suffered several serious wounds, and was at the time living in a particularly unhealthy region (Babylonia) at the hottest time of the year, his death should not have been a surprise. His mental condition was clearly by now strongly affected by the arrogance brought on by his successes, and of the conviction of his divine descent; to this may be attributed his failure to obey the sensible advices of his doctor (or doctors), something he had earlier in his life usually accepted. This is of a piece with his general unwillingness to buckle down to organize his empire properly, and his stated intention to go off on at least two more great new expeditions in the next years. As much as any causes, his death might be best described as due to suicide by carelessness.

His death, of course, created disputes and confusion whenever it was announced. In Babylonia it was some weeks before a new political arrangement was achieved.[1] Antipater, in Macedon, could not affect the outcome, despite his sons' presence at court – only Kassander might have been influential, but without having taken part in the great expedition he was ignored. He stayed, however, so it seems, until some sort of settled distribution of power had emerged, then returned to Macedon.[2] Probably Iolaos and Philip went with him or left even earlier – there was no place for the royal pages in the new scheme of things. It may be assumed that all three left for Babylon in the summer or late summer of 323.

Two decisions by the various authorities in Babylon had an effect on Antipater. One was the cancellation of Alexander's intentions, his 'last plans', which more pertinently ended the possibility of the Arabian and Mediterranean expeditions, but also involved cancelling the replacement of Antipater by Krateros.[3] Krateros in fact was appointed guardian (*prostates*) of King Philip III Arrhidaios, but since he stayed in Kilikia while Philip was in Babylon, he remained out of touch with events; his appointment as guardian of the king was effectively a dead letter from the start, since the king remained in Babylon under the control and influence of the Chiliarch Perdikkas.[4]

As soon as he was more or less firmly in position, Perdikkas sent word to Antipatros asking for one of his daughters in marriage. The message may have been carried by Kassander or one of his brothers to Macedon, though it seems that Kassander at least may have left Babylon before the issue of Perdikkas' position had been finally settled.

Not long after Alexander's death a new satrap for Kilikia arrived. This was Philotas, a former colleague of Krateros and a friend, who had in fact been appointed by Alexander before he died but had been caught up in the Babylonian crisis, though possibly he had delayed taking up his post because Krateros was there.[5] He was able to inform Krateros of what was happening in Babylon in some detail, but Krateros still stayed on in Kilikia.

Antipater's continuation in office in Macedon was now secure, and the offer of marriage of a daughter with the new controller of the empire must have been encouraging. In Greece he might have expected that the news would firm up his recently weakened authority, but the news of Alexander's death had the effect of largely destroying Macedonian authority in Greece, and not just Antipater's. The two major states, Athens and Aitolia, which were directly affected by the Exiles' Decree, took the removal of the king as the chance to escape Macedonian domination entirely. They were joined by many others.

The Athenians had already begun the process of arming themselves before the news of Alexander's death arrived. Some exiled Samians living near the island on the mainland had returned to the island even before Alexander's death, taking the Exiles' Decree as permission. The Athenians reacted by ordering the *strategos* on the island to arrest them, and then send them to Athens for imprisonment, and probable execution. They were rescued by Antileon of Chalkis, who provided a ransom and brought the captives to Chalkis. (It must be recalled that Chalkis had a Macedonian garrison; it is reasonable to assume that Antileon was acting in concert with its commander.[6]) This indicates Athenian determination, at that point, to fight the return of Samian exiles, but by making active preparations for war the city was also assuming that its appeal to Alexander would fail.

It is at this point, still before the news of Alexander's death had arrived in Athens, that Leosthenes emerged into prominence. He had apparently been one of Alexander's mercenaries and when they were all dismissed he had organized large numbers of them and transported them to Cape Tainaron.[7] (He had probably done so in part through Kilikia – another source of confusion in that afflicted province; Harpalos had also recruited 6,000 mercenaries there earlier.) Leosthenes then contacted the Athenian authorities, who were already beginning the process of mobilizing the citizen army.

Internally, half of the citizens liable to military service were mobilized, partly into a defensive force, to deal with raids from the sea or from the neighbours, but mainly into a force to be used to assault the Macedonians.[8] Meanwhile, externally Leosthenes was given fifty talents and sent back to Cape Tainaron to organize a mercenary army.[9] (The money came from that left behind by Harpalos when he 'escaped'.) Demosthenes, who was in exile after being condemned for having, so it was said, been bribed by Harpalos, toured the Peloponnese drumming up opposition to Macedon, and enlisting states into an alliance with Athens.[10] Leosthenes contacted the Aitolians, proposing an alliance.[11]

As a result of these discussions, decisions and manoeuvres a Greek version of the League of Corinth was formed, though it was more an alliance than a league; it was less restrictive, and essentially temporary, for the purpose and duration of the war. If it was compared with the alliance formed to drive out the Persians a century and a half before, some would have worried that Athens was trying again to convert it into an empire. Leosthenes was elected its general. The Athenians conducted a purge of those deemed to be too attached to, or sympathetic towards, Macedon – Demosthenes had taken Harpalos' money, Demades was deprived of his civil rights, Pytheas left the city, Aristotle was virtually expelled. The Athenian navy was got ready. In other cities, the change in political orientation will no doubt have also resulted in changes in political control, as pro–Macedonian politicians were ousted by their pro-alliance enemies.

This took until the autumn of 323, by which time the new regime at Babylon was in place and functioning. Much of the preparations by the Greek states had been diplomatic until this point or were actually secret. Antipater no doubt knew that something was being developed, but probably he was not sure just what; he sent groups of his supporters touring the Greek cities, just as Demosthenes and the Athenians did – he met Pytheas in oratorical combat at one point.[12] This would also allow Antipater to gain some information, though it is likely that decisions in individual cities were made slowly and piecemeal. It cannot have been clear for some time which side any particular city would come down on.

There were also distractions in and around Macedon. The return of his three sons from Babylon probably occurred in the late summer, assuming they left in June, and they could provide him with information about who was in charge at Babylon. New satraps arrived in the neighbouring provinces – Lysimachos in Thrace, Leonnatos in Hellespontine Phrygia, and Philotas in Kilikia.[13]

Lysimachos was faced with a disturbed province in the aftermath of Zopyrion's disaster, and immediately involved himself in a war with Seuthes, the Odrysian king, presumably to bring him back under Macedonian suzerainty, which he had recently renounced. He attacked Seuthes' army of 8,000 cavalry and 20,000 infantry with a Macedonian army of a quarter of that number. He was so far successful, though not actually victorious – his men were veterans of Alexander's war, after all – that he reduced Seuthes once more to accepting Macedonian suzerainty, returning the situation therefore to its condition before Zopyrion began his own campaign.[14]

The Greek alliance was composed of a mixture of states, several of whom had fought against each other in the Spartan War. Apart from Athens (which had been neutral) and Aitolia (nominally pro-Spartan), Argos and Messene had been pro-Macedonian, while Argos and Elis had been pro-Spartan. Several of the Peloponnesian cities – Sikyon, Epidauros, Phlious, Troezen – joined the alliance, as did the island city of Leukas in the west. The Athamanes, some of the Molossians, and some Illyrians from the mountains west and north of Macedon were also part of the alliance. Rhodes had risen against its Macedonian garrison even before Alexander's death, and had driven it out. Karystos in Euboia joined the Greeks, though the rest of the island (where there were ancestral and unpleasant memories of Athenian control, and a Macedonian garrison at Chalkis) took the Macedonian side. Next door the Boiotians as a group were vehemently pro-Macedonian. And yet in the Aegean Islands and along the Asian coast neutrality was the norm, which in the circumstances was effectively a pro-Macedonian policy.[15]

The western and northern allies were an even more curious group, and they emphasize that the one element of unity in the alliance was to be against Macedon; nothing permanent was intended, and no post-war planning was made. The only enemies in the Greeks' sights were Antipater and 'Macedon'. Yet it cannot have escaped their notice that 'Macedon' was now an empire stretching as far as India – plenty of mercenaries in Athenian service were veterans and could inform them of this. So the eventual aims of the Greeks were surely vague in the extreme. Could they even have expected to win their war? The tribal contingents in the north and west only emphasize the very limited nature of the purposes of the alliance. The Athamanes were a small community, geographically squashed between Macedon and Aitolia, struggling to survive inimical attentions from both. The Molossians were one of the constituents of the Epeiros kingdom, where Olympias was still extremely influential; it would seem that they were acting independently of her; Epeiros was not given a truly centralized monarchic system until Pyrrhos was king. The Illyrians were hereditary enemies of Macedon, and they launched an invasion whenever a Macedonian king died. It seems evident that this group of allies were less concerned at overthrowing Macedonian control of Greece than indulging in the usual raids. From the start the alliance was composed of discordant, even antagonistic, elements: some were sworn enemies of Macedon, some were former friends of Macedon, others were traditional raiders into Macedon. Such a heterogeneous group would probably have difficulty in staying united for very long, and some will have been less than enthusiastic from the start, and liable to fade away, especially when things dragged out or went wrong.

The allies contributed their city armies as separate units. Leosthenes had hired about 8,000 mercenaries at Cape Tainaron, which he put on board ships and transported to Aitolia. (Probably at least some of those ships had been Harpalos', just as the money used to pay the mercenaries had been his; it must have pleased many people to know that the 'rebellion' against Macedon was being funded by money and ships stolen from the Macedonian treasury.) Aitolia contributed 7,000 men, Athens 5,500 city troops and 2,000 mercenaries – Harpalos' money being put to good use once again – and smaller contingents came from the other allies. Athens launched 240 warships – 200 triremes and 40 quadriremes, which were manned by perhaps 30,000 men.[16] Athens at least was putting forth a maximum effort.

Leosthenes and his mercenaries were joined by the Aitolian contingent (7,000 men) to take up the position at Thermopylai, which was still the best defensive position for those blocking any attack from the north. Behind them, that is to the south, Boiotia was solidly pro-Macedonian because the several cities of the Boiotian League had profited from the destruction of Thebes by taking over slices of (former) Theban land. They had also been exempted from the Exiles' Decree, so there was no intention to restore and repopulate Thebes. Together with most of the cities of Euboia, and the Macedonian garrisons of the Kadmeia and Chalkis they were able to put a considerable force into the field, and drew together to camp at Plataia, just north of the Attikan border. It is not clear if the Athenian expeditionary force of 7,500 soldiers had actually left Attika at the time, but it would seem that the Plataian force was a distinct threat to Attika. Leosthenes executed a swift march from Thermopylai, apparently with his own mercenary force, leaving the Aitolians to defend the pass (though there was no danger of an attack there yet) and, perhaps in combination with the Athenian forces, defeated the Boiotians and Euboians at Plataia. Then he was able to march back to Thermopylai in full force. No doubt some of the Greeks, recalling the Persian Wars, took heart that the victory took place at Plataia. Leosthenes now commanded the whole allied army of 30,000 men.[17]

Antipater was not able to counter any of these moves militarily for some time, in part because he was effectively surrounded by enemies, though, of course, he had some idea what was being organized against him. It may be Lysimachos' semi-victory over Seuthes in Thrace that released him, since it meant that he was free from any threat of an invasion from the Thracians – another northern people addicted to raiding into Macedon in moments of the kingdom's weakness.[18] He also had to be very careful of his own forces, since he was outnumbered. On the other hand, he did command battle-hardened Macedonians, whereas many of the Greeks had not fought for years. Time was probably on his side as well, given that he faced a rickety alliance, and that it was likely he would be able to call up reinforcements from the rest of the Macedonian Empire. The real danger was that Macedon itself might be invaded, which would significantly reduce his manpower and his resources. He did, however, have much greater monetary reserves than the allies, and he had a good notion of how to apply them. This was, after all, the second Greek war he was fighting, and the fourth he had taken part in.

His dispositions were essentially defensive: detachments were placed to deter Illyrian and Molossian raids. We do not know when these were sent, or who commanded them, but a guess would suggest that Kassander was their commander; but he is called 'Sippas' in Diodoros, a name that is otherwise unknown, and it is assumed to be a mistake for another name.[19] Antipater's main force had to be deployed to the south, whence the main threat emanated. Since the Greek army had stopped at Thermopylai, this meant a march through Thessaly. This was a region he could not be wholly sure of. It had been part of the Macedonian kingdom for only a generation, and it may have hoped for independence once more, like the other Greeks.

Antipater took his time, just as he had in the Spartan War. His deputy in command of the northern border defences was given orders to recruit as many men as possible. His own army comprised 13,000 infantry, but only 600 cavalry.[20] He is said to have been short of 'citizen soldiers' – that is, trained Macedonians – but he had been instructed to send a force of reinforcements in exchange for Krateros' men. Krateros commanded 10,000 infantry, 1,500 cavalry and 1,000 Persian archers and slingers, more or less equal to the force Antipater had been left with when Alexander set out on his adventure. It is difficult to believe that Antipater was expected to take virtually the whole of his Macedonian command to Babylon, so the arrival of Krateros would have increased the force in Macedon; Antipater's contingent will have been the annual crop of new soldiers.

Antipater was counting on recruiting Thessalians, particularly cavalry, to bring his numbers up to a force large enough to face the Greeks. He may not have known the size of that army until he came face-to-face with it. By taking up the Thermopylai position, Leosthenes had negated his advantage in numbers, for the narrow area for fighting at the pass gave an advantage to the Macedonians with their long spears, but it may also have disguised the size of Leosthenes' force. Antipater cannot have expected the Thessalians to produce enough soldiers to give him parity of numbers, but a cavalry reinforcement would be especially valuable given the, surely unanticipated, superiority of the Greeks in this arm.

Some Thessalians did join Antipater on the march south, to the number of about 2,000, but when he squared off against Leosthenes' army at Thermopylai, they changed sides.[21] It would seem that Leosthenes had come out of the pass to take advantage of his greater numbers, and this cavalry reinforcement made defeat for Antipater's army inevitable. He thereupon withdrew. It is possible that Leosthenes or 'the Athenians', as Diodoros says, had sent messages into Thessaly, with Greek propaganda about freedom. The Thessalian system was semi-feudal, and the real military strength of the region lay in its horsemen. The appeal would be to them, and the freedom for them would be of two elements: a freedom from Macedonian control, and the freedom to exploit the peasantry. They may well not have been too keen to fight for old Antipater, in preference to the young, glamorous Alexander.

Antipater withdrew carefully enough to deter any Greek attack or pursuit. His lack of numbers could only be redressed by reinforcements from outside, for it would be suicide to bring the northern guard south and leave the borders unwatched. These reinforcements must therefore come from the army in Asia, from the forces under the command of the generals in Asia Minor. Lysimachos were still occupied with gaining control of Thrace, and anyway his small army would not be enough. The new forces must come from the Leonnatos in Hellespontine Phrygia, or from Antigonos in Phrygia, or from Krateros in Kilikia. Leonnatos had orders from Perdikkas to invade Kappadokia, which had been assigned to Alexander's Greek secretary Eumenes as his satrapy, and he had ignored Antipater's first appeal, made before he had marched south.[22]

Antipater's retreat took him past the city of Herakleia-by-Oeta, which had sided with Macedon, then over the Spercheios River to the city of Lamia, a march of less than 20km, which could have taken only a day, but more likely two. Polyainos has an anecdote that Antipater was faced by a Thessalian force at the crossing of the Specheios, from which he withdrew. The Thessalians then galloped off for their dinner, and he crossed the river then seized Lamia.[23] This was the main city of Malis, and was fortified. He set his men to strengthen the walls and gathered what supplies he could find.[24] A message went to the Hellespont, to the tyrant of the city of Kardia,

Hekataios (the murderer of Attalos), for him to deliver yet another appeal to Leonnatos.[25]

Leonnatos was distantly related to the Argead royal family, and the death of Alexander and the succession of Philip III Arrhidaios and the infant Alexander IV had stirred his ambition. He is said to have reacted to the news that Antipater had appealed to him by confiding to Eumenes, whom he was supposed to be helping to take up his position as satrap in Kappadokia, that he had received a letter from Alexander's sister Kleopatra, the widow of the Epeirote king, proposing marriage. This notion is supposed to have persuaded him that he might be able to replace Antipater in control of Macedon and perhaps make himself king. The arrival of Hekataios partly derailed these plans, if that was what they were, for he and Eumenes were mortal enemies, both being from Kardia, where Hekataios was tyrant. Eumenes took his own forces away from Leonnatos' camp and reported to Perdikkas on Leonnatos' ambitions. One result was that Perdikkas proposed himself as a husband for Kleopatra.[26]

What negotiations had been conducted between Antipatros and Perdikkas are not known but at some point, in late 323 or early 322, Antipater's daughter Nikaia was sent, escorted by her brother Iolaos and a man called Archias, who may have been a former actor from Thourioi in Italy, with the intention of her marrying Perdikkas wherever he was, probably at Babylon still.

The point here is that the death of Alexander had opened up the possibility for several high-ranking Macedonians of usurping the throne. Perdikkas' proposal to Kleopatra was seen as another man aiming to become king. (The succession of Argead kings had been punctuated by several similar usurpations in the previous century or so.) In Kilikia Krateros, who had no connection with the royal family, consciously posed as a kingly figure, dressing in the Alexander style, and receiving visitors seated on a golden throne;[27] Leonnatos' hairstyle and clothing was reminiscent of Alexander's as well; Ptolemy in Egypt took on the position of a pharaoh – and so on. The chances of Alexander IV actually operating as an effective king when he became adult were virtually nil from the moment he was born.

While Leonnatos was considering his options, and while Nikaia was on her way to Babylon, the Greek army followed up Antipater's force in its retreat, but it had plenty of time to stock up with food and munitions, and work on improving and repairing the Lamian fortifications. It seems quite probable that there had been discussions among the Greeks over what to do. The position at Thermopylai seemed to have been successful, at least as a base, and the Macedonians had not been able to pass into Greece proper; the pro-Macedonians in Greece had been defeated. One obvious option would be to go on holding Thermopylai and continue to defy Antipater to attack them. But the Greek army now included a large Thessalian contingent commanded by Menon of Pharsalos, and their homeland was now vulnerable to Macedonian attack, either from Lamia or from Macedon. The area of the Greek alliance had therefore expanded, and the proper base for the defence of its territory should now be on the northern borders of Thessaly – the Mount Olympos position. Antipater would soon be reinforced, even if the precise details of his appeals to the Asian generals were unknown, and then he would return to the attack with much greater strength. The decision was made to attack him in Lamia.

By the time the Greek army reached the city it was strongly held, and their immediate assaults failed. Antipater suggested negotiations. Again, one must assume that there was discussion among the Greek contingents over possible terms, and quite likely there was considerable disagreement. The result was that the Greeks demanded Antipater's unconditional surrender, which is probably the only terms the Greeks could agree on – the lowest common denominator, in effect. Inevitably Antipater rejected such an idea. His assaults having failed, Leosthenes resorted to a blockade, digging a ditch and building a wall of circumvallation, intending to starve the Macedonians out.[28] This was a likely war-winning tactic, since the Macedonian force was large and penned into a small city, and it could be presumed that it would rapidly use up whatever supplies it had had found in the city. But Antipater appears to have been able to feed his men – and any citizens who were still in the city – out of the stores he had collected and those he found in the city. Once the blockade was complete he could expect no supplies to reach him, and there is no record of supplies being sent from the fleet; the distance from the sea was far too great.

Antipater's appeals to Leonnatos and Krateros succeeded. Krateros had much further to come, and so Leonnatos arrived first, despite his initial hesitation, perhaps eventually urged on by his ambition. Krateros also, however, had a fleet at his disposal, the ships gathered from the Phoenician, Cypriot, and Kilikian ports in anticipation of the western expeditions planned by Alexander. These were put under the command of 'White' Kleitos.[29] But he could not sail in 323. The war on land did not start until well after September, and Krateros could not have received Antipater's appeal until perhaps the November or December, and winter was no time to sail in the Mediterranean. Antipater, however, already had at his disposal the fleet of 110 ships that had been sent at Alexander's orders to transport the treasure to Macedon. The ships (and the treasure) had arrived after the king's death, and so in the late summer of 323, before the war had begun. These were clearly available to be used in the autumn, though it seems most likely that the ships were kept in port during the winter.

Athens was the only Greek power with any naval capability. The years of peace since 336 had seen the fleet built up to about 400 vessels, which were held in the dockyard and shipsheds at Peiraios. In the preparations for the war the city's assembly had authorized 240 ships to be manned,[30] but it seems that the simultaneous mobilization of the army restricted the manpower available for the fleet, and the largest Athenian fleet at sea during the war was only 170 ships; there were, however, no doubt others at sea on other missions. The Athenian fleet was probably at sea in the summer and autumn of 323, perhaps assisting the grain fleet through the Straits.

The winter of 323/322 restricted operations both on land and at sea. Antipater was locked up in Lamia, and, according to Diodoros, his forces were running short of supplies, though this may only be Diodoros' assumption, for it was to be expected that a siege would produce privations among the besieged.[31] The Macedonian and Athenian fleets were held in harbour by the winter weather. The fleet under Kleitos could not arrive until the spring. Outside Lamia the Greek army shrank, in particular when the Aitolian contingent returned home, supposedly on some national business, which may have centred on the issue of Oiniadai, or Ambrakia.[32] In a skirmish in the lines at Lamia, Leosthenes was killed, and was replaced by Antiphilos, but the blockade continued.[33]

Leonnatos got his forces across the Hellespont in the spring, perhaps assisted and guarded by the ships that had brought the treasure the year before. Kleitos' fleet was approaching, and Krateros apparently set out to march his men to Macedon through Asia Minor, though he could not do so until the passes were open, and it would take some time for him to cross the 600–700km from Kilikia as far as the Hellespont. Leonnatos collected further forces from those in Macedon to bring his army up to 20,000 infantry, but he had only 1,500 cavalry. He then marched past Olympos and into Thessaly.[34]

When he heard of the approach of this army Antiphilos lifted the blockade of Lamia and marched the Greek forces north to meet it. He burnt the Greek camp, which was a clear signal to Antipater that the Greek army had gone. The Greek camp followers were put into Melitaia, a day's march north of Lamia. Antipater at once organized the evacuation of Lamia, and took his army north by hill paths, no doubt through Magnesia, hoping both to avoid Antiphilos' army, and to join that of Leonnatos, wherever he was. Antiphilos had 22,000 infantry and 3,500 cavalry, including the Thessalians under Menon.[35]

The two armies met somewhere in Thessaly, well north of Melitaia. The superior cavalry of the Greeks had the advantage and drove off the Macedonian cavalry, leaving the infantry vulnerable – and Leonnatos was killed in the cavalry fight. The Macedonian phalanx retreated to some nearby hills and beat off the Greeks' cavalry attacks. Antiphilos claimed the victory and then pulled back. Antipater's force joined with Leonnatos' army next day. He had clearly marched more or less parallel with the Greek army, and it might have been the knowledge of his proximity that persuaded Antiphilos to pull back. Antipater now withdrew the whole Macedonian army into Macedon, moving carefully through the hills to avoid the Greeks. He now had to defend the Olympos position.[36]

Antipater now had the stronger infantry force, but was still deterred by the more powerful Greek cavalry, a curious reversal in military affairs. He evidently determined to await Krateros' arrival. Leonnatos' death had also put an end to Kleopatra's attempts at a new marriage. It is not known how far the negotiations between these two had progressed, but the latter's death in the spring of 322 certainly occurred before Nikaia had married Perdikkas for she sent a message to him offering herself in marriage to him just as she had to Leonnatos.

The sequence of events at Babylon appears to have been, first, the betrothal of Nikaia and Perdikkas being agreed; second, Nikaia herself arrived. Perdikkas was now tempted by Kleopatra's offer, which would give him a clear shot at the throne, perhaps as official guardian for the incapable kings, rather as Philip II had been guardian for Amyntas, and had then made himself king. The temptation was clearly very strong, but there were obstacles in the way: Nikaia, Antipater, and Perdikkas' promise, not to mention the strong suspicion of his intentions. Then followed a cold-blooded debate at his headquarters over which woman he should choose.

Perdikkas' offer to marry one of Antipater's daughters was clearly intended as a stage in the construction of a major political alliance between the ruler of Macedon (and Greece), and the man who controlled the kings (only one, Philip III, at the time of the offer, but Alexander IV was soon born) and the government of the empire. Perdikkas had emerged as Chiliarch of the empire – the military chief – but his position was by no means secure, and it depended above all on his control of the kings. An alliance with the ruler of the homeland, who had won wars by his own efforts, and who had kept a firm grip on Macedon for a dozen years, would clearly be advantageous. Leonnatos had had the same idea when he chose to obey Antipater's appeal for help rather than Perdikkas' orders to put Eumenes in control of Kappadokia.

On the other hand, marriage with Kleopatra would make him a member of the Argead family, for he would become the uncle of the new two kings. The choice between the women was debated between Eumenes (who had joined him when Hekataios arrived from Antipater) and Alketas, Perdikkas' brother. Alketas argued for marriage to Nikaia, Eumenes for Kleopatra, each of them arguing in fact from their own political positions, preferences, and ambitions.

Into this complexity came the news of the Greek War. Antipater became fully preoccupied with the crisis, suffered an early defeat, and for a time it seemed he might not survive the siege of Lamia. So an alliance with him would not necessarily be of any value, and yet to betray him at that crisis would be much criticized; Perdikkas' decision was delayed. Meanwhile Antipater's appeal to Krateros brought him and his army to Macedon. And with him Krateros brought Phila, Antipater's daughter, the widow of Balakros, returning from Kilikia. It is not known what the relations were between Krateros and Phila at this point, but they had both been in Kilikia for a year or more, and were probably by now well acquainted. Krateros was renowned as one of the most handsome men of his day; he had been one of Alexander's favourite commanders, and in the share-out of posts at Babylon after Alexander's death he had been given the (mostly honorary) position of *prostates* for the king or kings. He was not a particularly skilful political operator, as was shown by his failure to profit from his new post, but he had the devoted loyalty of the men he commanded, which in the circumstances of the time was probably somewhat more valuable than a rather theoretical post. Further, he had enough sense, unlike the more arrogant Leonnatos, to put himself willingly under Antipater's orders; in the final months of the Lamian War he was a loyal and sensible second in command. One wonders if Phila had influence here: she was renowned as an intelligent observer of political affairs, valued by her father even in her youth; Krateros was no doubt susceptible.

Meanwhile the war at sea brought an overall result closer, though it was also a major problem. Diodoros reports that Kleitos' fleet fought two battles against the Athenian fleet commanded by Euetion, winning victories, though most of the Athenian ships survived.[37] This would be expected, since Kleitos seems to have had more ships, and was perhaps a more imaginative commander. But Diodoros places the fighting in or near the Echinades Islands. These are off the coast of Akarnania, and considerable disbelief is voiced that this could have been the correct location for the battles. This in fact would make the encounters near to Oiniadai, one of the prime Macedonian objects of the war (though the city is not mentioned in the accounts of the war). The presence of a Macedonian fleet in these waters might be behind the withdrawal of the Aitolian forces from Lamia to attend to some 'national business'. However, none of this is specified, and it is not directly connected with any of the sea fights.

The alternative to a naval campaign off Akarnania seems to be fighting in the Malian Gulf, near Lamia, where there were a group of islands called the Licinades, which name could have been mangled in Diodoros' account; perhaps also in the Malian Gulf, there may have been some islands off the town of Echinos, but if so these have now vanished. So the only authentically named islands seem unlikely, while the others are named only by amending the name or have disappeared.

Not only that, but neither of the general conditions suggested for the fighting are satisfactory. The Aitolians were surely concerned about Oiniadai, but nearby also was a Macedonian garrison in Ambrakia. Oiniadian exiles and Macedonian soldiers would constitute a serious threat to the Aitolian homeland if the whole Aitolian armed forces were at Lamia. When next heard of, in 314, Oiniadai was again Akarnanian, and so presumably the exiles had returned to reclaim their city; it would seem that Aitolian concerns at their 'national business' were fully justified; but it would not necessarily call for two naval battles for the city to change hands.[38]

Antipater left Lamia in the early spring of 322, so there would be little point in fighting a sea battle in the Malian Gulf. There were certainly raids by Macedonian ships on places on the Athenian coast – one took place at Rhamnos[39] – and these presuppose the absence of the Athenian fleet. There was also some fighting at the Hellespont, which is attested by two Athenian inscriptions from some years later. When or how large the fighting was is as unknown as other sea war details. But given that the passage of the Hellespont was vital for Athens, it was presumably to assist the grain fleet in getting through, probably in 322 (that of 323 will have got through before the fighting started). All the raids are undated. It is all fairly unsatisfactory.[40]

It seems most likely, therefore, that Kleitos had taken his fleet from Kilikia into the Aegean and had fought Euetion's fleet in that sea. The crucial point in the spring of 322 was not Akarnania, nor the Malian Gulf, but the Hellespont. Krateros needed ships to get his force across into Europe, and the Athenians needed to bring their grain ships through. The two fleets met once more at Amorgos, in the southern Aegean, quite possibly on their rival ways to the Hellespont, or perhaps it was an Athenian attempt to intercept Kleitos' fleet. Kleitos may have united his Kilikian fleet with the ships already in Macedonian ports, and the combined force defeated the Athenians. Diodoros reports that in the summer of 322 the Macedonian fleet was supreme at sea. Kleitos dressed himself as Poseidon and wielded a trident.[41]

The war at sea was largely an auxiliary to that on land. The main target was control of the Hellespont, and this the Macedonians achieved, probably because they had more (and perhaps bigger and better) ships than the Athenians, but also that they had control of both sides of the Strait, the Gallipoli Peninsula and the Troad. Wherever the battles at sea were fought, they were essentially part of naval campaigns to gain or seize control of the Straits – in fact, to maintain Macedonian control as opposed to Athenian attempts to seize control, would be the better formulation. There is no real sign that any of this affected the war on land. It cannot be argued either that the absence of the Aitolians from the land war after the start of the Lamian siege was important, since even had they been present in the last battle, the Macedonians would probably have won. Whatever their 'national business' was, it did not affect the main issue any more than did the sea war.

Antipater had already united his original army with that of Leonnatos, giving him at least a numerical equality with Antiphilos' army, but the latter needed to reunite his original forces – that is, bring back those Greek units that had gone home, including the Aitolians. But the Aitolians had probably become stuck at Oiniadai, or maybe Ambrakia, and other Greek cities had lost interest, perhaps assuming that they had won the war after driving Antipater out of Greece and Thessaly and into Macedon – they had, after all, now 'freed' all Greece by that point.

When Krateros brought his force to join Antipater, the latter then had a superiority 3 to 2 in infantry, and an approximate equality in cavalry. Krateros brought 6,000 of his original force, had collected 4,000 more on the way, and also brought his 1,000 Persian archers and slingers; but most importantly he also had 1,500 cavalry. Antipater had already moved back into Thessaly from the north, and Krateros joined him there. The joint Macedonian force now numbered 40,000 heavy infantry, 5,000 cavalry, and 3,000 archers and slingers. These men met Antiphilos' reduced army near the city of Krannon in north-central Thessaly. Several Greek units had rejoined their army in the crisis, but Antiphilos commanded only 25,000 hoplites and 3,500 cavalry.[42]

Krateros gracefully accepted Antipater being in command, which was also intelligent of him, for Antipater had at least some experience of commanding a large army, and he was by now familiar with the probable tactics Antiphilos and the Greeks would adopt; Antiphilos put his cavalry in front of his infantry phalanx, assuming it would be able to drive off the Macedonian cavalry, as he had earlier, leaving the infantry phalanx vulnerable once more. But this did not work a third time. Antipater did not wait for the end of the cavalry fight, which clearly took longer than before, for the Greeks were now outnumbered in horsemen and so the Macedonians were able to prolong the fight, but the Greek cavalry did actually prevail, possibly by Antipater using his own cavalry to draw off the Greeks. The fighting between the rival cavalry forces drew away to one side, leaving the space between the two phalanxes open, and Antipater set his phalanx to attack, while his cavalry preoccupied the Greek cavalry. The sheer weight, and the long spears, of the Macedonians succeeded in driving the Greek phalanx back, but not in breaking it. As the Macedonians had done in the earlier fights, the Greeks drew back on to higher ground, having lost 500 men; Macedonian casualties were 130.

That, and the Macedonian supremacy in numbers, persuaded the Greeks that the battle had been lost, as had that at sea. It was now the turn of the Greek commanders to ask for terms. Menon and Antiphilos did have the option of waiting until some of their still missing units arrived, though they were unlikely to do so after the defeat; even so, their numbers would still not be sufficient to allow them to renew the battle. Meanwhile the Macedonians would no doubt drive them back, and possibly starve them out. Antipater, when terms were asked of him, insisted that these would only be agreed with each city individually, thereby denying the legitimacy of their alliance and their Congress. Menon and Antiphilos refused these terms.

Antipater had demonstrated a flexibility in command which had eluded Leonnatos, and was particularly admirable for a man in his seventies, though it has to be said that having a large numerical advantage at Krannon clearly helped. When the Greek commanders refused the terms suggested, he was able to use his numerical superiority to detach forces to attack nearby cities, thus implementing the terms he had stated without overall agreement.[43] At least that is what we must assume. All that we are told is that he and Krateros attacked the Thessalian cities. This does presuppose making substantial detachments, while the Greek army remained locked in its new position. This was a dangerous manoeuvre and could have left the Macedonian army vulnerable to a new strike from the enemy; the great majority of the Macedonian army must have been left facing the Greeks.

However, once the nearby Thessalian cities came under attack, the Greek soldiers would become nervous. Any city that was captured would have terms imposed on it, and these would necessarily include the withdrawal of any of its troops with the Greek army – and since these were Thessalian cities, the cavalry would be the first to be reduced. Some cities were taken by assault, but others negotiated terms of surrender when threatened. The terms imposed by Antipater were said to have been 'easy', though none of the individual treaties are on record. The effect was to reduce the Greek army unit by unit until it was no longer capable of fighting. And the more cities who made terms, the faster the army disintegrated.[44]

The exceptions to all this were Athens and the Aitolian League. (It must be assumed that the Peloponnesian cities in the Greek alliance surrendered by sending heralds to do so; there is no sign that the Macedonian army went beyond Corinth.) The two main Macedonian enemies could have made a serious fight of it, as the Athenians had previously shown, and as the Aitolians would soon show. But Attika was a much more vulnerable country than Aitolia, and Athens was as ever riven by antagonistic parties. As the Macedonians approached – and once they were in Boiotia, any concerted action by Athens and the Aitolians was impossible – the leading anti-Macedonian politicians, above all, Demosthenes and Hypereides, fled the city.[45] The Assembly swiftly restored Demades' civil rights, and appointed him and Phokion as the chief negotiators to make terms with the two Macedonian generals. They met at the Macedonian garrison at the Kadmeia, Antipater presumably making another very obvious point.[46]

Antipater was insistent on carrying out his programme. If all the other Greek states must accept his terms, however 'easy', so must Athens, no matter that the negotiators sent by the city were supposed to be his friends. Antipater had spent much of his adult life fighting Athens, and all the previous peace agreements had left the city largely untouched, and capable, as it had just proved, of going to war again with some confidence of winning. This may have been acceptable to Philip or Alexander, both of whom had their minds fixed on further wars, and wanted their full forces available to be under their command for the next campaign, and Athenian forces as well. But Antipater ruled only Macedon, and he had no intention of going on a foreign campaign, so he was quite willing to impose disabling terms on Athens, which in effect pushed the city into a military and political dependence on Macedon. On the other hand, Krateros was even more determined to reduce Athenian power, and proposed an invasion of Attika, citing the unfairness of the Macedonian army camping in Boiotia, which was friendly territory, rather than ravaging the enemy, Attika. At this, the Athenian delegates swiftly accepted Antipater's terms, which effectively amounted to unconditional surrender, and permitted him to change the city as he wished. This was possibly intended as a deliberate reminder to the Athenians of the terms they had demanded from him at the beginning of the Lamian siege.[47]

Identifying the democracy as the engine of Athenian war-making power, and of hostility to Macedon, Antipater imposed a new constitution. The membership of the Assembly was to be restricted to the middle class – technically to those with assets of 2,000 drachmas or more; this still left 9,000 full citizens, but removed 12,000 others from that category. In territorial terms Oropos, which Athens had gained in 336, was removed once more, and Samos' fate (it was still in Athenian control) was referred to the kings, which effectively meant Perdikkas.

These terms, despite the surrender of Athens, were actually the result of negotiations. Antipater, perhaps conscious of Krateros watching him, put on a display of anger, but when it came down to detail he was quite willing to adopt suggestions from Phokion. (Demades appears to have taken little part in the talks.) His initial demands were a reduction of the franchise, the surrender of Demosthenes and Hypereides, a Macedonian garrison placed in the Munychia fort in the Peiraios, and Athens to pay the cost of the war, and a fine on top of that.

Phokion succeeded in deflecting the suggestion that a Macedonian garrison be placed in the city itself – one such garrison in the Peiraios would be intimidating enough – and it seems probable the demand for a financial reparation was dropped; in the matter of the reduction of the citizen body it seems to have been Phokion's suggestion as to where the new limits should lie. Further, no doubt as Antipater could have predicted, Demosthenes and Hypereides fled the city before they could be handed over to him.[48]

Once they were back in Athens Phokion and Demades had to put the details of the terms to the Assembly, and they put forward the motion to condemn those who had proposed the war, especially Demosthenes and Hypereides. On the other hand, the islands in the north-east Aegean that Athens held – Lemnos especially – remained hers.

The result for Athens was a drastic reduction in the city's power. Half the fleet had gone as a result of the defeats in the battles (though Antipater made no demand for its further reduction); the number of citizens was now reduced to those who were never in favour of imperialist adventures; the leading populist orators were gone and would soon be dead. And the city had a Macedonian garrison imposed on it: in mid-September a Macedonian force commanded by Menyllos occupied the Munychia fort.

The end of the war came suddenly. The battle at Krannon took place at the beginning of September; within a fortnight Athens had succumbed to Macedonian threats, and had been reduced to an occupied city dominated by Macedonian orders. The disfranchised suffered both in the loss of their civil status, and in the disappearance of much of the fleet, in which they had been paid as rowers. Antipater organized an emigration for any who wished to go to a 'town and territory' in Thrace. This was not, of course, generosity on his part, for it worked to weaken the city still more.[49]

The 'Lamian' War, which at the time was called the 'Hellenic' War, was not yet over. There was a campaign of murder to remove the anti-Macedonian politicians, not just those of Athens, but those in other states as well; this may be counted as a continuing military mopping-up operation. Archias was put in charge of this operation, accounting for Hypereides, though Demosthenes committed suicide before arrest. The final blow to Athens came at the end of 322, when it was confirmed that Samos was no longer Athenian; the Athenians in the island had to be removed to the city, and the Samian exiles returned to their island.[50] This cannot have been unexpected, but it hurt nevertheless. Meanwhile, the Aitolians were not willing to accept any of Antipater's terms, and certainly not unconditional surrender. They continued fighting.

Chapter 6

Triparadeisos

The reduction of Athens in 322 marked the end of the Greek alliance. This was the fourth time in the last sixteen years that most of Greece had submitted to the Macedonian power – Khaironeia, Thebes, Megalopolis, Krannon were the moments of defeat. There was, however, still one state, the Aitolian League, which remained in arms against the Macedonians. It is probable that Antipater assumed that now the Aitolians would quickly succumb and make peace. If so, he was wrong. But for the moment he was now preoccupied with a new problem.

The Aitolians had been only marginally involved in any of the wars of conquest by Macedonian armies until this war, but had suffered nonetheless. In Philip's war an Aitolian garrison in Naupaktos was butchered by a joint Macedonian-Achaian force that had captured the city;[1] in the Theban War of Alexander, the several Aitolian tribes had submitted individually to him, which implies that their league had been dissolved, probably by Philip after Naupaktos.[2] In Agis' War the Aitolians took Agis' part, but were largely ignored.[3] The basic reason for this repeated minimal involvement was the instability of the Aitolian League, which was largely dismantled and then reconstituted several times during these wars. It was as separate tribes that they were members of Philip's League of Corinth in 338 and submitted to Alexander in 336. It seems that Philip had broken up the league when he captured Naupaktos – just as Antipater dealt with the Greek alliance by making peace with each city individually. Alexander did so again after the Theban War, and once more at about the time of Agis' War. The league was repeatedly revived, however, and it was a league action that led to the capture of Oiniadai.[4] Probably it was this double defiance that so angered Alexander. Antipater, on the other hand, acquiesced in this, even though Alexander vowed to reverse the action, and made diplomatic efforts to resolve their differences. It seems likely that Antipater felt that he could not afford to become involved in a war in Aitolia, a difficult and mountainous country, while his grip on Greece was based only on military power so recently imposed, with the Greek cities resentful and restless, and while his own armed forces were so exiguous. The army of 40,000 he had gathered to fight Agis was quickly reduced in the aftermath of victory; in 323, and no doubt much earlier, he was back to the 13,000 men Alexander had left with him, but in 322, with Greece subdued, that Macedonian army stood once more at 40,000 men. The aftermath of the war included Archias hunting down and killing anti-Macedonian politicians. The balance of power had drastically changed, and this was marked by the new Aitolian War, and by Antipater arranging the marriages of two of his daughters. This came first.

When Perdikkas realized that Antipater had been victorious in Greece, and that he had control not only of his own original army, but those of Leonnatos and Krateros as well, and that he was firmly allied with Krateros, his own marriage decision inevitably was for Nikaia, rather than Kleopatra. When he and Nikaia were actually married is not clear, but it would fit best with the general political situation in late 322. Perdikkas had spent the earlier part of 322 campaigning with success in Kappadokia (to seat Eumenes in his satrapy) and Pisidia (to subdue the Larandians and others who had rebelled against and killed Balakros).[5] He now encountered the problem of Kleopatra once more, but also that of Antigonos, who had not obeyed the instructions he had given to campaign on behalf of Eumenes earlier.

Antipater had also arranged, or agreed to, the marriage of Krateros and Phila. This will have been negotiated during the time Krateros was in Europe, the summer of 322, during their joint campaign which ended at Krannon, though it seems probable that Antipater only set his seal on an agreement that the two parties, Krateros and Phila, had made between themselves. Perhaps unusually for betrothed people at the time, they already knew each other fairly well, and had been in each other's company for the past year; she had travelled back to her father from Kilikia with Krateros. Krateros had had to divorce his Persian princess-wife, Amastris, before marrying his new wife, and he did so long enough before his second marriage to have been able to arrange for her to marry the tyrant of Herakleia Pontike, Dionysios.[6] It appears he was one of the few Macedonian lords who accepted the notion of monogamy – or perhaps it was Antipater's influence, or even Phila's.

Krateros and Phila were married in Macedon as soon as Antipater and Krateros had finished with Athens, that is, in late 322,[7] probably more or less at the same time that Nikaia was finally married to Perdikkas. At that point three of the most powerful men in the empire, Antipater, Krateros and Perdikkas, were linked into a political alliance by those marriages. It must have seemed to observers that here was a political alliance that could successfully control the empire, though how firm an alliance this could be when based only on marriages is difficult to gauge: political priorities always overwhelmed such relationships.[8]

Perdikkas successfully conciliated Kleopatra by making her governor of Lydia – she had already moved to Sardis at this point.[9] This involved the demotion of the satrap Menandros who had been appointed to Lydia at the Babylon settlement; he now became *strategos* of Lydia, Kleopatra's military commander, and he was not pleased. Perdikkas made it clear that he expected to deal with Antigonos, presumably believing that his alliance with Antipater was firm enough to allow him to do so. Antigonos did not wait, but, late in 322, fled to take refuge with Antipater.

Perdikkas had to be careful in these moves. He will have been alert to the fact that Antipater and Antigonos were well acquainted. They had been governing neighbours in Macedon and Phrygia for ten years, and they will have communicated frequently. Antipater regularly dispatched groups of new recruits for Alexander's army through Phrygia, where Antigonos was responsible for feeding them and sending them onwards; to do this the two men will have had to make careful administrative arrangements. They were of Philip's political generation, and though the record of neither man during Philip's reign is known in any detail there can be no doubt that it was under Philip that they had risen to importance and developed their military and administrative capabilities. In Alexander's empire they were the two most important elements of stability in the West while he ventured into the distant East. In displacing Antigonos Perdikkas was striking at one of the foundations of the whole empire.

But Antigonos fled his satrapy before he could be caught, and Perdikkas perhaps thought he had already succeeded in displacing and eliminating him. So in the winter of 322/321 the Perdikkan regime appeared to be well emplaced. Perdikkas had enlarged the empire into Kappadokia, his lieutenant Peithon had crushed a Greek settler/mercenary rebellion in the east, just as Antipater, Perdikkas' ally, had crushed the Greek rebellion in Greece, and now a disobedient subordinate had fled. And yet Perdikkas had, in the process of all this, manifested ambitions that were incompatible with the position of regent of the empire, and he had accumulated some awkward enemies.

That winter was therefore a busy time. The question of the Aitolians was probably uppermost in the thoughts of the Macedonian generals, but there was also now the issue of Antigonos. He was left in Phrygia when Alexander moved further east, and had a difficult time for a couple of years as the Persians had revived and sent several armies into his territory to recover control of Asia Minor and cut Alexander's westward communications. Antigonos prevailed with the assistance of Kalas in Hellespontine Phrygia and Balakros in Kilikia. By about 330 Antigonos' satrapy was safe enough for his wife Stratonike and their children to join him, just as Kilikia was safe for Phila to join Balakros.[10]

Antigonos retailed stories to Antipater and Krateros about Perdikkas' intentions, which may have been true, or may have been exaggerated or possibly even invented, but which carried conviction.[11] He could certainly explain Perdikkas' intentions towards himself, which amounted to dispossession of his satrapy, if not worse. Then there was the issue of Kynnane, the widow of Amyntas Perdikka. She had remained quietly in Macedon until Alexander's death, but the emergence of Alexander's half-brother Arrhidaios as Philip III brought her to plan a revival of her fortunes. She collected a small army and marched eastwards, evading Antipater's prohibition, crossed the River Strymon (and so into Thrace) and then across the Hellespont and into Asia.[12] Her intention was to marry her daughter Adea to King Philip III Arrhidaios. It seems unlikely that she had much of an army with her, an enlarged bodyguard perhaps, and she must have been relying primarily on her status as a daughter of Philip II for protection. But she was also an accomplished soldier, and one would have to assume that she was an object of admiration for the soldiers. Perdikkas was at the time still preoccupied in or near Kappadokia, but his brother Alketas was operating as his deputy, and he intercepted Kynnane near Ephesos. There she faced up to him, though his army was reluctant to fight her. However, when she faced up to Alketas personally, he murdered her. At this his troops mutinied. This was suppressed only when it was agreed that Adea, Kynanne's daughter, should after all marry Philip III.[13]

The ineptness of the conduct of Perdikkas and Alketas over Antigonos and Kynnane was another indication of the essential political weakness of

Perdikkas' position. All this was explained to Antipater when Antigonos arrived at Pella. It was all very disturbing to Antipater and Krateros, but there was not yet anything either of them needed to do. Perdikkas did have a good reason for going after Antigonos, after all, and Adea's marriage to Philip was what Kynanne had wished. Meanwhile they had to attend to Aitolia.

We have no information about the terms offered to Aitolia, though it is probable that some sort of unconditional surrender preparatory to some internal adjustment of the league would be involved. The obvious model was the terms imposed on Athens (and probably the other Greek cities as well). The release of Oiniadai would certainly be demanded, as with Samos; on the pattern of the demand that the Athenian constitutional system be altered, some sort of change to the Aitolian constitution would be demanded; some territories might be detached, but the obvious penalty would be to break up the league, as Philip and Alexander had done previously. The Aitolians were not popular in Greece, having a probably undeserved reputation for banditry and piracy. Since Athens had been so drastically and humiliatingly reduced in power, so it must be expected that Antipater and Krateros would aim to reduce or destroy Aitolian power as well; this would automatically extend Macedonian power and authority over all Greece, and so render the possibility of yet another 'rebellion' highly unlikely, at least for the immediate future.

This could not be accepted by the Aitolians. They had not, unlike the Athenians, been defeated in the fighting, unless Oiniadai had already been taken from them. They were, as a people, quite used to fighting their own wars, a preference presumably confirmed by the failure of the recent wider Greek alliance. Their antipathy towards Macedon was further fuelled by the arrival of exiles and refugees from the terror being visited upon other cities. And when they refused Antipater's terms they knew well enough what the consequences would be.

Whatever preliminary negotiations took place probably did not last long; the Macedonian terms were clearly unacceptable, so the Aitolians probably returned a blank refusal. The Macedonian invasion of Aitolia began in the summer or autumn of 322, and continued well into 321.[14] Both Krateros and Antipater commanded, though it seems that it was Krateros alone who was in command towards the end of the campaign; no doubt Antipater had responsibilities in Macedon that called him back. The Aitolians, either adopting traditional defensive tactics, or taking note of the difficulties the Greeks had usually encountered in capturing fortified places – as at Lamia – withdrew to their more remote areas, abandoned their towns, and defended their hill forts, meanwhile harassing the attackers with guerrilla raids. The invaders came with 30,000 infantry and 2,500 cavalry: the Aitolians could muster no more than 10,000 men, but it was not a war in which superior numbers would easily prevail. The campaign went on late into the winter, when Krateros got his men to build shelters against the winter weather. There was, no doubt, little or no food available for the Macedonians, the defenders having removed it all to their fastnesses; but there was still less available for the defenders.[15]

Winter was very harsh to both sides, but it seems likely that the Aitolians suffered the more. The cold of winter will have been worse on the hills than in the valleys, which the Macedonians seem to have controlled. The food supply for the invaders was negligible from local resources, but this was an army that had subsisted throughout Asia, and it had a fully competent logistical system. It is said that the Aitolians had almost decided that they would have to come down out of the mountains and fight the invaders in the valleys – though this may be the usual rhetorical assumptions of the historians looking to increase the tension – when it became evident to them that the Macedonian invasion was being suspended.[16]

Antigonos arrived to take refuge with Antipater in 321, and further news came about Perdikkas. He had decided to repudiate Nikaia and marry Kleopatra.[17] This was when Perdikkas' authority began to disintegrate. Antigonos now defied and escaped him, and Asandros, the satrap of Karia (he was some relative to Antigonos), and Menandros the former satrap of Lydia, who had been displaced by Kleopatra, both indicated that they supported Antigonos. Their messages to Antigonos reported the up-to-date situation of Perdikkas, which included not only the repudiation of Nikaia, which Antipater could regard as a gross personal insult, but also the courting of Kleopatra, which was clearly a bid for the kingship. They could also report that Perdikkas aimed to remove Antipater from the government of Macedon.[18]

Perdikkas could perhaps claim that this was in accordance with Alexander's wishes, and that since Krateros was now in Macedon, and had thereby accomplished Alexander's orders, Antipater was surplus to requirements. The Macedonian commanders, having heard the news from Menandros, and taken in Antigonos' explanation, met in conference to discuss the problem of Perdikkas.

The political ambitions of Perdikkas were mixed in with his marital intentions, but these latter should not hide the fact that his main aim was to overthrow not just Antigonos, but Antipater now also. Antipater had taken note of Perdikkas' work in Asia Minor, and presumably approved of his conquest of Kappadokia, and of his punishment of the Pisidians, who had killed his son-in-law. It seems probable that, given his constant involvement in Greek affairs over the past fifteen years, Antipater was less than up-to-date with the wider context of the empire. No one had yet threatened his position in Macedon, and his succession of victories should have rendered him politically invulnerable. But Antigonos, from his position in Asia Minor, was clearly much more familiar with imperial matters. The joint shock of the repudiation of his daughter and the apparent intention of Perdikkas to attack him, finally brought the full realization of his vulnerable situation home to Antipater.

The eventual result of the dispute that was about to begin in the later part of 321 has been explained as the overthrow, by Antipater and his confederates, of the Babylon settlement, and this, so as far as it goes, is correct – the Babylon settlement was replaced by another. But it had been Perdikkas' ambitions that had first tilted the Babylon settlement towards collapse. He had driven out one of the main satraps; he had altered Alexander's intentions with regard to his burial place; he was intending to remove the governor of Macedon, the other senior figure in the empire; his brother had killed one of Alexander's sisters; and he was aiming to marry another of those sisters as part of a campaign, of which all these other elements in the case were a part, to make himself king. This amounted to a campaign of altering the Babylon settlement piece by piece; by his threat to remove Antipater, whose position in Macedonia had been confirmed at Babylon, he was definitively overthrowing that settlement.

It is worth pausing here to consider what might have resulted if Antipater and his allies had allowed Perdikkas to continue on his path. First there would have been a major civil war, since it is highly unlikely that Antipater would have permitted Perdikkas to remove him. But before then it would have become obvious to every other satrap what Perdikkas was doing, and many of them would have resisted him – more civil warfare. On the other hand, supposing Perdikkas had won all these wars and made himself king. It seems unlikely that his rule would have been powerful or long, given the methods he had used to reach that position. He could clearly see that to make himself king it was necessary to overthrow the Babylon settlement; he had been doing so first by insidious means, but persisting in such methods would certainly lead to war. And in the process Philip III and Alexander IV would probably die.

Antipater's reply to the challenge was essentially aimed at stopping any of this from happening, and that maintaining the Babylon settlement; having eliminated Perdikkas' threat the battered Babylon settlement must be restored by means of another conference. Had he been able to live longer, or had he been younger, this conference system might have been institutionalized. It was not to be.

At the council in Macedon between Antipater, Krateros, Antigonos, Polyperchon and their advisers, it was decided that the Aitolian War should be immediately suspended, no doubt to the relief of everyone involved, commanders and soldiers, Macedonians and Aitolians alike.[19] An expedition was to be organized to move to Asia in the spring to confront Perdikkas, and to restore Antigonos. Contact was also made with Ptolemy, satrap of Egypt, with Kleitos the White, and with Dionysios the tyrant of Herakleia Pontike, both of whom had squadrons of ships.

The date of these contacts is not known, except that contacting Ptolemy was a result of Antipater's council; contacting the other two would be easy. Ptolemy was known to be already antagonistic towards Perdikkas; they had disagreed at Babylon, and Ptolemy had eliminated Kleomenes, the man who Perdikkas had hoped would report to him. Ptolemy had also conquered Cyrenaica, apparently independently, and so quite possibly in defiance of Perdikkas, whose approach rather suggests that displays of independence by any subordinate were unwelcome. He was an obvious man to contact for anyone who was in Perdikkas' sights. And it turned out that Ptolemy had a very effective ploy available.

Perdikkas had set Alexander's corpse in motion in its monstrous funeral cart, intending to conduct the funeral himself in Macedon, at Aigai where Philip II and earlier kings had their tombs. By doing so he was, once again, marking out his claim to the kingship, for it was one of the duties of a new king to cremate the body of his predecessor and construct his tomb. But to do this he would need to move into Macedon, and this was another aspect of his threat to remove, or attack, Antipater. Perdikkas would clearly only be able to conduct the funeral after forcing his way into Macedon against Antipater's own forces. By contacting Ptolemy, Antipater was clearly hoping he would be able to do something to distract Perdikkas.

Ptolemy did so by taking control of the hearse of Alexander at Damascus. The task of moving the unwieldy cart had been given to Arrhidaios, an almost unknown Macedonian officer, and it is evident that his original instructions had been to take it to Egypt. This is the significance of the fact that he had reached Damascus on his way when he was interrupted. It is sometimes claimed that it was always intended to bring Alexander to Aigai in Macedon, to bury him alongside his father, but Arrhidaios' arrival at Damascus shows that he was going to Egypt.

Perdikkas must have been informed of the route taken by the hearse, perhaps when Arrhidaios refused his orders to go to Macedon instead, an order possibly issued only when the hearse was in north Syria. Ptolemy was also informed, perhaps when Arrhidaios, reasonably afraid of what Perdikkas would do, reported his whereabouts. Two Macedonian forces therefore had been dispatched to secure control of the hearse. One was sent by Perdikkas; it was commanded by two brothers, Polemon and Attalos, sons of Andromenes; the other was brought by Ptolemy personally. (Attalos was married to Perdikkas' sister Atalante, another wing of the marriage system being constructed by Perdikkas.)

Ptolemy won the contest, and took the funeral cart to Egypt, where it rested in Memphis for the next dozen years or so. He is often said to have 'stolen' or 'hijacked' the hearse, but the fact that he took it over at Damascus is a clear indication that the hearse was already on its way to Egypt; had Polemon and Attalos succeeded in taking it over, their action would really have been a hijacking. Polemon and Attalos had to report failure to Perdikkas, a report that must have arrived at much the same time that he heard of the approach of the army of Antipater and Krateros coming from Macedon.[20]

Perdikkas was thus faced by defiance from Antigonos, Asandros and Menandros, from the well-armed Antipater and Krateros, and at the same time from Ptolemy; Ptolemy's enmity was the more important because it directly affected his intention to seize the kingship. Antipater and Krateros had not yet made any open moves and could not do so until free of the Aitolian War. If he was to have any chance of securing the kingship – which his efforts regarding Kleopatra and Alexander's body do strongly imply – Perdikkas needed to bury Alexander and marry Kleopatra, preferably in that order. Now he was going to have to fight to realize his ambition. It was a war that he could blame on his opponents, but which was in reality the product of his own policies.

The issues involved in this war included both the future of the Macedonian Empire and outrage at the way Perdikkas had behaved to his enemies personally, though it was clearly the former that was the more important, as is shown by their delayed reaction – none of them acted against Perdikkas until it was clear that he aimed to overthrow the political arrangements made at Babylon. Antigonos was essentially appealing to the fact that he had been made satrap of Phrygia by Alexander, had fought for and defended that territory, and that his occupation of the post of satrap had been confirmed by the conference at Babylon after Alexander died, the same conference at which Perdikkas had been appointed to his present position; he was thus insisting that, whatever grievances Perdikkas had with him, it did not justify arresting him or chasing him out of his province; he was thus appealing over Perdikkas' head to the assembly of Macedonians, and to the memory of Alexander.

Antipater was similarly denying Perdikkas' authority in a matter of the appointments to governing posts, and was also appealing to the assembly of the Macedonians, or at least to a conference of the Macedonian army chiefs, against Perdikkas' ambitions and intentions. Krateros would appear to be to have agreed with both men, though what post he was hoping for is unclear; probably he aimed to make his position as *prostates* of the kings effective. Krateros' second in command, Polyperchon, who had not appeared in any of the events since his appointment to that situation by Alexander, may or may not have agreed with them, though his later policies suggest he was equally in favour of maintaining the Babylon settlement, and was apparently content to take the position of temporary governor in Macedon while Antipater went on a long campaign to deal with Perdikkas.

The first task, however, was to disentangle the Macedonian army from its Aitolian campaign. This turned out to be fairly easy, though no doubt it took some negotiation. The essential point was that the Macedonian army was to evacuate Aitolia, but the treaty that was made solved none of the issues between the two parties involved. An unusual degree of hatred had apparently been built up by the Macedonian attack, and the invaders set down in writing that they would resume the war later with the object of complete conquest, followed by the removal of the entire Aitolian population to 'the most distant desert of Asia'.[21] Diodoros' words imply that this was part of the agreement with the Aitolians, though this seems highly unlikely; when he says it was set out in a decree, be must be referring to an internal Macedonian document, or a private agreement between the three commanders to come back later to attend to the Aitolian issue, as they may have thought of it. There is no doubt that, whatever the details of the treaty it was in reality no more than an armistice. The Aitolians both fully understood that and resolved to take early countermeasures.

Perdikkas held his own council meeting as the various challenges to his authority became clear.[22] There were two main military problems: the enmity of Antipater and his group, and that of Ptolemy. The main danger came from Macedon, where Antipater's army was a formidable force, the size of Alexander's at Gaugamela, and it was commanded by a victorious general. Perdikkas, however, may have assumed that the war with the Aitolians would pin down Antipater's Macedonian forces for some time yet. Ptolemy did not seem strong enough militarily to do him serious damage: an invasion of Syria by him would not be a serious threat. All Perdikkas' commanders wanted to attack Ptolemy first, presumably fitting in with Perdikkas' own inclinations. The theft, as he would have put it, of Alexander's funeral cart was a personal defiance, a challenge to his authority, and a clear setback to his ambitions. Ptolemy's military weakness meant he could be dealt with fairly quickly. It may also be that Predikkas knew that his troops would be distinctly unhappy at having to fight with Macedonians in Macedon itself; this was in part the lesson of Alketas' confrontation with Kynnane.

Perdikkas needed to consider the wishes of his soldiers. The one major force in the Macedonian Empire, which seemed to be intent on holding the empire together despite the disputes of the generals, was the Macedonian soldiers and they understood that the symbol of that unity must be the Argead royal family. Perdikkas had shown that he knew the soldiers' preferences, for he had given way to Alketas' men over the marriage of Adea with Philip III.

If he could go into battle with the aim of conducting the delayed funeral of Alexander, they might be less reluctant. However, it also seems that his desire to become king was capable of overriding his common and political senses. He decided to attack Ptolemy first, but he also made no attempt to deal diplomatically with Antipater; quite the reverse, for he was contacted by the Aitolians and made an alliance with them. He urged them to resume their war at once, which he must have known would be a severe threat to the Macedonian homeland.

Perdikkas took part of his army south into Syria to attack Ptolemy in Egypt, leaving Eumenes in command in Asia Minor with what Diodoros calls 'a suitable army'.[23] It is not at all clear how many troops he had or how the whole army was divided among the commanders, but it is probable that Antipater's and Krateros' forces were larger than Eumenes' army. It was obvious, however, that Antipater would need to divide his forces in view of the hostility of the Aitolians, and to supervise the conquered Greeks.

As the most aggrieved party, Antigonos with 3,000 men, collected ten triremes from the Athenian dockyard, courtesy presumably of Antipater, and sailed across the Aegean to land in Karia. The satrap there, his relative Asandros, welcomed him, and Menandros in Lydia did the same – both had already indicated their support for Antipater and so for Antigonos, and were inimical to Perdikkas. The speed of events does suggest that their defections were prearranged.[24]

Perdikkas, on his way to Egypt, gave further indications that he regarded the arrangements made at Babylon to be changeable at his whim. He removed Philotas from Kilikia as being too friendly with Krateros, replacing him with Philoxenos (not the man who had been in authority in Asia earlier, but a man of no apparent earlier attainments).[25] It could be that Perdikkas' plan was to replace notable Macedonians with nonentities who were dependent solely on himself (though if so it did not apparently work with Philoxenos). He also replaced the satrap of Babylon, Archon, with Dokimos, who had to fight to gain possession, killing Archon in the process; Dokimos was another Macedonian of no previous attainments, and, like Philoxenos, of very pliable loyalty.[26] He sent a naval force to Cyprus under Aristonous to prevent the Cypriot kings leaguing with Ptolemy.[27] Aristonous had at least served with Alexander and had been awarded a golden crown at Susa in 324, but all three of these commanders clearly owed their new importance to Perdikkas.

Antigonos collected a force of infantry – probably his original 3,000 men – and a small fleet that included ten Athenian triremes, together with some reinforcements from Dionysios of Herakleia Pontike, and sailed to recover Cyprus from Aristonous. He was successful in a naval fight – which the Athenians claimed as a victory for their ships – and defeated and captured Aristonous' land forces. Aristonous was allowed to return to Macedon on parole.[28]

The forces left to defend Asia under Eumenes' command were still in the Pisidian area. Eumenes himself was at Sardis seeing Kleopatra when Antigonos arrived and was taken by surprise, but he was warned by Kleopatra and escaped.[29] He had difficulty in gathering together all the forces assigned to him by Perdikkas: Alketas refused to join him, arguing that his Macedonian soldiers would not fight Krateros' Macedonians – these were the men who had already refused to fight Kynanne's little army.[30] The unsuccessful would-be satrap of Armenia, Neoptolemos, did join Eumenes, but does not seem to have commanded many soldiers, and proved to be very susceptible to Antipater's intriguing messages.[31] Antipater and Krateros brought their army to the Hellespont – no doubt assisted once more by Hekataios at Kardia.

Polyperchon was left in Macedon to defend the kingdom.

The arrival of Antigonos and the defection of Menandros and Asandros seriously weakened the Perdikkan position in western Asia Minor. Antipater and Krateros crossed the Hellespont when they persuaded Kleitos the White to change sides, and bring his ships with him.[32] Eumenes quarrelled with Neoptolemos, who had been invited also to join Antipater, and they fell to fighting; Neoptolemos was defeated and escaped with only a few soldiers to join Antipater. Eumenes retreated eastwards, and was tackled by Krateros, with Neoptolemos, while Antipater marched on after Perdikkas.

Krateros and Eumenes squared off in battle 'near Kappadokia', Neoptolemos persuaded Krateros that Eumenes' Macedonians would not fight him, and all Krateros had to do when the battle began was to show himself and they would desist. This very idea no doubt greatly appealed to the highly self-regarding Krateros. Eumenes got wind of the scheme, and clearly understood its likely efficacy. He changed his dispositions so that in the battle Krateros found he was facing a 'barbarian' contingent of Paphlagonians, who had been recruited by Eumenes. These were quite happy to fight (and kill) Macedonians. One of those who died was Krateros. Neoptolemos also died, this time by Eumenes in a hand-to-hand fight between them. Neoptolemos had been disloyal to the very end.[33]

The battle is difficult to understand from Diodoros' account, for he is fixated on supposed combat between Neoptolemos and Eumenes, but it seems that Krateros' hoplite infantry phalanx was badly damaged, but the other wing was hardly involved. (This amounted to a defeat of Macedonian infantry by Paphlagonians.) Eumenes followed the survivors as they retreated, hoping to persuade them to surrender, but they broke an agreement and marched off in the night, and succeeded in joining Antipater.[34]

Meanwhile in Macedon, Polyperchon had been left in command of the remaining forces, a 'considerable army', probably the usual 13,000 infantry and 1,500 cavalry. He faced an immediate renewal of the Aitolian War as soon as Antipater's army had crossed into Asia. The Aitolians mustered a force of 12,000 infantry and 400 horse – a larger force than they had deployed to resist the Macedonian attacks, and almost twice what they had contributed in the Lamian War, so they had presumably either gathered allies or had recruited mercenaries, or, more likely, this time they put their full force in the field, without leaving a strong homeland guard for defence. They attacked and captured Amphissa in Lokris, and other towns in that country, and then defeated a Macedonian force in the area commanded by a general called Polykles, who was killed. They then turned north and invaded Thessaly, where most of the Thessalians joined them, producing an army of 25,000 infantry and 1,500 horse. Thessaly was horse country and its armed forces were usually mainly cavalry; it is unlikely that the Thessalian infantry was well-trained.

It may be presumed that the Aitolians intended to continue north to invade Macedon, but were prevented by an attack on their homeland by the Akarnanians from the west, which was provoked by diplomacy from Macedon, and perhaps by the removal of so many Aitolian troops to the east. At once, the Aitolian forces were recalled, leaving their allies, commanded by Menon of Pharsalos, to face Polyperchon and the Macedonian army. The Akarnanians had clearly waited until the Aitolians were deeply involved in Thessaly before striking, just as the Aitolians had seized the moment of Antipater's departure to mount their own attack. It is to be presumed that the inciting of the Akarnanians was Antipater's work; it was a repeat of the situation in the Lamian War, when the Aitolians had left the siege of Lamia to attend to their 'national business'.

Polyperchon similarly used the temporary absence of the Aitolians from the main front (they drove off the Akarnanians quickly) to attack Menon's army, of which the Macedonians made short work. It looks very much as though Menon's instant army, produced when the Aitolians arrived, was large but barely competent. Menon was killed; his army was 'cut to pieces', as Diodoros says. Polyperchon reimposed Macedonian control over their country.[35]

The two enemies in Europe do not seem to have resumed their fighting. With an army only a third of the size of that which had failed to conquer Aitolia in the winter campaign, Polyperchon could not hope to succeed; the Aitolians, threatened from the west and east simultaneously as before, and having secured control of Amphissa, were not going to risk another campaign, and a possible defeat – the destruction of the Thessalians was a sobering thought. This war stopped, though it is not likely that any definitive peace treaty was made.

It is also probable that the fighting stopped because the news arrived that Perdikkas had attacked Ptolemy in Egypt, and had been fended off; a conspiracy among his officers had then brought his murder, carried out by Peithon and Seleukos (his second in command) and others.[36] The war had been Perdikkas' War, and so now with his death it was over. All the combatants could stop, take a breath, and reconsider. It had cost the lives of Perdikkas, Krateros, Neoptolemos, Menon, Archon and Polykles among the senior Macedonian commanders, and several thousands of soldiers.

The result was to put Antipater in command, for the moment.

He had reached Kilikia when he heard that Perdikkas was dead, having already heard of Krateros' defeat and death. He then, having probably collected the men from Krateros' army who had escaped from Eumenes, moved on south. Perdikkas' army, purged of his main supporters by proscribing fifty or more men, elected two new guardians for the kings, Peithon and Arrhidaios. Conveying the kings and Adea, now married to King Philip and renamed Eurydike, the army moved north to meet Antipater. A great conference was held at a place in central Syria called Triparadeisos, which from its name was a large hunting reserve originally organized for the Persian aristocrats living in Syria – and so, no doubt, complete with the sort of well-appointed accommodation suitable for a set of luxury-loving Macedonian generals. Antipater was joined by many of those generals, several of whom were in command of troops: Antigonos had won his victory in Cyprus and had his own small force; the Perdikkan army that Ptolemy had beaten was now led by the two men elected as guardians, Peithon, who had beaten the Greek rebels in the east, and Arrhidaios, who had commanded the funeral cart. These were to be the 'temporary' guardians of the two kings, while Seleukos and Antigenes, former Perdikkans who had murdered their chief, now had actual command of the army. Adea-Eurydike began to act vigorously in her husband's name, demanding the right to confirm any orders given by the guardians. She was no more than 17 years old, but like her mother a trained warrior and capable of commanding troops.

The army itself was in a disgruntled mood, having been beaten, seen its commander murdered, suffered the murderous purge of fifty of its officers, and claimed not to have been paid. The arrival also of Attalos, Perdikkas' brother-in-law, who had commanded his fleet, was a further complication; his wife Atalante had been one of the victims of the purge, and Attalos was justifiably angry; he also had command of a major fleet. He landed at Tyre, secured a treasure of 800 talents from the commander there, and received many of those who escaped from the army's anger, so that he soon commanded a considerable force, said to be 10,000 strong.[37] There were thus at least three armies present at the meeting when Antipater's force arrived – Attalos', Antipater's, ex-Perdikkas' – and each was loyal to a different commander or commanders; in addition there were other smaller forces, such as that of Antigonos.

It seems that Antipater and his army were the last to arrive. In Kilikia he probably had to wait for the refugees from Krateros' army to join him. He had been welcomed by Philoxenos, recently appointed by Perdikkas, but who proved fully amenable to Antipater's authority, even before news of Perdikkas' death arrived.[38] This may well have given Antipater a taste of the condition of affairs. With the elimination of several of the greater commanders, the second-level commanders such as Philoxenos were freed of any allegiance; they could therefore accept the supremacy of any man with a large army. That is, none of such men was predictable, nor could they be relied on.

When he reached Triparadeisos, Antipater found that Peithon and Arrhidaios, faced with disputes with the army, conflicting loyalties, and perhaps most unnerving of all, the fierce demands and authority of Adea-Eurydike, acting for Philip III, had resigned their posts. (Or perhaps they had only been appointed for the brief march from Egypt to the meeting.) Antipater appears to have been made guardian of the kings in their place, even before he arrived at the camp, though this is not altogether certain.[39] The soldiers were mainly concerned, so they said, to secure their pay, which they appear to have expected would be the same as that which Alexander had given to the veterans who had made the march from Babylon to Kilikia with Krateros – that is, full back pay plus a talent for each man.[40] This, apart from being barely affordable, would be impossible to provide in the short term since the main treasury of the empire was still at Susa in Iran; also to pay off the soldiers might mean the disintegration of the army, as the men took the money and went home. But it was a very useful political tool in the hands of those who might aim to deny the control of the army to Antipater: Eurydike used it and was supported by Attalos for his own reasons. Many men of the Perdikkan army now supported Eurydike.

It was at this point that Antipater and his army arrived. He encamped his own army near to, but separate from, the former Perdikkans. The two forces occupied opposite sides of a river, probably the Orontes, which was wide enough to need to be crossed by a bridge (which rather puts it some way north of the Bekaa Valley, perhaps in the plain below the later Apameia). The events that followed are retailed in very different ways by the three sources that have survived, but the main incidents are clear, though much of the intermediary and explicatory details are missing.[41] This, in fact, is clearly the result of the conditions at the meeting, which must have been confusing for all involved, until the moment when Antipater finally gained control.

It is evident that he had not expected an unruly army to confront him with an angry teenage queen at its head. But she was the wife of the legitimate king, and Antipater was loyal to two things, Macedon, and the royal house of Philip II. What he cannot have expected was that the army would be vociferously demanding an issue of pay to which the men were not entitled. They looked back, probably repeatedly, to the generosity of Alexander, and when Antipater said he would look into the matter, he simply provoked their anger, since it sounded like, and probably was, an evasion. Either then or at a later confrontation, he had to get through an angry Perdikkan group to get to his own base, but the mob of soldiers blocked his way, and seemed intent on killing him if he challenged them. (This confrontation is strange: why should they wish to kill him? One must suspect that someone had egged them on, presumably Attalos, possibly Eurydike; but it was only a minority who were involved; the rest of the men were fairly reasonable.) Antigonos and Seleukos faced them down, and Antigonos talked to them, probably addressing the great majority who were not so antagonistic, and persuaded them to let Antipater through.[42] It was, after all, only reasonable for Antipater to investigate the condition of the local treasury before making promises to pay the soldiers, and he was experienced enough not to make promises he might not be able to keep. And the fact that the soldiers were amenable to Antigonos' words suggests that the threat to kill Antipater was unlikely to have been all that serious and had perhaps only been made by a relatively small group.

Antipater, having reached the safety of his own camp, held a meeting of his own commanders.[43] The fact that Antigonos and Seleukos had spoken to the mutineers in separate groups, suggests that they were not really united, and could therefore be dominated by the united command. Antipater's commanders, however they did it, together with the authority of all (no doubt) the other major commanders, with the exception of Attalos, succeeded, perhaps over a period of several days, in quelling the trouble. None of the commanders will have been pleased at the rank-and-file's activities and agitations. We lack all details of this process, but it seems safe to assume that, like Alexander in a similar situation at Babylon, the ringleaders of the troops were identified and killed. Antipater could evidently rely on the cavalry, and on his own men (which included those of Krateros' men who had survived, and who had been given the original pay awarded by Alexander) as against the Perdikkans. Quite probably the soldiers who had come from Europe despised the unruliness of the Perdikkans for their failure in Egypt, their unpleasant killing of Perdikkas' people, and their propensity to indiscipline.

Once he was securely in command, Antipater addressed the troops. He appears to have been confronted by Eurydike again, but it is said that he frightened her into silence. The only threat that could do that would be one of instant death.[44] Eurydike had witnessed the murder of her own mother in a similar situation, and Antipater had dealt in death as ruler of Macedon for the past fifteen years; any threat he uttered would carry full conviction; he had probably organized the killing of the soldiers' agitators, the men who had been Eurydike's instruments, and he was clearly quite willing to kill others; any threat he uttered would have been fully believable. He might also have promised her honour and protection, and he was certainly solicitous of her and her husband, and of the other king and his mother, in the next months. Eurydike's meeting with him was the last chance she had of exercising open influence and given the fact that Antipater had clearly regained control of the whole camp, she must have known that it was bound to fail. All credit to her for her persistence, however.

Antipater had been appointed, or elected, as the replacement for Perdikkas (and Peithon and Arrhidaios) as guardian of the kings – that is, regent of the kingdom. This had, of course, actually been Krateros' position, and had he survived the battle with Eumenes his presence at Triparadeisos might have made a significant difference. Without him, the only man who was of sufficient authority and political stature to take the position was Antipater. When he was given the post, and exactly how, is one of those details that has vanished. The most likely occasion is when Peithon and Arrhidaios resigned, that is, before Antipater had arrived at the meeting. He is said in one source to have been 're-elected' to the post, which has been interpreted as meaning that he had been elected before he arrived, then deposed by the riotous army, then re-elected after gaining control, though this sequence seems unlikely. His only way of gaining control was to exercise his authority, so a new election after actually establishing his control makes little sense. It is therefore likely that the 're-election' was a reference to his appointment, a confirmation of his original election at Triparadeisos.

Chapter 7

The Problems of Empire

A ntipater had been accompanied to Triparadeisos by his eldest son Kassander. By this time Antipater was in his late seventies and it is probable that Kassander was doing diplomatic tasks for him. The recent crisis had had a powerful effect on the other members of his family: Phila's second husband Krateros had been killed in battle – as had her first, of course, four years before. It is not known if Krateros ever saw his son, but Phila gave birth during 321 and named the child after his father. Her sister Nikaia had been married and perhaps repudiated (or not repudiated, it is not clear what the situation was exactly) by Perdikkas; either way, he was now dead as well, and she was the third of Antipater's daughters to be widowed. Part of the negotiations, or at least the contacts, Antipater had with Ptolemy had been over another marriage, that of Antipater's youngest daughter Eurydike, to the Egyptian ruler; the marriage took place in 321.[1] At or before the meeting at Triparadeisos Phila, the recent widow, was married to the son of Antigonos, Demetrios.[2] This was a curious alliance: Phila was now twice widowed, had two young children (one born earlier that year) and was about 30 years old: Demetrios was an inexperienced boy of only 17. Such were the exigencies of politics. Both of these marriages were clearly connected with the political relations of the crisis over Perdikkas; they may have taken place at any time in 321 until the meeting at Triparadeisos.[3] And Nikaia, widowed or repudiated (or both), was now also quickly remarried, to Antipater's neighbour Lysimachos. It has been suggested that this was a great enhancement of Lysimachos' status, and so it may be, but it may also be well to recall that the groom had been *somatophylax* of both Philip and Alexander. Socially among the Macedonians, he was already remarkable.[4]

All this has an air of some desperation about it. It was all in large part political, as the hasty marriage of Phila to an adolescent boy shows. But to marry off three of his daughters in one year is more than politics; at nearly 80 it seems likely that Antipater was feeling that he could not last much longer. (In fact, he lasted two more years.) He must have hoped that this marital generosity, spraying the political world with his daughters, would have a beneficial effect on the empire's affairs.

If that was Antipater's intention he was, of course, wrong. There is no case in the ancient world where a marriage alliance became a political alliance for more than a brief period after the ceremony. This was, for the men involved, one of the benefits of the general practice of immuring wives into the household, where they could be ignored, and the husbands could pursue their own, frequently selfish, agendas without restraint. Antipater surely knew this. He had seen Philip and Alexander use themselves in the same way, with little or no effect on political affairs; his own marriage had produced many children, but there is no glimpse ever of his wife; indeed, it is not known what her name was or even if there was more than one wife. Alexander's marriage to Roxanne had no effect in Baktria, other than to enhance the importance of her father Oxyartes, but that might well have happened anyway. The women in these marriages were certainly seen as eligible, but not as people of power, unless they were able to exploit the security of their marital status to exert influence; they were more useful as a means of enhancing the prestige of the husbands, and in this, as it happens, Antipater's daughters carried an exceptionally high value, and Antipater clearly spent some time in or before the Triparadeisos meeting in attending to this marital diplomacy.

At the same time, this generation of women, and perhaps the next, were exceptionally active politically, a factor which is partly due to the families, but also to their own forceful characters. Kynanne and Adea-Eurydike are good examples, but Olympias was perhaps the most notable. Phila's marriage to Demetrios was also a particularly good example; Eurydike in Egypt later proved to be just as assertive. This characteristic carried through into the following generation and set the pattern for several women over the next couple of centuries. (This aspect of the Antipatrid family will be discussed in more detail in Chapter 13.)

Antipater also now had three grandchildren. Phila's sons by Balakros and Krateros – Antipater and Krateros – joined his eldest daughter's son by Alexander Lynkestis, Arrhabaios. (The widow of Alexander is not heard of; presumably she was either dead or living silently in Antipater's household; it is noticeable that he made no attempt to marry her off to a second husband, though he did so for her sisters.) This eldest grandson, Arrhabaios, was about 15 years old at the time of Triparadeisos, while Antipater son of Balakros was about 10. So far as is known, none of Antipater's sons was yet married, but the eldest, Kassander, was still no more than 35, perhaps less, and the age of marriage for such men was, as apparently it had been with Antipater himself, only after they could afford to set up their own households, and it may be that Antipater's unusually long life was preventing that. His son Iolaos is the only other one who is recorded as doing anything at this period. He had escorted Nikaia to her marriage with Perdikkas, which took place during his campaigns in Kappadokia and Pisidia.[5]

Antipater's other major activity at Triparadeisos was to allocate satraps to their provinces.[6] It is here that his essentially conservative policy reveals itself. Antipater had made war on Perdikkas with the aim of restoring the Babylon settlement after Perdikkas' assault on it in pursuit of his personal ambitions. This meant returning as far as possible to the conditions and personnel arrangements agreed in 323. In most cases this meant confirming in office those who had held their posts since the settlement at Babylon, or in some cases before that, wherever it was possible. Mostly it was in the east that no changes were necessary, since those governors had hardly been involved in the recent crisis. The changes that did take place therefore were only in a relatively few provinces. Eumenes, still in arms after defeating Krateros, was, naturally enough, to lose Kappadokia, and to be replaced by Nikanor. The large number of Nikanors at large at this time prohibits any clear identification of this man, but it is virtually certain that he was a supporter of Antipater, possibly one of his commanders. He might well need to fight to gain control of his satrapy, as it had only just recently been conquered by Perdikkas, so a man with some military ability would be needed.

His neighbour to the south-east was to be Amphimachos, in the satrapy of Mesopotamia, to which Arbelitis in northern Babylonia was now attached. This man has been mistakenly identified as a son of Philinna, one of Philip II's wives; rather he was probably the brother of Arrhidaios, the funeral cart man and former joint-guardian, who was also given a satrapy at this distribution. Amphimachos replaced a satrap called Archelaos, who had probably been originally appointed by Alexander. He had – also apparently, for he is scarcely known – been a supporter of Perdikkas.

There were several posts available for new appointments in Asia Minor as a result of the fighting there, and the divided allegiances of the governors. Antigonos would, of course, continue to be satrap of Phrygia, to which Lykia and Pamphylia had been added some time before. This was a large satrapy, in effect one of perhaps four of equivalent size and importance in the empire – Egypt, Babylonia and Media were the others, along with Macedon itself. But it would seem that Antipater was already suspicious of the ambition Antigonos was displaying. Ambition was, of course, a familiar trait in all the Macedonian commanders, indeed it might be a necessary element in their characters, but Antigonos' ambition was linked to his holding a large satrapy. Ptolemy had demonstrated, by his defence of Egypt and his subsequent refusal of any imperial post after the death of Perdikkas, that he was certainly ambitious, but only to hold Egypt. The satrap of Media, Peithon, one of the kings' guardians appointed to convey the army to the Triparadeisos meeting, had earlier clashed with Perdikkas over the treatment of the defeated Greek colonists in the east. Perdikkas had ordered them to be massacred rather than allow Peithon to recruit them into his own satrapal forces. Peithon would later show and demonstrate an awkward ability to expand his control over his neighbouring territories. Neither of these men was Antipater's current problem. But Antigonos in Phrygia was. It was not far from Macedon, it was strategically placed in regard to the control of the western part of the empire, and it had both a considerable army and an ambitious and capable governor. In addition, Antigonos had been given two other imperial tasks: he was given charge of the kings, rather as Perdikkas had been. Antipater was now *prostates*, but just as Krateros' position as *prostates* had been separated from the control of the kings, so it seems Antipater was also in that position. Antigonos had also been given charge of the war against Eumenes, now designated as a rebel. Thus Antigonos in effect took over Perdikkas' task, and Eumenes' territory, in Kappadokia: but now he would need to remove Eumenes in order to install Nikanor, the new satrap, just as Perdikkas had had to conquer Kappadokia to install Eumenes.

Antipater clearly understood that it needed a man like Antigonos to take on this latter task, a capable commander and administrator. Eumenes, after all, had already won two battles. Of capable commanders there were not many in the empire – Antipater was one, possibly Ptolemy was another, but most of the many commanders of units had never displayed any real military command ability of their own. Take, for example, Leonnatos and Krateros, whose lack of expertise had led to two defeats and to their deaths. Krateros had been beaten by a simple manoeuvre that he had not been quick enough to detect. It took more than mere ambition, personal beauty and a commanding presence to win battles in the Hellenistic World; subtlety and manoeuvring were still required. Alexander was the model, and perhaps Philip. Antigonos had shown those qualities, in his war to defend Phrygia against the Persian attacks, and in his campaign against the Perdikkans in Cyprus.[7] Antigonos was familiar with the territory and had shown good and inventive command abilities, so his appointment to suppress Eumenes made sense. Eumenes, of course, was another highly capable commander, though probably this was not yet understood, despite his defeating both Neoptolemos and Krateros. It turned out that Antigonos had a major task on his hands.

At the same time, Antipater had to limit Antigonos' scope. To do this he appointed a series of men to the satrapies next to and around Phrygia, only one of whom was a friend of Antigonos; the rest were Antipater's men. Nikanor in Kappadokia was one, chosen by Antipater and owing all to him; Arrhidaios, appointed to Hellespontine Phrygia, was another, an associate of Ptolemy, and a brother to Amphimachos in Mesopotamia, all three of whom were linked to Antipater. To Lydia, where it seems that Kleopatra was no longer governor, though she continued to live in Sardis, went Kleitos the White, the victor of the battle of Amorgos, who had deserted Perdikkas during the crisis. He was also as arrogant and self-regarding as Antigonos; they were unlikely to be friendly. In Karia, Asandros was confirmed, the only man in the area who was linked with Antigonos; he had joined the anti-Perdikkan movement from the start of the crisis and so he could hardly be removed. He had also, soon after the end of the Triparadeisos meeting, come under attack by Attalos, Perdikkas' brother-in-law, who had sailed from Tyre with his fleet and his adherents to attack Rhodes, which resisted successfully, and the coastal cities of Knidos and Kaunos, both in Asandros' satrapy. Even suggesting replacing Asandros while he was under attack would be unthinkable. The opportune shift of Philoxenos in Kilikia to support Antipater was rewarded by his confirmation in office. It is noticeable that both Kleitos and Philoxenos had been Perdikkans until the crisis but were preferred by Antipater in their new jobs to men whom he might have considered to be earlier supporters. Menandros, the former Lydian governor, for example, who had been helpful in the crisis, suffered another demotion; he had been, like Asandros, an associate of Antigonos before the crisis.

Antipater, therefore, ringed Antigonos round with satraps who were less than friendly to him in the imperial political system; this was a condition of which Antigonos must have been aware from the start. It may have been intended to compel him to concentrate on his main task, which was the elimination of Eumenes, though a more straightforward interpretation would be that these appointments were intended to prevent him from expanding his control over these neighbours. No doubt Antigonos would end up in control of Kappadokia, either in person or through Nikanor, whose obligations would therefore shift from the distant Antipater to the nearby Antigonos, but that was a minor problem that could eventually be controlled by imposing a new satrap. This interpretation is encouraged by the appointment of Antipater's eldest son Kassander as Antigonos' Chiliarch, his subordinate commander of cavalry.[8] It is clear that Kassander's role was to report on Antigonos' activities to his father, and that this was publicly understood. It was unlikely to be effective; one is reminded of Perdikkas' attempt to have Kleomenes of Naukratis operate in the same way with Ptolemy; Ptolemy soon disposed of him. It is unlikely that Antigonos could have executed Kassander, but the fact is that they soon parted company. The installation of Phila as the wife of Demetrios may well have had a similar intention on Antipater's part, but Phila was loyal to her husband above her father and certainly above her brother, as she proved repeatedly in the next thirty years, and Antipater surely understood this, so perhaps we can discount the idea of Phila as a spy in Antigonos' household.

Antigonos will have understood precisely what Antipater was doing. There is no indication that he contested the situation – indeed Antigonos is said to have requested the task of dealing with Eumenes and his party.[9] Antipater compensated for intimidating encirclement of Phrygia by two further measures. In order to pursue Eumenes, and a number of other former Perdikkan supporters who were at large in Asia Minor, including Dokimos from Babylon, Antigonos was given charge of the former Perdikkan army, a commission as '*strategos* over Asia', and the custody of the two kings. Holding the two kings would make it clear to any Macedonians on Eumenes' side that Antigonos was operating as an imperial agent, and that the army he was leading was the royal army, so that fighting against him would clearly be treason. It might also act to persuade Eumenes' Macedonian soldiers to stop fighting.

The Perdikkan army was therefore now being given the chance to demonstrate that it was truly loyal to the Macedonian Empire. Furthermore, chasing the ex-Perdikkans, and above all Eumenes, though he was not the only one, would clearly keep Antigonos busy for some time to come, and it actually did so for the rest of Antipater's life. It did, however, have some unexpected consequences. Antigonos' new task was some compensation for the evident suspicion shown by Antipater's appointment of inimical men to his neighbouring satrapies. The whole arrangement was also clearly a return to what had been the situation before Perdikkas upset the Babylon settlement: Antipater remained in control in Europe, Antigonos in Asia Minor, with a particular task to accomplish; one must, of course, understand that '*strategos* over Asia' referred to Asia Minor and not to the whole continent, though Antigonos proved capable of expanding that definition when Eumenes moved further east. It was not intended that Antigonos should move out of the circumscribed territory of Phrygia, of which he was satrap, but the exigencies of war eventually pulled him away. It was hardly expected that his commission to suppress Eumenes would take him all the way to central Iran.

Antipater made two more new appointments to major eastern satrapies, while leaving the rest unchanged. Seleukos was rewarded for having murdered Perdikkas, and perhaps for having intervened on Antipater's behalf at Triparadeisos, by appointment as satrap of Babylonia. This was one of the richest satrapies, but like Egypt, it was a proud land of long traditions and might be difficult to govern if the satrap was arrogant and careless of its lifestyle. Arrogant Seleukos probably was – he was a Macedonian general after all – but careless he could rarely be accused of being. The anti-Perdikkan satrap Archon, who had been appointed by Alexander when he returned from the east, had died in the fighting when Dokimos had been appointed to replace him by Perdikkas.[10] Seleukos had to drive Dokimos out to secure his satrapy, which was greeted as a relief by the Babylonians – Dokimos had been oppressive – so getting Seleukos off to a good start. Dokimos fled to Asia Minor to join Eumenes.

Next door to Babylonia, Antigenes, Seleukos' fellow murderer, was appointed as satrap of Susiana. One cannot help wondering if Antipater deliberately posted these two men as far away from Macedon as he could, contriving a political murder tainted a man, and he might get a taste for it; sending them far from Macedon might make Antipater himself safer. Susiana had had several satraps in the recent past, and Antigenes proved to be absent more often than present; in Susa itself Xenophilos had been garrison commander under the previous three satraps and seems to have continued in that office; in effect he was Antigenes' deputy and substitute satrap.[11]

Antigenes also had another task, which was to begin transporting the treasure held at Susa westwards.[12] It was clearly, as the recent crisis had demonstrated, in an awkward place at Susa, and moving it to the west would render it more accessible, and therefore useful, especially since the bulk of the army was now in Phrygia and Macedon. Antigenes already commanded a potent regiment, the Argyraspides, the 'Silver Shields', a large force, 3,000 strong, of highly competent hoplites. They had originally been part of Krateros' army, and he had left them in Kilikia when he marched to Macedon to join Antipater; Perdikkas had taken them to Egypt to attack Ptolemy. They were exceptionally loyal to Alexander's memory, and to the royal house generally, so they could be trusted, as perhaps could Antigenes himself, with the task of transporting the treasure without losing, or looting, too much of it on the journey.

The detachment of the Argyraspides on a particular task was only one of the several further decisions made at Triparadeisos concerning the army. By this time there were in fact a number of separate armies, usually identified by their commander's names – Antipater's, Attalos', Antigonos' and so on – and it is probable by now that the Macedonians were outnumbered overall in the total of soldiers. In the battle between Eumenes and Krateros at least half of Eumenes' army was composed of Paphlagonians, and the world from Greece to India was populated with, and garrisoned by, detachments of Greek mercenaries. In the Far East it seems highly likely that the local armies of the satraps were, like Eumenes' force, a mixture of Greeks and locals, the Macedonians having been largely taken away by Alexander. Alexander had recruited 30,000 Persian youths and trained them in the Macedonian methods, though how far they were still mobilized is not clear. Krateros had brought with him from the east 1,000 Persian slingers and archers. It followed from such work that the army as a whole was no longer anywhere near wholly Macedonian, and yet it was the Macedonian troops who made the political running, largely because they were concentrated, had their own agenda, and were commanded by the generals who were the real political animals.[13]

Antipater now had on his hands the royal family, consisting of the two kings, Philip's wife Eurydike (who appears to have accepted her new situation) and Alexander's mother Roxanne. He already knew Philip, and presumably was acquainted with Eurydike before she married Philip. Antipater's opinion of all this is quite unknown, but one of the measures he now took was to appoint bodyguards for the kings, that is *somatophylakes*. Alexander III had had seven of these, until late in his career, when an eighth was appointed. Antipater now appointed seven once more.

Of course, he also had to consider that there were two kings. That the traditional number of seven was repeated, and not eight, may be a matter of Antipater's traditionalism and conservatism, but it may also be a subtler matter. He divided the seven into two groups, assigning four of them to King Philip, and three to King Alexander. He chose the sons of prominent men to fill these posts. The four assigned to Philip were: Autodikos, who was a younger brother of Lysimachos; Amyntas, the brother of Peukestas, who had been *somatophylax* of Alexander III and now was governor of Persis; Alexander, the son of Antipater's second in command, Polyperchon; Ptolemaios son of Ptolemaios, who is probably to be identified as a nephew of Antigonos. These were thus all relatives of associates of Antipater, except for Peukestas.

It is more difficult to identify the three *somatophylakes* of Alexander IV. One of them is totally unknown even by name; the others are Philip and Iolaos, who are identified as *somatophylakes* in an Athenian document dated to between 307 and 301, though their families cannot be identified.[14] This might suggest that the three assigned to Alexander were from much less socially prominent families than the four with Philip; if so, no doubt Eurydike was pleased.

These differences between the numbers assigned to each king and the manifest difference between the social status of the two groups has plausibly been interpreted as a deliberate statement by their appointer, Antipater, about the status of the two kings: that is, that Philip III was regarded as by far the more important of them. This seems quite reasonable. Philip, even as a lackwit, was an adult (and had a more than capable wife), whereas Alexander IV was both an infant and half-Iranian. One of the reasons Philip was originally made king was that he was Macedonian. (One wonders if Eurydike's opinions were taken into account – was this higher status one of the elements in the agreement between her and Antipater at Triparadeisos, which resulted in her acquiescence?)[15]

The army that Antipater commanded was probably very largely composed of Macedonians, but he took only part of it back to Macedon. Antigonos had some Macedonians, but in view of the army constructed by Eumenes, and its success, he no doubt also recruited Greeks and Asian reinforcements. The army of King Alexander, the one coherent force whose priority was the maintenance of rule by the Argead family and the unity of the empire, had been largely broken up, the largest fragment being with Antipater.

Antipater set off with his own forces to return to Macedon. It appears to have been a fairly slow journey, or perhaps merely one which was repeatedly interrupted. He had work to do on the way, and contacts to renew and decisions to take. The essential problem was the activities of Eumenes. He had been condemned as a traitor, so meriting death, and so he had a powerful motive for building an army, and since an army requires pay and supplies, an equally powerful motive for raiding and plundering. There were also others in the region who had been similarly condemned as Perdikkan partisans, including Alketas, Perdikkas' brother, and Attalos, his brother-in-law; Dokimos had joined them.

The sources for all this tend to be partial and fragmentary, but a few items stand out. One of those who had emerged as a serious problem was Alketas, who had been recruiting in Pisidia after defeating Asandros and joining with Attalos.[16] Antipater arranged for Asandros from Karia to campaign against him.[17] Eumenes raided for horses in a royal stud near Mount Ida in the Troad, leaving a note for the official in charge as though he was simply acting in a lawful manner.[18] He contacted Kleopatra in Sardis, presumably to get her approval for his actions, though it does not seem that he was successful in this: Kleopatra was adjusting her position as the political winds changed.[19] At some point he also raided to gather plunder and impose 'fines' and 'ransoms' so as to build up a war chest.[20] In the midst of all this, at one point his and Antipater's armies were not far apart, but Antipater did not attack and Eumenes sheared off.[21]

Antipater also interviewed Kleopatra, who was sensible enough of her own interests to defend her own conduct but also to accept a reconciliation with the most powerful man in the empire.[22] He met again with Antigonos. The relationship between Antigonos and Kassander had inevitably begun badly and got worse. Antigonos reasonably resented the imposition upon him of a man he could only see as a spy; and given that Kassander was the commander of his cavalry he could hardly trust him to support him in a fight; it was not a position in which any commander could be confident when seeking battle. Kassander had come to the conclusion, whether or not it was justified, that Antigonos had greater ambitions than simply suppressing Eumenes. Antigonos had as yet done very little or nothing about Eumenes, though this was very likely due to his shortage of troops – as well as Kassander's hindering presence, not to mention the unreliability of his army. Like Antipater he had no intention of engaging in a fight unless he could expect to win. All this inevitably reflected back on the relationship of Antipater and Antigonos, aggravating the distrust both felt for each other that had been obvious in Antipater's satrapal appointments.

Kassander met his father and increased his earlier suspicions about Antigonos, which had been indicated already by the satrapal dispositions. Then Antipater met Antigonos, near the Hellespont, which Antipater had reached in his march towards Macedon. They may have distrusted each other, and Kassander's words may have had their effect, but the two men were intelligent politicians and commanders, and for the present were effectively on the same side, as well as having differing geographical priorities, and a history of early cooperation. It was probably not difficult to reach an agreement. Antipater took over control and protection of the two kings, plus Eurydike and Roxanne. It may be that he was convinced that the disorder in Asia Minor would at some point result in the capture of the kings by Eumenes. Antigonos' army was, after all, composed of Perdikkas' former force, and it was noisy, vocal, and no longer well-disciplined. It would not be difficult for a faction within the army to seize the kings and ride off to join Eumenes. Also if they stayed in Asia Minor, they could well link up with Kleopatra, in which case almost the whole royal family would have joined together, and the man who protected them would be in an exceptionally strong political position. Such a grouping would be an irresistible target, attracting both the royal loyalists, and their homicidal enemies.

In exchange, Antipater handed over a section of his army. Arrian reports this as 8,500 Macedonian infantry, plus a large contingent – he says an 'equal' force, which must mean several thousands of men – of 'foreign' cavalry, and seventy elephants.[23]

This will have improved the discipline and loyalty of Antigonos' army; Antipater apparently took over part of Antigonos' forces, taking some of the men originally Perdikkas', judging by the troops' later behaviour. Antipater also removed Kassander from Antigonos' service.[24]

The whole episode of Antipater in Asia Minor shows that he was concerned above all to be conciliatory – with Antigonos, with Kleopatra, with the kings, with the army, even with his son. But his army now included an element that had developed a taste for mutiny. When they almost met Eumenes' army, but he avoided a fight, his army was annoyed and demanded that he fight. He had refused, for whatever reason, perhaps because he was outnumbered, but the refusal also fits with his whole conduct in this march to Macedon: he was concerned to put the measures agreed at Triparadeisos into operation, and to make a serious attempt to see that they worked, yet at the same time he was anxious to avoid military conflict, partly because of the casualties that would result, but also perhaps because without fighting the various antagonisms might fade.

Soon after parting from Antigonos, when he and the army prepared to cross the Hellespont, the army began demanding money. This was the tactic used by the old royal army that he had taken in exchange for those men who had been 'given' to Antigonos. But the old fox still could play his tricks. He simply rose early in the morning and carried the kings across the Hellespont, leaving the army on the other bank. Lysimachos, presumably with his own army, met him. The mutinous troops could stay in Asia, leaderless and at the mercy of other satraps, or they could accept the situation and cross to Europe where they would land in single boatloads under the eyes of Lysimachos' forces.[25] And one is reminded that Antipater must have marched through Lysimachos' satrapy to begin his journey to Triparadeisos, and that since then Lysimachos had become his son-in-law.[26] The mutineers were outmanoeuvred.

When he got back to Macedon, Antipater had less than a year to live. (Probably inability to move about with ease is another explanation available for his unwillingness to fight.) He appears to have kept a firm grip on Macedonian affairs and issues during that time, and his Triparadeisos settlement did not begin to break down until after his death. In Greece, he found, for example, that Polyperchon's reconquest of Thessaly been quite sufficient to prevent any further trouble with Aitolia. Aitolia's attempt to gain revenge for its near-conquest by Krateros had perhaps developed into a realization of the difficulties likely to be involved. And despite the Macedonian civil war in Asia and Syria, and Antipater's absence for much of 320, no Greek 'rebellions' had taken place. Of course, it helped that internally most Greek states were now in the hands of pro-Macedonian parties, either tyrannies or oligarchies. And Krateros, who was perhaps the Macedonian whom the Aitolians most identified as their main enemy – they had probably by now heard of the Macedonian compact aimed at transporting them entirely to an Asian desert – was dead. It is likely that the return of Antipater will have reassured them. He had failed to attack them in the past over Oiniadai, and if Oiniadai was now freed – as it was certainly by 314 – the main cause of war between Macedon and Aitolia had been removed. And Aitolia apparently kept control of Amphissa.

This crisis of survival was the beginning of the rise of the Aitolian League to power as one of the two major Greek states, which it maintained for the next century; it was also an opponent of Macedon during any Greek crisis. Its fellow Greek power in the Lamian War, Athens, was simultaneously beginning its steady decline. It is, in fact, only at Athens that any comments on Antipater's control of Greece can be made. This may be attributed to Athens' still potent strength in the immediate aftermath of the Lamian War, but it is also the case that most Greek cities were busy organizing the return of their exiles.

This is another almost blank area in Greek history. The decree compelling the cities to accept returning exiles was only announced in August of 324, ten months before Alexander's death, and we know that Athens protested to the king.[27] It was not therefore until Perdikkas' ratification of Antipater's terms concluding the Lamian War – in 321 – that the return of Samians to Samos became possible on a serious scale. It seems probable that Athens' appeal may well have led to the general suspension of exile returns in the rest of Greece, in the hope that the decree might well be cancelled, though Athens was principally concerned with the order that Samos should be 'returned' to the Samian exiles. If other restorations had been suspended, then Perdikkas' decision on Samos will have made it clear that both he and Antipater were determined to carry out Alexander's intentions. For Athens this meant the return of Athenian cleruchs and their descendants from Samos to live in the city; there was therefore serious social, political and economic disruption in both places, as the returnees to Samos reclaimed their former properties, or in Athens sought land and employment in their 'new' homes.

This happened everywhere. We have an indication of the difficulties from legislation at Tegea in the Peloponnese, at Mitylene in Lesbos, and, of course, at Samos.[28] It always convulsed the community and often required the perpetuation of injustices, or at least the application of rough justice. When the decree was announced at Olympia in 324 it was said that '20,000' exiles turned up to hear it and to celebrate, and this can be no more than a proportion – large, perhaps – of those who were affected.[29] Many of the Greek mercenaries on both sides in Alexander's wars were exiles, and were then entitled to return 'home'; any man who had might have a case to recover confiscated lands; if they had been bought by another he in turn would have a case for compensation.[30] The fact that we hear only of internal difficulties or political measures to accommodate the returning exiles does, however, suggest that most cities made serious efforts to deal with the situation in a peaceable and more or less just manner, but the Lamian War will clearly also have disrupted that process.

One of the results of the Greek defeats, in both Agis' War and the Lamian War, was internal revolutions in the defeated cities – and by listing the defeated cities of the battles of 331 and 322 we would include virtually every Greek state. These revolutions will probably have created a new set of exiles. Athens had the experience of undergoing a forced reduction in the franchise together with the offer of land for any poor Athenians who wanted to move to Thrace.[31] This obviously involved further disruption. The city also found that, because of their connections with Antipater, Demades and Phokion were the most influential politicians, but that those very connections rendered them deeply unpopular, a matter that became clear later.

The period of Antipater's domination following the Lamian War cannot therefore be considered peaceful, except in the sense of an absence of war; internally every Greek state was upset. It was necessary to maintain Macedonian armed garrisons at several places to demonstrate that domination. Peiraios and Akrokorinth were the main ones, but there also seems to have been a garrison on the Kadmeia at ruined Thebes – the Theban exiles had been excluded from returning according to the original

Exiles' Decree – and, of course, with Macedon back in control of Thessaly, its forces were no more than two or three days' march from Boiotia and Attika. A garrison that Philip and Alexander had put into Ambrakia had been withdrawn, but Ambrakia, faced by Aitolian hostility, was a firm Macedonian friend – as was, probably, all Akarnania, including Oiniadai, as Aitolia discovered in 320. Every city, in fact, where a new, usually oligarchic, government was in control, was automatically a Macedonian friend.

Antipater's measures in Asia had at last allowed Antigonos to make serious headway against the surviving Perdikkan partisans. He was assisted by their personal rivalries, and none of the Macedonian leaders was prepared to serve under, or indeed with, Eumenes. Eumenes was defeated in battle and then penned up in the fortress of Nora.[32] Alketas and Attalos had joined in resisting an attack by Asandros, satrap of Karia, but then headed off to recruit in Pisidia.[33] There, at Cretopolis, they were attacked by Antigonos, who had more men and was superior in cavalry and now had elephants; neither phalanx was seriously engaged until the end, when the Perdikkan phalanx was surrounded and forced to surrender. The cavalry and the elephants were the forces handed over to him by Antipater and they were the instruments of his victory. In the fighting, Alketas died, Eumenes was now locked up under siege, and the others, including Attalos and Dokimos, had been captured and imprisoned.[34]

More significantly, the defeated armies, both that of Eumenes and that defeated at Cretopolis, when detached from their leaders and commanders, had willingly enlisted with Antigonos, whose army therefore quickly expanded to 60,000 infantry, 10,000 cavalry and the squadron of elephants, originally seventy in number.[35] He had suddenly become the most powerful of the Macedonian commanders.

This, of course, had not been Antipater's intention, but, given the willingness of the soldiers to switch sides to avoid worse treatment, it is not surprising, and something like this might have been expected. But it had the same effect on the Triparadeisos settlement as had Perdikkas' grasp at power by threatening Antipater in Macedon; the concentration of military power in Antigonos' hands unbalanced the settlement, and this time there was no mechanism available by which it could be restored, above all because Antipater died at about the time of the Cretopolis battle, and Antigonos' ambition grew by what it had fed on.[36]

There were more reactions elsewhere. Ptolemy in Egypt, contemplating Antigonos' power, moved into Syria even before the battle of Cretopolis had so enlarged his army. Ptolemy had been a friend of Laomedon of Mitylene, the Syrian satrap, who had been appointed at Babylon and had then been confirmed at Triparadeisos, where he was, in a sense, the host of that meeting. He must also have been involved in ensuring that Alexander's hearse went to Egypt. None of this affected Ptolemy's actions, and Laomedon, whose forces were apparently few, and were probably scattered over his satrapy, resisted this invasion of his authority and was driven out. Ptolemy only took control of the southern half of the Syrian satrapy, but Laomedon abandoned his charge, and took refuge with the Perdikkans in Asia Minor, presumably hoping to get assistance in returning, but he joined them just in time to (probably) become one of the casualties in the battle at Cretopolis.[37]

Ptolemy was clearly aiming at controlling the approaches to his Egyptian satrapy, and his seizure of southern Syria (probably as far north as the Eleutheros River, his later boundary) could be seen as a similar move to his earlier conquest of Cyrenaica. It was, however, carried out in defiance of Antipater, or at least of the Triparadeisos settlement, just as he had moved into Cyrenaica in defiance of Perdikkas. He may have been Antipater's son-in-law, and his ally against Perdikkas, but he clearly cared nothing for the old man's achievement at Triparadeisos, any more than his friendship with Laomedon, or any more than did Antigonos now that he was wealthy in soldiers. That the two men now intent on overthrowing the Triparadeisos settlement were also mortal enemies for the next twenty years only compounded the situation and ensured that their actions destroyed both the Triparadeisos settlement and what remained of that at Babylon.

Cretopolis appears to have been fought in mid-319. By that time Asandros had been defeated, Eumenes had been locked up in the siege of Nora, Laomedon had been evicted from Syria, and Ptolemy had seized control of southern Syria.

As Antipater's life faded during the summer of 319, his authority similarly declined, and his physical inability to intervene in events meant that he could not insist on the Triparadeisos settlement being continued. By the time he died, sometime in the late summer or autumn of 319, that settlement had clearly been disrupted, and it was his allies, Antigonos and Ptolemy, who had broken it.

When Antipater died he had been in sole control of Macedon for fifteen years, a longer 'reign' than Alexander's, and two thirds the length of Philip II, of which it appears to be very much a continuity. In that time he had been conspicuously loyal to his king, only to find that his king planned to remove him; but he had also become disillusioned over Alexander's practices, over his claim to divine honours, his decision to return Oiniadai and Samos, and probably over the Exiles' Decree. He had won two wars in Greece, and probably another in Thrace, by which he had maintained the settlement that Philip and Alexander had organized, though he got rid of the League of Corinth, reasonably enough as it had failed. He had endured the enmity of the king's mother while protecting several members of the royal family, including a son of Philip and the son of Alexander, neither capable of ruling, and many of the family was now collected in Macedon, where he may well have thought they should have been all along.

He had dutifully delivered large numbers of soldiers to Alexander in Asia, very few of whom ever returned, so much so that there was a distinct shortage of manpower in Macedon when both of his Greek wars broke out. He had seen several of his friends and colleagues die in the battles he had fought, and three of his sons-in-law had died in the wars he and Alexander had fought. Probably one of his daughters had died as well; all three of his surviving daughters were now successfully married to others of his colleagues, none of whom was particularly loyal to him. He had clearly done his best, at the age of nearly 80, to sort out the problems of the empire at the conference at Triparadeisos. That he had failed in the face of the vigorous rivalry and ambitions of these 'colleagues' was hardly his fault. That he could not find a successor who could carry on his work was also hardly his fault given those same rivalries and ambitions. In the next two generations, there were to be two major attempts made to reunite Alexander's empire, by Antigonos and by Seleukos, neither of which succeeded, and the major obstacles to these enterprises were Antipater's sons-in-law, and his Macedonians.

Part II

Kassander

Chapter 8

Kassander to Power

During Antipater's final illness Kassander exercised some of his father's power as his deputy. This is the conclusion to be drawn from the trial and killing of Demades, the Athenian politician. One of the parts of the baggage transported from Triparadeisos to Macedon was the archive of royal correspondence. It was not examined, it seems, until the cavalcade reached Macedon, but then letters were found that had been sent by Demades to Perdikkas during the crisis, in which the Athenian was insulting about Antipater: he was called an old and rotten rope, though this was not unusually insulting, at least in Athenian political-rhetoric terms. More importantly, Demades had also asked Perdikkas to attack Antipater in Macedon.[1]

A tribunal presided over by Kassander was constituted when Demades and his son Demeas arrived in Macedon to request that the Macedonian garrison be removed from the Munychia. He had been sent officially by the Athenian Assembly, and so technically he had protection as a diplomat. Demades was voicing a constant Athenian complaint-cum-request, which Demades appears on the occasion to have accompanied with threats against the garrison. If the garrison was taken away, however, it was obvious to Antipater and Kassander that there would follow agitation to restore the full democratic constitution that Antipater had limited, and if that happened Macedon would be faced once more by a very hostile Athens. Demades was accused, by Deinarchos of Corinth, of treason – against Macedon, that is. Such a charge was nonsense, of course, since Demades was not Macedonian, just as the evidence of the letters to Perdikkas was a mere pretext; on the other hand, Demades could justifiably be accused of treachery towards his Macedonian supporters.[2] It must have been this that led the Macedonians to ignore Demades' diplomatic status.

It was not Demades who was the real target in all this, however, but rather Athenian opinion, which had to be intimidated, both by the continued presence of the garrison in the Munychia fort and by the fate of Demades. Kassander, seeing his father was dying, and probably assuming that his death would be the signal for an uprising of some sort, had determined to sacrifice Demades (who Antipater by now characterized as being 'no more than blood and guts', and like a victim that had been dismembered for sacrifice).[3] He was apparently no longer seen as useful to Macedon, and so could be cast aside; yet the brutality of his death is not the sort of thing usually attributed to Antipater; it seems to have been Kassander's contribution to the proceedings. Demades was condemned, and, so it is said, so was his son, who was killed before his eyes; then Demades was killed.[4]

The savagery of the executions became well-known and was presumably deliberately broadcast and publicized. (Kassander demonstrated later that he was quite capable of carrying out secret murders, so the publicity was clearly deliberate.) The sentence of death is variously attributed to having been delivered by either Antipater or Kassander.[5] Technically the responsibility must be Antipater's, and he was surely involved in Demades' condemnation. But Antipater was ill and dying, so Kassander is usually selected as the agent of death; besides, Kassander was also the target for other denigratory stories, not all of which were undeserved. Certainly, Kassander was involved in the whole process, and this is, of course, the key to understanding the episode. Kassander expected to be Antipater's successor, not only in personal terms, but in political terms as well, as the ruler of Macedon. This display of power on his part was therefore intended to warn those who might feel like taking advantage of the interregnum, a message to them that such action could and would be dangerous to them. Kassander was making his bid for a smooth transition.

Kassander's assumption in this matter was based on succession by heredity, but he also claimed to have given proof of his ability and courage.[6] Of these latter qualities in fact we have no proof at this point, other than his rapid break with Antigonos and his apparent substitution for his father in such matters as Demades' trial and killing, which certainly argues decisiveness. He did, however, demonstrate considerable political and military abilities in the next years, so it may well be that he had also already done so. In the question of the succession to his father's office, however, he was passed over precisely because his claim to that office was based on heredity. So far none of the offices of the Macedonian Empire had been passed by such a means to another, other than the monarchy, and even there the process, as with the usurpation of Philip II, and as the events at Babylon had shown, was not necessarily automatic. It must have been obvious to any man who was capable of seeing the empire as a whole that to allow hereditary succession in such offices as the regency would lead fairly rapidly to the disintegration of the empire into separate monarchies, or at least into independent satrapies, and the withering of the central authority, which in 319 was represented by Antipater. It was this that Antipater and the Macedonian Council that ratified his nominee was trying to avoid.

So Kassander's bid to succeed his father was unsuccessful, and it might be that his display of anger and savagery over the death of Demades was one of the factors that helped to persuade his father and the council not to make him his successor. On his deathbed, probably in autumn 319, and so after Kassander's killing of Demades and Demeas, Antipater nominated Polyerchon as his political successor. This was accepted by the council, who then named Kassander as Polyperchon's Chiliarch.[7] Given the obvious attempt earlier by Kassander to persuade his father to make him his political heir, it is not surprising that this pairing did not work, any more than had that of Antigonos and Kassander a year before.

The choice of Polyperchon, however, was scarcely based on an assessment of his ability. He had risen only to battalion commander under Alexander and had been sent with Krateros on the march to Macedon because Krateros was ill, and Polyperchon could be relied on by Alexander to obey orders and not take any initiatives – this was probably the reason Krateros was given the command. He became Antipater's second in command in Macedon, after Krateros and he went east, and was seen as a sufficiently safe pair of hands to be left in command in Macedon when the regent went off to sort out the empire at Triparadeisos; that is, he was not expected to have to do anything. His one individual achievement was to defeat the scratch Thessalian army that had sprung into existence as an ally of Aitolia – and perhaps to instigate the attack by the Akarnanians that compelled the Aitolians to withdraw (though that success seems likely to be either Antipater's or Kassander's work). He was also one of the oldest of the Macedonian leaders, having been born about 380.[8] He was thus of the generation of Philip II and Antigonos, and this may well have been one of the factors influencing Antipater to nominate him. It is hardly surprising that Kassander was annoyed to find this old second-rater preferred to him.

The feud between Polyperchon and Kassander following Antipater's death was enough to bring down the last remnants of the Triparadeisos settlement, one of the elements of which must have been the ability of the regent to fill vacant offices, such as his own, by men of his own choice. Heredity would have destroyed that power. Two men were the main proximate agents for the dissolution: Kassander and Antigonos; in the longer term, however, Eumenes and Polyperchon contributed as much to its destruction, and ironically, it was Polyperchon who seems to have begun the process, by his conduct and his encouragement of Eumenes.

Polyperchon sent to Olympias, who was in Epeiros again, having revived her antagonism towards Antipater and all his family, and invited her to return to Macedon to take charge of the kings and their courts, and supervise the education of the young Alexander.[9] She did not respond for some time, but did assume a power of interfering in affairs. Kassander gathered a group of friends and associates and persuaded them to go with him in breaking with Polyperchon, though, like Olympias, he did not do so immediately, though he did intrigue. Before the news of Antipater's death and his own effective demotion reached Athens, he sent a new commander for the Munychia garrison in the Peiraios, Nikanor, to replace Menyllos; he communicated with Ptolemy, asking him for the use of part of his fleet; messages were also sent to 'commanders and cities', which means the agents and soldiers of Antipater in the Greek lands, asking for their support.[10] He was aiming to seize power in Greece, and control of the soldiers there, before Polyperchon could do so.

In Asia, Antigonos was also actively pressing on with intrigues and diplomacy but in his case, he was backed up by a great military power, and his aim was to enlarge his own power. The satrapal arrangements made by Antipater to hem him in were his target. He sent Hieronymos of Kardia to contact Eumenes, who was also from Kardia, and was still holed up in Nora, with the offer of an alliance; he sent envoys into Kleitos the White's Lydian satrapy, above all to Ephesos, to undermine the authority of the satrap; when Arrhidaios in Hellespontine Phrygia attempted to force garrisons onto the Greek cities in his area, he found himself opposed by Antigonos, whose pressure reduced Arrhidaios to control of the city of Kios only, where he held out.[11]

The result of these manoeuvres was that Eumenes seemed to accept his approach and remained quiet, though he was gathering support at the same time.[12] Both Kleitos and Arrhidaios effectively succumbed; Kleitos fled from his satrapy to take refuge with Polyperchon; Antigonos also seized a shipment of 600 talents that was being taken to Macedon, when the ships put in at Ephesos.[13] In his demands on his victims and in his own actions, Antigonos made it clear that he regarded his authority as '*strategos* over Asia' to be above that of other satraps. Antigonos had therefore as decisively dismantled the Triparadeisos distribution of satrapies as Ptolemy had done in Syria. He does not, however, seem to have appointed replacement satraps for Arrhidaios and Kleitos; that is, he seems to have still accepted the authority of the regent, while presenting him with a major geopolitical change and in effect defying him.

Kassander had moved quickly after his father's death by installing Nikanor as commander of the Munychia garrison in Athens in place of Menyllos. Nikanor cannot be certainly identified with any of the other contemporary Nikanors, though it would suit Kassander's situation that he was a relative, possibly a brother or nephew of Phila's first husband Balakros.[14] Kassander elsewhere could probably count on the other partisans of Antipater in cities in central and southern Greece with whom he communicated as soon as he could, if warily, until what was probably a confused situation clarified. He thus held a number of garrisons in Greece but had no field army. He went to see Antigonos, probably once it became clear by the latter's invasion of Lydia and Hellespontine Phrygia that he was willing to oppose Polyperchon. After some negotiation – they had a disputatious history – Antigonos responded with a loan of 4,000 soldiers and 35 ships.[15] This was not charity on Antigonos' part; he was interested in further undermining Polyperchon's authority; the small force he had delivered to Kassander was enough to keep the fighting going in Greece, but perhaps not enough, he must have calculated, to give Kassander the victory.

Polyperchon now offered as a policy the 'freedom of the Greeks'. He proclaimed it in a decree, which is quoted, apparently verbatim, by Diodoros. Addressed to the Greek states, it begins with a rewriting of recent history, claiming that 'you and your government' enjoyed peace under Philip and Alexander, and this was to be revived under the new regime. To do this Polyperchon ordered that those who had been exiled 'by our generals from the time Alexander crossed into Asia' – meaning by Antipater – shall be returned to their homes, their property, and their citizen rights. He made exceptions of five cities – Megalopolis and Amphissa, and three of the Thessalians.

The significance of naming these cities as exceptions gives away his real aim. Megalopolis was a notorious partisan of Antipater's ever since the Spartan War, when he rescued it from Agis' siege. Amphissa was Aitolia's prize in the late war in Thessaly, and it seems that Polyperchon was looking for an Aitolian alliance, once more reversing a Macedonian policy. The Thessalian cities might take the restoration of anti-Macedonian exiles as a signal of Macedonian weakness. It is evidence that Thessaly was still in a disturbed condition after the defeat of its forces by Polyperchon. Friendship with Aitolia was a useful brake on such Thessalian activity. All these exceptions were therefore in Macedon's particular interest; the concept of the 'freedom of the Greeks' was more a matter of the power of Macedon rather than for the benefit of the Greeks.

In other items in the decree, Samos was to be returned to Athens, but not Oropos. All cities were to 'pass a decree that no one shall engage either in war or in public activity in opposition to us'.[16] This was a direct negation of 'freedom' to the Greeks, since one of the freedoms Greek cities relished was that of conducting their own foreign policy, and of fighting their enemies; this item meant that Macedon would control both of these.

So much for the 'freedom' that Polyperchon pretended to be awarding to the Greek cities. This decree was obviously primarily designed to undercut Kassander, whose support outside Macedon lay essentially among the oligarchies and garrisons that had been installed by his father. It was also a repudiation of many of Antipater's policies towards Greece, while by the five exceptions Polyperchon was trying to avoid stirring up trouble with the Aitolians and among the Thessalians. It was as much a Macedonian display of power as anything done by Philip, Alexander, or Antipater, but for the Greeks the concept of 'freedom' for the Greek cities served to override all Polyperchon's divisiveness and exceptions, at least for the moment.

Kassander's man Nikanor held on in the Peiraios, while the Athenian regime set up by Antipater succumbed to Polyperchon's proclamation and to democratic pressure. To the Antipatrid party in Macedon this result was not, as Polyperchon had suggested would happen, a return to the partnership of Macedon and Greeks that he claimed had been produced by Philip II, but which was perhaps an echo of Philip's propaganda that Polyperchon had naïvely absorbed. Actually, of course, it marked the beginning of the crumbling of the Macedonian position in Greece, and a return to the Greek 'rebelliousness' of the latter years of Antipater's rule; the Greeks had sensed Macedon's weakness.

A case can be made for Polyperchon's policy in the sense that he did seem to be reviving a version of Philip's system, but in fact he was being driven to adopt several new measures in a rather desperate attempt to gather support for himself. His planned reimportation of Olympias to Macedon was intended to shore up his support among the Argead royalists by bringing all the royal family under his own control and protection. (This had been one of Antipater's gestures as well when he collected the kings from Antigonos.) The 'freedom of the Greeks' was aimed to bring him Greek support. And when it became clear that Kassander had secured the support of Antigonos, Polyperchon sent a commission to Eumenes in his name as regent and in that of Olympias, appointing him a representative of the regent, and instructions to the Argyraspides, then in Kilikia, also in his and Olympias' name, to obey Eumenes.[17] This was aimed to derail Antigonos, just as his policy towards the Greek cities was aimed at Kassander. By this time Polyperchon's policy had therefore developed into a divisive series of gestures intended to destroy Kassander and Antigonos; it produced a civil war in Europe and Asia that lasted for the next four years – 'the Second War of the Successors'.

It is at about this stage in the conflict between Polyperchon and Kassander that the curious document usually called *The Last Days and Testament of Alexander the Great* was produced. It is clear from its contents that this is a piece of fiction, fairly artfully including some credible elements of fact.[18] It centres on the accusation that King Alexander was murdered by poisoned wine delivered to him by Iolaos, Antipater's son and Kassander's younger brother. Kassander was also in Babylon at the time, having been sent there by his father, and the further accusation is therefore made possible that he was carrying instructions from Antipater to Iolaos for the murder.

The author has been plausibly identified as Holkias, perhaps an Illyrian, who had been one of Alexander's soldiers, and claimed to have been in Babylon when the king died. He had racketed around from one loyalty to another since then, ending up in Macedon under Polyperchon in 319/318.[19] The thesis is that Holkias concocted his document on behalf of Polyperchon, and perhaps Olympias, as a means of denigrating and subverting Kassander and his whole family as part of their internecine conflict. Iolaos was, in fact, probably dead by the time it was written, as was Antipater, of course, so that neither of those designated as the principals in the poisoning could contradict the story.[20] Any denials Kassander might make would be dismissed. The story was clearly current by 317 when it affected Olympias' actions, and since damaging Kassander was something which would benefit Polyperchon, and probably only him, the period of the forgery's production must have been between 319 and 317, though, of course, the author might have been working on it for years before it was published.

There is no record of any reaction to this by Kassander, probably because to deny anything would be pointless, since he would not be believed, and to do so would provide publicity for the accusations, but it is very likely that it had its effect on his behaviour. His frustration at being denied power, first by his father, then by Polyperchon, had perhaps already been seen in his savage treatment of Demades and Demeas, accused of 'treachery', and it later came out in his occasional unusual viciousness towards his enemies; there would be further frustration at his inability to counter the denigratory story.

The accusation may also be one of the roots of the stories of Kassander's dislike, even hatred, of Alexander or at least of his memory. Here we may well be entering fiction's territory again. Several stories are told that are supposed to illustrate that the enmity of Kassander towards Alexander lasted into his later life. Plutarch collected them and included them in his essay on Alexander, and included another in his *Moralia*.[21] Kassander is said to have burst out laughing at the sight of grown men prostrating themselves before the king – surely a reasonable reaction if he had not been long at Alexander's court – at which Alexander grabbed him by the hair and banged his head on the wall. This story may very well be true, or at least based on an actual incident, for Alexander was particularly sensitive in the matter of prostration, and Kassander, fresh from Macedon, where this was never the practice, might well have found it comic and ludicrous. He might well also resent such treatment even by the king – he was at that time a full adult not much younger than the king himself. Such treatment was clearly humiliating, and clearly it took place before an audience. (It says a good deal about Alexander as well, of course.)

This is hardly enough to produce lifelong hatred, but it may have come on top of tension and fear at Antipater's court in Macedon at the news that

Antipater had been commanded to Babylon, and that Krateros had been dispatched to Macedon to replace him. Given Alexander's record, such a summons might mean anything from extravagant honours to execution. As Antipater pointed out when he heard of the killing of Parmenion: 'If Parmenion plotted against Alexander, who is to be trusted? And if he did not, what is to be done?'[22] This could be turned against Alexander, and if Alexander had heard the comment, he would probably, in his paranoia, take it as a threat. Kassander is said to have gone to Babylon to answer charges against his father, though it is perhaps more likely he was to make his father's excuses for delaying his departure from Macedon until Krateros arrived to take over directly, and to give a first-hand report on conditions there and in Greece.[23] Apprehension must have certainly existed: approaching the court of a violent autocrat such as Alexander could never be less than fear-inducing; if he was then beaten up and several times insulted by Alexander, it is hardly surprising that Kassander retained a detestation for his memory.

The other stories, however, are more in the nature of verbal disputes in which Alexander is said to have ticked Kassander off. The clear impression is that Kassander is portrayed as the country boy rather at sea in the king's sophisticated court. Apart from the headbanging, none of these stories are serious enough to account for Kassander's repeated reaction later in life that 'the mere sight of a statue of Alexander struck him with horror'.[24] One wonders how much of this set of anecdotes is the product of the atmosphere of tale-telling and invention produced by the fiction of *The Last Days*. Kassander's later (later than 318, that is) conduct does indicate a certain rivalry with Alexander, but there were attempts to link himself with him as well.

Polyperchon sent an army into Greece commanded by his son Alexander with the aim of driving off Kassander's supporters, which could well mean the seizure of the cities. The pro-Macedonians in Athens, headed by Phokion, attempted to persuade Alexander to join with Nikanor – and so confirm the Macedonian presence at Peiraios – since the eviction of the Macedonian garrison, which was Polyperchon's apparent intention, and that of the Athenians generally, would remove their own main support and leave them exposed to their internal enemies. The democratic upsurge in Athens was too strong, however, and Phokion and his party had to take refuge with Alexander, who sent them on to Polyperchon.[25]

When he received them in his camp at Phokis (south of Thermopylai, therefore, and so somewhat threatening), in the presence of King Philip, who was enthroned under a golden canopy, Polyperchon proved to be all too true to his policy. He had already seized Deinarchos of Corinth, who had been a prominent supporter of Antipater, and was presumed to support Kassander now – he had been the accuser of Demades. (Polyperchon was thus no more a respecter of the sacredness of envoys than Kassander.) The message of Demades' killing was directed at any others who were associated with Kassander, just as Kassander's killing of Demades had been. Alexander had pointed out to his father the advantages of protecting Phokion but at the meeting with Polyperchon the Athenians soon began arguing with each other, shouting and contradicting each other at the tops of their voices. They were invited to state their individual cases, but when it came to Phokion's turn he was repeatedly interrupted by Polyperchon, presumably because his presentation of the case was all too persuasive; eventually he simply refrained from speaking at all. Polyperchon identified another of the Athenians, Hegemon, as a supporter of Kassander, and when Hegemon therefore claimed to have been insulted, this provoked King Philip to lunge at him with his spear. In the end Polyperchon handed them all over to Kleitos the White to be returned to Athens as prisoners, and into the hands of their enemies. They were condemned in a tumultuous trial in the Assembly, and immediately executed.[26] Phokion had been an elected general of the city more than forty times, was notoriously uncorrupt, and was now 83 years of age; the cruelty and lack of proportion of the Athenians was as shameful as that of Polyperchon and Kassander.

At this point Kassander reappeared, with the ships and soldiers provided by Antigonos. He landed at Peiraios and secured control of the whole town, including the harbours, and this now became his main base.[27] His presence attracted Polyperchon himself with his main army down from Phokis. He was unable to make headway against the defence of the Peiraios, and then a shortage of supplies forced him to head further south; he marched into the Peloponnese in order to dismantle Kassander's support in that area.[28] Kassander seized control of Aigina but failed in an attack on Salamis when Polyperchon sent a relieving force to rescue the island.[29]

In the Peloponnese Polyperchon convened a meeting of representatives from many of the cities in which Antipater had placed oligarchies in power.

This developed as an amiable meeting, but then Polyperchon did have an army at his back, and he promoted revolutions in many cities to unseat the Antipatrid oligarchs, with the accompaniment of the usual massacres and men driven into exile; some of the cities made alliances with Polyperchon, though for protection rather than offering enthusiastic support: this was again the 'freedom of the Greeks'.[30]

Megalopolis, however, proved recalcitrant and busily organized itself for defence, and succeeded in collecting an army of 15,000 to face Polyperchon's, which was not much larger. Polyperchon made a serious attempt at a siege, involving a blockade and mining beneath the walls, which brought down three towers and the intervening wall. An infantry assault was foiled by well-thought-out preparations inside the city, which involved blocking the streets with palisades and so forcing the attackers to fight in small units. A second assault using elephants also failed when the Megalopolitan commander Damis, experienced in such warfare under Alexander, planted spikes to damage the elephants' feet. With the animals reeling in pain, the Megalopolitans threw missiles to fell the mahouts, and, out of control, the animals ran amok among their own side.[31]

Polyperchon displayed one of his weaknesses at this point. The siege having apparently failed after his two assaults, he withdrew part of his army, leaving another part to continue a siege that must have declined to the status of a blockade, and went off on other business, probably trying to secure other cities in the area. By this time he had divided his army, never all that large, into three parts, none of which was big enough to have a serious effect or to succeed in its task. He appears to have been a man of short attention span, always willing to be distracted, and unable to decide the relative importance of the several tasks before him – that is, he was essentially out of his depth. The fight against Megalopolis was clearly the most important task he faced in the Peloponnese since victory there would have been convincing to any waverers; an absence of victory made him seem weak and indecisive, which would have been an accurate diagnosis.

Kassander's visit to Asia had accomplished more than a loan of ships and soldiers: contacts between Antigonos and Kassander had expanded into an alliance of both men with Lysimachos in Thrace and Ptolemy in Egypt. All four felt that they were threatened by Polyperchon, especially when he switched the royal support to Eumenes; this was a clear threat to both Antigonos and Ptolemy and put them openly at enmity with him, to add to his current dispute with Kassander. Antigonos began preparing to cross into Europe to attack him in Macedon, but apparently he needed more ships.

Polyperchon sent his own fleet, commanded by Kleitos the White, the exiled satrap of Lydia (who had experience of sea warfare) to patrol the Straits and to prevent Antigonos from crossing over. (This could count as yet another division of Polyperchon's forces.) Kassander, in control of the Peiraios, was able to collect Athenian ships to add to those that Antigonos had lent him and so form a fleet of ships large enough to pose a serious challenge to Kleitos' ships; he put Nikanor, the commander of the Munychia garrison, in command of the fleet. Kleitos meanwhile had contacted Arrhidaios, Antigonos' other Asian victim, at Kios, and had evacuated him and his forces; he now had a considerable force of both ships and soldiers under his control. This operation brought both fleets to the neighbourhood of Byzantion and the Bosporos. The two fleets collided and in the battle Kleitos' fleet sank seventeen and captured forty of Nikanor's ships. At a stroke half of Kassander's fleet had gone.[32]

Nikanor's survivors took refuge in Chalkedon's harbour, to the east of the Bosporos entrance, where presumably they were watched by Kleitos' ships, at least during the day. The rest of Kleitos' ships were beached and the men made camp on the shore on the western side, probably somewhere along the Bosporos. Antigonos contacted the Byzantine government, who provided a fleet of small ships to transport Antigonos' forces – 'bowmen, slingers, and light armed troops' – across the Strait. (The bowmen and slingers may well be the men handed over to Antigonos by Antipater earlier, and earlier still had marched with Krateros from Babylon to Macedon.) A night attack by missiles and by surprise panicked Kleitos' men on shore and drove them to take refuge in the ships, and in confusion. Nikanor's fleet, and those warships that Antigonos still had, now attacked the disorganized fleet from the sea. All of Kleitos' fleet was sunk or captured, and only Kleitos' own ship escaped; when he landed he was intercepted by some of Lysimachos' men and killed, presumably by Lysimachos' orders.[33]

Polyperchon's fortunes had therefore suffered three defeats in a very short time. He had failed to capture Peiraios, he had been clearly defeated by the Megalopolitans, and his fleet had been sunk, and none of these enemies had been of any real strength. In the Peloponnese, as the realization of all this spread, he found that the initial lack of enthusiasm for him developed into open hostility, and many of the cities in his 'alliance' abandoned him to return to independence and to friendship towards Kassander. It had become quite clear that his 'freedom of the Greeks' was no more than another fig leaf to hide the reality of Macedonian control and domination – but in Polyperchon's hands that was no more than an army thrashing about doing damage, and so bringing neither freedom nor peace.

Kassander returned to the attack at Salamis, successfully this time, though he had to beat an Athenian fleet to do so. No doubt the Athenians would attempt to seize the moment when Kassander's fleet was away under Nikanor – and Nikanor must have taken some of his troops from the fort with him. Kassander also gained control of the fortress at Panakton on the border of Attika and Boiotia.[34] The city was thus partly cut off by land, and almost entirely cut off from its main port; shortage of food would soon result, if it had not yet. Athenian voices were now raised that it would be better to negotiate with Kassander while the city still functioned. Contacts were made between Athenians in Athens and the Athenians who had taken refuge in the Peiraios, largely friends of Phokion; Kassander's officers then got involved, and eventually Kassander himself. On the refugees' side the lead was taken by the philosopher Demetrios of Phaleron, who was actually under sentence of death in the city at the time.

An agreement was reached on the usual terms, which included an alteration in the Athenian constitution in an oligarchic direction, and alliance with Kassander, whose troops would continue to garrison Munychia, and the execution of particularly recalcitrant democrats, especially those who had forced through the condemnation of Phokion. Athens and Peiraios would be reunited under a single government, a measure that would instantly relieve the pressure on food supplies, especially with friendly ships controlling the Straits. Much of this was clearly agreed between the various groups of Athenians, with Kassander's ratification. Kassander's input included that the garrison would stay in Munychia 'while the war lasted'.[35] Athens had thus succumbed once more to Macedonian power, this time most feebly, for no more than a fragment of Macedonian strength had been exerted. Kassander was even able to ensure that Demetrios of Phaleron headed the government of the city, a quasi-tyrant overseeing a limited democratic constitution.

Nikanor returned from the Bosporos, having developed large ideas of his abilities and status, even though he had suffered one defeat and the eventual victory was all due to Antigonos' scheming. Kassander did not like such presumption. The settlement with Athens had burnished Kassander's power, and the collapse of Polyperchon's prestige allowed him to look about for new opportunities. Nikanor, whose command of the garrison had included bringing in soldiers who appeared to have been loyal particularly to him, was assassinated, and Kassander' base was therefore once more secure.[36]

Antigonos had now shown that there was another result of the waning of Polyperchon, in that he now had no need to campaign against him in Macedon, and he would now concentrate in Asia, which meant he could go after Eumenes, who in turn was the new military support for Olympias. Eumenes got out of his near prison and would soon link with the Argyraspides to become a major menace. There were in fact two separate wars now going on, linked loosely by the alliance of Kassander and Antigonos – while Antigonos fought Eumenes in a campaign spread from Asia Minor to central Iran, Kassander fought Polyperchon from Megalopolis to Epeiros.

Kassander, in Athens, received an appeal from Adea-Eurydike in Macedon. The siege of Megalopolis, the naval battles, the Athens agreement, took place close together in the spring of 317, and were followed by Eurydike's appeal, which was presumably provoked by Polyperchon's collapse, since it must have seemed he would no longer be able to protect her properly. With Athens subdued and Polyperchon apparently immobilized in the Peloponnese, Kassander was able to respond to Eurydike's appeal and went to Macedon. There the two made an agreement that he would assume the position of guardian of King Philip, the post Polyperchon held until then; she even ordered Polyperchon to hand over the royal army to Kassander.[37] This brought Polyperchon north, and finally induced Olympias to respond to his earlier summons to return to Macedon.

The two warlords appear to have avoided each other. Kassander at some point secured control of many of Polyperchon's elephants, though no battle is recorded; perhaps Polyperchon was separated from the animals at the time.[38] Kassander went back to the south and, with Polyperchon and most of his army removed, he was able to campaign successfully to restore much of the position his father had held in the Peloponnese, though, like Polyperchon, he became held up by a recalcitrant city, in this case Tegea, which he besieged. He was sufficiently successful and threatening that the Spartans decided that their city should be fortified for the first time, though the actual wall was a flimsy affair, hardly likely to interrupt the march of a Hellenistic army.[39] Meanwhile Polyperchon marched into Epeiros to escort Olympias to Macedon.[40] He had also allied with Aitolia, and so had compiled a considerable alliance, consisting of Macedon, Epeiros, and the Aitolians, virtually the whole of the northern Greek lands. The Aitolians had clearly been watching all these manoeuvres somewhat apprehensively; they had in the end allied with the strongest Macedonian party of the moment, that of Polyperchon.

It seemed that Kassander in the Peloponnese was now cut off from Macedon, for Alexander son of Polyperchon with a part of his father's army was in a position to move into the Peloponnese when Kassander left. He had been left in Attika with his force, though he had not been able to interfere with events in Athens once Kassander had arrived; his force was presumably just too small. Alexander occupied the Isthmus, so that if Kassander moved out of the Peloponnese, Alexander would be able to move in. The Aitolians now occupied the pass of Thermopylai, so Polyperchon's forces blocked the two main choke points in Greece. However, Kassander was able to get past Alexander, probably because he had the greater numbers and control of most of Attika, and he was able to pass Thermopylai by moving his army by sea after having requisitioned boats and barges from Boiotia and Euboia and Lokris. He landed in southern Thessaly, probably not far from the city of Lamia, the scene of his father's fight.[41]

While Kassander was in the south, Polyperchon had brought Olympias back to Macedon. She was opposed by Eurydike, who, in Kassander's absence, 'had assumed the administration of the regency', as Diodoros primly puts it.[42] It was by a messenger from her that Kassander heard of Olympias' return. The two women gathered their forces. Polyperchon, on behalf of Olympias, with Epeirote and Macedonian forces, confronted Eurydike's and Philip's forces at a place called Euia. The Macedonian soldiers refused to fight each other, or against Olympias, and King Philip was captured. This may have been a refusal to fight against Olympias, as Philip II's widow and Alexander's mother, but it is just as likely to be a more careful calculation of the odds – Macedonians fighting each other might well cause heavy casualties to both sides. Eurydike cannot have had much of an army, and she was a 20-year-old woman commanding against two kings, their joint forces, and an experienced Macedonian commander. To Eurydike's troops it must have seemed they were heading for a swift defeat, followed by obloquy from the rest of the Macedonians, so capitulation was their best option.

Eurydike got away together with one of her commanders, Polykles, but they were captured.[43] Olympias mistreated her captives and finally got some Thracians to kill the king – no doubt she could not trust Macedonians to do so. Eurydike she compelled to commit suicide.[44] She also found Nikanor, Antipater's son and Kassander's brother, and killed him for his father's supposed involvement in the death of Alexander. And she dug up and scattered the bones of Iolaos, on the grounds that he was said to have poisoned her son.[45] Beyond that she organized the murders of any adherents of Kassander she could find, supposedly to the number of about 100.[46] Polyperchon apparently did nothing to prevent or stop any of this carnage. He was clearly outmatched, but he was also Kassander's enemy and probably felt much the same anger at him.

While this went on in Macedon, Kassander was on his way from the Peloponnese. How much he had heard of what was happening in Macedon is not known, but when he got to Thessaly – arriving by sea having evaded the Aitolians' block at Thermopylai, though they apparently took no part in the fighting – he found that both Polyperchon and Olympias had taken measures to block his further progress, Polyperchon with his army in Perrhaibia in the north of Thessaly, while Olympias was sending troops to gain control of 'the defiles', that is, the passes from Thessaly into Macedon. This strategy failed. Kassander sent part of his forces under Kallas to contain Polyperchon, while another commander, Deinias, moved ahead to seize control of the passes before Olympias' men could do so.[47] Without difficulty he took the main part of his army past both of these enemy forces and entered Macedon.

Olympias appointed Aristonous (who had been Antigonos' opponent in Cyprus in 320) as her general and moved herself, King Alexander and Roxanne, and her supporters, into Pydna on the coast, with a substantial garrison, including elephants. Kassander laid siege to the city, but also had to cope with Aristonous and an army, Polyperchon's army, one of Olympias' commanders holding Pella, and the forces of Aiakides, king of the Epeirotes (and Olympias' nephew) who had assisted at the Euia fight against Eurydike.

It is unlikely that the siege of Pydna under the circumstances was more than a fairly loose blockade, though it did include a sea blockade.[48]

The contrast between the generalship of Polyperchon and Kassander becomes clear in this war. Both were confronted with a whole series of enemy forces spread from Amphipolis to Epeiros and from Pydna to Thermopylai. But Polyperchon did not move any of his forces and made no attempt to coordinate their activities. Kassander on the other hand occupied the central ground – Macedon – and from there was able to deploy his forces to take several initiatives. He clearly identified Olympias in Pydna as the main target, even though Polyperchon was probably in command of a larger force, though once again he had divided it. The tactics he used were well adapted to the situation, which by this time was essentially a Macedonian civil war.

Polyperchon in Perrhaibia was watched by Kallas, and Monimos in Pella and Aristonous in Amphipolis were isolated and presumably blockaded, while Olympias in Pydna simply sat besieged, apparently waiting for somebody else to release her. This allowed Kassander to concentrate on what turned out to be the real danger: the Epeirote army under King Aiakides. Kassander's' general Atarrhias blocked Aiakides from reaching Macedon by occupying the passes of the Pindos Mountains. This enforced delay gave the men of the Epeirote army time to consider what they were being asked to do, and invading Macedon to support Olympias was not their choice. They made their feelings clear.

Faced by these mutineers, Aiakides, who was perhaps convinced that Kassander's distribution of his forces showed that he was weak everywhere – which was a reasonable military conclusion to reach – gave those who were disaffected leave to abscond. As a result, however, he was so weakened that he was unable either to carry out his plan or to hold on to his position. He was also ignoring the character of the war, and the threat posed to his position by his own weakness. He must have assumed that he would need only a small force to make a substantial impact in Macedon. He was now dethroned by an uprising in favour of a rival branch of the royal family, the 'sons of Neoptolemos', probably as a result of an intrigue promoted by Atarrhias and Kassander. Kassander evidently understood the dynamics of this war better than Aiakides. He forthwith installed as regent (*epimelites* and *strategos*) one of his men, Lykiskos, who was to control the Epeirote kingdom in alliance with him. The speed of this action suggests strongly that Kassander was involved in the overthrow of Aiakides and the suborning of his army.[49]

This assumption is encouraged by the way Kassander dealt with Polyperchon, for Kallas operated in the same way against his army in Perrhaibia. Supposedly he bribed many of the soldiers to change sides, but it was probably more the general incompetence of Polyperchon, and the revulsion at Olympias' conduct in the moment of victory that persuaded most of Polyperchon's men to switch sides. Polyperchon was left with only a fragment of his original force, just like Aiakides, and he retired from Thessaly into Aitolia; there he was joined by Aiakides.[50] The Aitolians themselves were taking no further part in the fighting, but by giving refuge to the two men they gained the possibility of using them if Kassander proved hostile.

These peripheral affairs having been removed from the board, there remained Olympias in Pydna, Aristonous, who had taken refuge in Amphipolis, and Monimos who held Pella. Aristonous was the only one who was strong enough to display any military activity, winning a small battle against a detachment of Kassander's army, but unless he could reach Pydna in force, and collect Olympias' army and that of Monimos, which he never could, he was only marginal to the overall situation.[51] The Pydna siege was pressed only to the extent that the city was starved of supplies, but Olympias held out until the spring of 316. When she made a final attempt to escape by breaking out in a quinquereme she was betrayed by a deserter and foiled. She then asked Kassander for terms, and bargained well enough to secure a promise of her personal safety.[52] At this, Monimos surrendered Pella.[53] Olympias' conduct in killing King Philip had clearly sapped support by those not wholly committed to her cause. Escapees from Pydna – allowed to go home by Kassander – had spread the news of her state in Pydna long before, and her support outside the city had faded away. There is no reason to suppose she was ever popular or well liked, and, like Polyperchon, her general incompetence as a politician had become quickly evident. There was nothing left, but she was still dangerous because she was the widow of Philip II, the mother of Alexander III, and the grandmother of Alexander IV, and she was always capable of disrupting her enemies' activities.

Kassander honoured his word about her personal safety to the extent of not killing her himself, but he did bring her before an assembly of Macedonians who had to decide what to do with her. It is said that he packed the meeting with relatives of those she had murdered, though it does not seem that they would have needed to be summoned to such a meeting to have the opportunity of revenge. She had the opportunity of escaping to Athens, with Kassander's contrivance, but refused to take it. It would seem that Kassander had therefore made several attempts to avoid having to either imprison or execute her. But the Assembly condemned her to death, which was to be carried out by a party of Kassander's soldiers, men 'who were best fitted for the task', whatever that might mean. These are said to have recoiled when actually confronted by the old woman, but relatives of her victims carried out the killing – the two groups, soldiers and relatives, are, of course, not necessarily different.[54]

With Olympias dead and Alexander IV and Roxanne in Kassander's hands, Aristonous had no cause left to fight for. Olympias had already ordered him to surrender and, having received promises, in the same way as Olympias, of his personal safety, he gave up. However, his conduct of the defence of Amphipolis had been too much admired for Kassander's taste, and he could not abide a rival. One of those who died fighting at Amphipolis was Krateuas, and his relatives were allowed to kill Aristonous.[55]

It was a mark of things to come when Kassander sent Alexander and Roxanne, under guard, to be kept at Amphipolis, which Aristonous' defence had shown to be a particularly strong fortress, and which he now garrisoned strongly.[56]

Chapter 9

Kassander, Lord of Macedon

The siege of Pydna and the capitulation of Amphipolis occupied Kassander into 315; the campaign of his ally Antigonos against Eumenes into the East was also finished by then, but Antigonos was moving only slowly back towards the west. The allies had achieved their victories, and so had overthrown both the Babylon and Triparadeisos settlements, although Kassander had not fully eliminated Polyperchon, whereas Antigonos had crushed and executed Eumenes. More, it was slowly revealed to those in the West that Antigonos had collected most of the forces in Asia under his command and had acquired control of the majority of the immense treasure of the Akhaimenids.

Kassander spent the immediate aftermath of his victory in settling Macedon after the civil war. The government system of the kingdom was fairly rudimentary, but with a decisive man in charge it could be operated well enough, if in a crude and possibly slapdash and negligent way. Kassander's experience of this government was based largely on the methods of his father, and more distantly on memories of the practices of King Philip II, under whom he had grown up. The more eccentric and innovative – and even more negligent – style of Alexander passed him by, so when he came to rule Macedon, it was like a return to a well-established and comfortable system.

The basis of his rule came essentially from his victory over Polyperchon and Olympias. He further burnished his authority by conducting the funerals of King Philip III, his wife Eurydike and Eurydike's mother Kynnane, daughter of Philip II, all of whom had been killed by Olympias.[1] Since conducting the funeral rites of a deceased king was the responsibility of his successor, this amounted to a claim by Kassander to royal authority, though he did not yet claim the royal title; Alexander IV still lived, though his association with the disastrous period of Olympias' savagery, plus his half-Iranian ancestry, made it highly unlikely he would ever be able to exercise royal power.

This veering away from the direct succession in the Temenid royal house was a condition to which the Macedonians were well used. Hereditary succession was the general assumption for the kings, but such a practice had been broken more than once in the previous century, including the intrusion of Philip II in place of Amyntas IV. Philip's father, Amyntas III, had also succeeded a distant cousin, while at least two non-Argeads had exercised royal power in the previous eighty years. Kassander in exercising the royal authority was thus quite within Macedonian expectations – quite apart from his succession to his father – and another of these expectations must have been that Alexander IV was not likely to take power, just as his father had ensured that Amyntas IV was killed. Alexander IV's arrival at adulthood would create a situation in which another Macedonian civil war would become threatening, unless Kassander was prepared to retire from power gracefully. Better the elimination of an adolescent boy than the deaths of many Macedonian men.

One of the other prisoners captured at Pydna was another daughter of Philip II, Thessalonike, whose mother had been the Thessalian Nikesipolis of Pherai.[2] It is supposed that she had been named after the country of her mother, and had been born probably no earlier than about 346, or maybe a little later.[3] Her mother had died shortly after her birth, and she appears to have been brought up in Olympias' household, but held away from any possible marriage by her foster mother or her father so as not to pose any competition for her half-brother Alexander or her half-sister Kleopatra. In fact, this is conjecture since no item of information exists about her between her birth and her marriage.[4]

She was, even if she was invisible and probably largely forgotten outside Olympias' household, an Argead, and a Thessalian. When he found her his prisoner, Kassander might have quietly killed her off. The stories of his hatred of Alexander and his dislike of the whole Argead family would have suggested this outcome. But it is unlikely that such stories were in any way accurate. Instead he married her – she probably had little choice in the matter, especially if execution or perpetual imprisonment were the likely alternatives.[5] Kassander would be unlikely to allow her to roam free; as a daughter of Philip she was very marriageable, just as was her half-sister Kleopatra. She was by this time (316 or 315) about 30 years old, a very late age at which a woman was first married in that time.

To Kassander the political advantages of this marriage were plentiful. She was, first of all, a daughter of Philip II, the last and most successful king of Macedon who had actually lived in and directly ruled the kingdom. She was probably descended from the family of a Thessalian hero, Jason of Pherai, which would stand him in good stead in Thessaly. Between 323 and 319 Thessaly had risen more than once against Macedonian domination. A connection with a leading family in one of the leading cities was one to be sought for; this was, of course, one of the reasons why Philip had married Nikesipolis. Thessalonike was also, as it soon turned out, fertile, giving birth in the next few years to no less than three male children, who were given the significant names of Philip, Antipater and Alexander. This will have bolstered Kassander's clear intention, in contrast to his father, of establishing a hereditary Antipatrid rule over Macedon, now that he had male children to succeed him. The marriage, the male children, and the boys' names, made it clear that a new dynasty was being established, a factor which seems not to have been at all unwelcome to the Macedonians, who were perfectly capable of protesting loudly at something they did not like.

Holding Thessaly had been one of Philip II's fundamental achievements and uniting it with Macedon was decisive in hoisting the joint state to a position of overwhelming power in the Balkans. Philip, of course, used that position to expand his kingdom into Thrace and into Greece, and could probably have expanded further north had he chosen to do so, but he was seduced by the prospects of conquests in the rich East, as was his son. Now Kassander had secured as important a position as that Philip had achieved after two decades of warfare: Macedon–plus–Thessaly, and domination of Greece. Thrace had escaped direct Macedonian control, but was currently, at least, in the hands of one of Kassander's allies, Lysimachos (a Thessalian), even though he had by no means full control of the province. In compensation, though, so to speak, Kassander had secured some control over Epeiros. From being a wandering warlord borrowing troops and ships from Antigonos in 317 he had become lord of Macedon, Thessaly, Greece and Epeiros only two years later.

We have no indication of what he intended to do with this powerful position. His career in the next twenty years suggests strongly that he was quite uninterested in emulating Alexander or Antigonos in great adventures overseas. He certainly had problems enough in Greece to keep him busy, both in confronting enemies and in maintaining his own position at home. Overall it would probably be a reasonable characterization of his aims to say that having reached a position comparable to that of his father, he hesitated to risk it.

This satiation was not, however, what his contemporary warlords had in mind for themselves. Antigonos spent the time while Kassander was finishing off his own war in moving slowly westwards. He had assumed the largest possible authority that the position of '*strategos* over Asia' might imply, and he had used it to rearrange the satraps and satrapies of the eastern provinces. Some men were executed and replaced, others were newly installed, still others were confirmed in office – all done by Antigonos as a function of his 'office', but actually as a result of his military victory.[6] Of course, this is something he had already done in Asia Minor, but his eastern work was on a much grander scale. (It may also be pointed out that it was his complaint at being expelled from his satrapy of Phrygia which he brought to Antipater and Krateros that began the whole collapse of the Macedonian Empire; it seems likely that this coincidence was something he ignored.)

In Asia Minor he had already expelled satraps when he drove out Kleitos and Arrhidaios from their satrapies of Lydia and Hellespontine Phrygia, but in the east he also appointed satraps to replace those he expelled, and it was this that marked his growing ambition and claims to authority. Until now satraps had been appointed by King Alexander, or by the conferences at Babylon and Triparadeisos; Antigonos' assumption of that power and authority was as decisive a move as was Kassander's conduct of the funeral rites for the dead King Philip III. Peithon the ambitious and troublesome satrap of Media, was enticed to Antigonos' camp and there killed; Antigenes of the Argyraspides, satrap of Susiana, was also executed; two distant enemies, Stasanor of Baktria and Tlepolemos of Karmania, were too far off to be dealt with and too weak militarily to be worth attacking, so they were confirmed in their offices, which confirmation they may or may not have publicly accepted, though Antigonos did not have the authority to do this; Peukestas of Persis was far too popular with his subjects to be allowed either to remain or to be killed, but he was deposed and carried off to the west. Media, Susiana, and Persis were all given new satraps by Antigonos' own authority. He had thus claimed superior authority over all the East from Babylonia to India.

Ptolemy had already driven out one satrap, Laomedon of Syria, though this was not a formal deposition, since Laomedon could be said to have abandoned his satrapy.[7] Nor did Ptolemy, so far as we are aware, appoint a successor, perhaps assuming that another conference would deal with the issue – or perhaps he did not care, since an absence of governing authority in northern Syria would suit him well enough; and he had occupied half of the satrapy and taken authority there himself – just as Antigonos had done in part of Asia Minor. But this was only one satrapy, and Laomedon at the time, as an adherent of Perdikkas and Eumenes, could be portrayed as an enemy of the Triparadeisos settlement. Antigonos was going much further, killing, confirming and appointing satraps on a much wider scale.

These events and changes were probably not known in any detail, if at all, in the western parts of the empire. There, the two men most interested would be Ptolemy in Egypt (and southern Syria) and Kassander in Macedon and Greece, who had been Antigonos' allies in the war just concluded. No doubt communications between the three men were poor. The dispatch of news from the east would be in Antigonos' hands, and he may not have been too keen to reveal all that he had been doing to his allies. Certainly, it became clear later that neither of the westerners really understood the extent of Antigonos' achievement in Iran, nor the ambition he was displaying in the aftermath of his victory; it is probable that Antigonos did his best to conceal both his achievement and his deeds from his allies.

This, if it was so, changed once Antigonos reached Babylon where Seleukos was satrap. Seleukos had endured the transition of both Eumenes' and Antigonos' armies through his satrapy, though he did help to secure Susiana in Antigonos' rear, and he was more supportive of Antigonos than Eumenes. Since he also remained quiet while Antigonos was fighting in Iran, when he could have intervened effectively, he had evidently leaned towards Antigonos' side. They had been allies at the Triparadeisos meeting in supporting Antipater, and this mutual support clearly continued, if without much enthusiasm on Seleukos' side. He certainly put forward an elaborate welcome for Antigonos and his army on their return to Babylon.[8]

Babylonia was a rich satrapy in manpower and resources, and so, as the controller of all that, Seleukos was a rich and potentially powerful man, on a par with Ptolemy in Egypt, though he did not control much of an army, certainly nothing capable of facing up to Antigonos' massive force. It was also clear that Seleukos was well liked among the Babylonians. This combination was what had led to Peukestas being removed from Persis, and it soon became clear that this was also the source of Antigonos' enmity towards Seleukos. The two men came into conflict over Antigonos' assumption of authority over Seleukos, by demanding an accounting of his revenues, and when he interfered in Seleukos' disciplining of a subordinate. Seleukos replied to all this by insisting that he and Antigonos both owed their positions to the Triparadeisos conference, and neither was superior to the other. They had both been allied in support of Antipater against the army agitators at that meeting, a past association which had no doubt been the source of Seleukos' support for Antigonos in the Iranian conflict.

This did not now influence Antigonos, who could well argue that conditions had changed since then, and no doubt flourished his assignment as '*strategos* over Asia'. But Seleukos was not yet entirely within Antigonos' grasp and was probably uncertain as to his abilities. Antigonos may have only intended to depose him from his satrapy and send him to the west, as he had done with Peukestas and others. But Seleukos did not accept such a solution to the quarrel, and probably did not trust Antigonos, having no doubt heard of the treatment of Eumenes and Peithon and Antigenes – the latter two had also been his own allies against Perdikkas. Suddenly Seleukos fled with his family and some close associates to the west, riding fast enough to evade all pursuit.[9] The move was sudden enough to take Antigonos by surprise, and it clearly required some advance preparation, so perhaps Seleukos had been planning it from early on in their meeting.

Kassander had been similarly busy during the year that Antigonos was moving west. He may have felt that he was repairing damage inflicted by his predecessors, but he was also acting to secure the kingdom that he now controlled. He founded three, perhaps four, cities in that year. On the site of the destroyed Potidaia, one of Philip II's victims in the Chalkidike, he founded a city named after himself, Kassandreia; he gathered survivors from the destruction of Potidaia and from those of destroyed Olynthos into the new city, together with the people of several local villages and small towns.[10] This may have healed a few open wounds in Macedonian Greek society, but it also fulfilled one of Alexander's policies – the return of exiles. Alexander probably did not even consider that it applied to these people when he formulated his decree, but by returning them to their homes, Kassander was clearly acting in the spirit of it. Diodoros makes the point that he named the city for himself, and this was an explicit complaint by Antigonos a year later; the practice was tantamount to using the authority of a king, just as he had at the funerals of his royal predecessors.

Nearby, he also founded a completely new city, named for his new wife, Thessalonika. This was populated by the people of a dozen or more local villages. It was planted at the head of the Thermaic Gulf, and one of the reasons for the choice of site must have been that the harbours of the older cities to the west were silting up from the deposits brought down by the rivers which reached the sea near Pydna and Pella.[11] Ironically, it was this city, rather than the one he named for himself, which became the greatest Macedonian city.[12]

Another exception Alexander had made to his Exiles' Decree had been the Thebans, who were not to be permitted to return. The problem here was hardly the exiles from the city, who were powerless, but the absence of the city itself, which left a major strategic gap in central Greece. Boiotia without Thebes was a land of small, weak cities, and so was an open invitation to any army – that of the Aitolians, for example. The smaller cities that had constituted the Boiotian League may have resented Theban control, but the absence of the city meant that they and the whole region had become extremely vulnerable. Every Macedonian ruler since Alexander had maintained a sizeable garrison at the Kadmeia, the Theban Acropolis, and one at Chalkis in Euboia. None of the local cities was large, none of them was easily defensible, all of them could be taken without much effort by a modern Hellenistic army, and most of them automatically surrendered when threatened. For real Macedonian control in Boiotia, the restoration of Thebes was clearly necessary, and by refounding it a founder would have influence over its affairs.[13]

These three cities appear to have been founded more or less simultaneously, probably in 315–314, once the fighting in Macedon was over. Two more cities were also founded, but the dates of neither are known. A town called Antipatreia, no doubt named for Kassander's father, was founded in the Aspros Valley, a route leading from Epeiros towards Macedon. It was not a major route, but could certainly be used, and the town was clearly aimed at blocking Epeirote invasions – it was in fact in Epeiros itself. The obvious time for its foundation would be in a brief period when Kassander was dominant in Epeiros, and so in the year or so after he drove out Aiakides.[14]

The fifth city was not Kassander's, but founded by his brother Alexarchos. It was built somewhere on the eastern Chalkidike Peninsula, Mount Athos, though its exact site is not known. It was a visionary project, called Ouranopolis – 'City of the Sun' – and it is interesting more for the indulgence Kassander evidently displayed towards his brother in allowing, and perhaps financing, the project. Like all such schemes it did not outlast its founder.[15] Alexarchos is regarded as eccentric, but Kassander clearly was prepared to indulge him; he is also known as a creator of Greek neologisms, but they did not catch on, and he was subject to scholarly ridicule for his efforts, as is only to be expected of an amateur's intrusion into scholarly exclusiveness.[16]

All the cities can be dated to the year or so after Kassander had secured control of Macedonia. Two conclusions may be reached. First, the whole series had evidently been in Kassander's mind earlier, possibly even when he had been his father's message boy. Second, they were intended above all to stamp his authority on the kingdom. As Antigonos later charged, this was work normally done by a king, though of all Alexander's successors, Kassander seems to have been the least anxious for a royal title; the cities were as much for Macedonian security as for his own fame.

And finally it may be noted that, whatever Antigonos' complaint, he and the other successors similarly founded cities with their own names well before taking royal titles themselves. In this activity Kassander was leading the way – and was also following in Alexander's footsteps, and correcting one of Alexander's nastier decisions. Was he criticizing Alexander, or following him? Was he berating Alexander, or going beyond him? It is no surprise that Kassander's relationship to the dead Alexander is a puzzle.

Late in 314 Kassander marched south from Macedon, intending to carry on his war against Polyperchon by attacking his son Alexander, who was still at large in the Peloponnese with his section of the old royal army. It may be that Kassander was opposed in his march through Thessaly, since Diodoros remarks that he got through 'without loss', which does imply some local hostility. If so it was obviously of little account. At Thermopylai, however, the Aitolians held the pass, and Kassander had to fight his way through; on the other hand, that he got through fairly easily suggests a less than stern resolution on the part of the Aitolians.[17]

In Boiotia, Kassander set about refounding Thebes. He must have persuaded his Boiotian allies to allow this.[18] The city had been destroyed by

Alexander, but the decision to do so had been referred by him to the Boiotian League. That league, without Thebes, was a feeble thing, but it would be diplomatically senseless to restore the city without the agreement of the neighbours, and he had to ensure that Thebes was not all-powerful locally; from Kassander's point of view it was required as an enlarged Macedonian ally and garrison. This he evidently achieved. The word went out that those Theban exiles who survived could now return to repopulate their city.

It proved to be a widely popular decision, attracting contributions for the rebuilding from all around Greece and the Mediterranean during the next generation; this is perhaps a mark of the dislike Alexander still evoked.[19] On the other hand, the city does not seem to have ever become as populous as before and it certainly was never powerful again.[20] For Kassander, of course, there was only gain in all this: he acquired renown as a city founder, as the refounder of one of the greater Greek cities and the rectifier of a widely perceived wrong, and he could then see a well-fortified centre for Boiotia, which could well be a Macedonian friend, and a restriction on the power of its greater neighbours; it is likely that the Aitolians were one of the powers he had in mind to restrict, especially as they were now permanently hostile.

Having begun the work, or rather having made the decision to begin the work – which took a generation to complete – Kassander marched on towards the Peloponnese. Alexander, son of Polyperchon, blocked the passage of the Isthmus, no doubt holding Corinth. Kassander stopped at Megara, constructed barges and boats, and moved his army, elephants and all, across the Saronic Gulf to land at Epidauros in the Argolid.[21]

Alexander had clearly made good use of the time Kassander had spent in Macedon, and it appears that he had secured control of most, if not all, of the places that had taken Kassander's side earlier, no doubt with the notable exception of Megalopolis. From Epidauros Kassander marched to Argos, where he compelled the city to change sides again, then marched across to Messene in the south-west corner of the peninsula, which also largely capitulated to him, with the exception of the citadel above Messene city, Mount Ithome. Back in the Argolid he gained control of the Hermionis, the extreme end of the peninsula, round the small city of Hermione.

It is evident from Diodoros' barely coherent account that Kassander had only partly accomplished his aims. Alexander was unable to face him in battle, but by remaining in Corinth he was effectively out of reach. Unless

Alexander's forces could be removed, Kassander could not be confident of holding what he had gained. But at that point he had to return to Macedon. He left a general called Molykkos with just 2,000 soldiers to hold what he had gained and left.[22] He abandoned the Peloponnesian work only partly done because envoys from the east had arrived, and a new threat had emerged.

Seleukos, when he escaped from Antigonos in Babylon, rode hard through Mesopotamia to Syria. The satrap of Mesopotamia was Blitor, who had been appointed, probably by Antigonos, when Amphimachos deserted his post to move east with Eumenes.[23] He assisted Seleukos in his flight, presumably in ignorance of the purpose of his journey, for which he was deposed by Antigonos, who apparently assumed that Blitor should have been at least suspicious of the fleeing satrap of Babylonia. Antigonos had in fact delayed sending men in pursuit, being quite satisfied at first to have driven Seleukos out of Babylon.[24] It looks as though he was taking out his bad temper on Blitor. Antigonos marched on westwards with his forces and his treasure, halting for winter quarters (winter of 315/314) in Kilikia.[25] Seleukos rode on further, into Ptolemy's part of Syria and on to Egypt.[26] Not long behind him came an envoy from Antigonos, who had quickly worked out what Seleukos would do. Other envoys went to Kassander and to Lysimachos.[27]

By the time Seleukos arrived Ptolemy had probably heard of Antigonos' march from the east, which was relatively slow, but Seleukos was able to provide details, full and graphic. His very arrival as a refugee from his satrapy was even more startling than the news he brought, which included information about the execution and replacement of satraps, the size of Antigonos' army, and the enormous wealth he had gathered. Antigonos' envoy arrived with the request that Ptolemy should remember their friendship and maintain their alliance, and this message had also gone to Kassander and Lysimachos.

Such a message to Ptolemy was probably wasted, given that Seleukos could inform him of the sheer power that Antigonos now possessed. To the other two, the message must have come out of the blue, without the context that Seleukos could provide to Ptolemy. Quite possibly Antigonos' envoys expanded on the power he now had; this, of course, would have had the effect of rousing their suspicions. The message suggesting the continuance of their alliance was soon followed by the revelation that Seleukos had been driven from his satrapy; this was hardly encouraging or reassuring; Seleukos had been an early ally of Antigonos. Whatever was actually said it must have become clear to the two westerners that Antigonos' message was actually a threat, coated in honeyed language. Ptolemy and Seleukos sent out envoys of their own to the two men. Travelling by sea they may well have been able to get to them even before Antigonos' men. No doubt with clear information the four men reached the conclusion that Antigonos was dangerous.

The timing of all these movements is difficult to discern, partly due to Diodoros' attempt to describe them in sections. By the time Antigonos began to move his forces from Kilikia southwards into Syria early in 314, Ptolemy, Lysimachos and Kassander had so coordinated their responses to Antigonos' messages that they were able to present him, by way of their own envoys, with their own suggested new distribution of authority and satrapies. By basing themselves on the practices at Babylon and Triparadeisos they recommended that the satrapies that were now in Antigonos' control be shared out among the four allies as well as Antigonos. Ptolemy was to have 'all Syria', that is from Sinai to the Euphrates and the Taurus Mountains; Lysimachos was to take over Hellespontine Phrygia as well as Thrace, which would also give him control of both sides of the Straits; Kassander to have Kappadokia and Lykia, the latter to supplement his control of the Aegean. The former would, along with Ptolemy in Syria, separate Antigonos' satrapy in Phrygia from that in Mesopotamia; Seleukos was to return to Babylonia.

This scheme is generally ignored or ridiculed in modern discussion, but it makes sense in a geopolitical way.[28] The aim was to reduce Antigonos to the basic territory with which he had begun his career as '*strategos* over Asia' in Asia Minor, and the treasure he had accumulated, claimed as common property of the empire, should be shared among them all.[29] Kassander, perhaps to nudge Antigonos in the direction of acceptance, had already sent an expedition, commanded by Asklepiodoros, into Kappadokia; he had begun by laying siege to the city of Amisos, whose capture would ensure his seaward communications.[30]

This was an interesting concept. It implied that the empire was a political unity still, governed by a set of major satraps, with a king as the nominal head of state, at least until he grew up. It also implied that the distribution of territorial power was not permanent, and that it was likely that another distribution of satrapies would be made later, such as when one of the satraps died. That is, they were in effect suggesting a new distribution on the pattern of the Babylon and Triparadeisos settlements. It was highly unlikely that Kassander would attempt to rule such a disparate set of provinces as Macedon, Lykia and Kappadokia personally, the implication was that subordinate satraps would be installed, presumably at the nomination of the overlords, just as Antigonos had done in the eastern territories and Mesopotamia. The empire was to be a group of major or super-satrapies, with subordinate provincial rulers removable at will – that is, a small oligarchy of overlords.

This suggestion has, of course, generally been ignored or dismissed by modern historians, who assume that it was merely put forward in order for Antigonos to reject it.[31] This is certainly what happened, but that is not to say that it was not seriously suggested as a solution to the empire's problem. It stands in comparison with any other empire, notably the later Roman Empire, and, of course, the British. The huge territory involved would obviously require satraps, as Alexander and Antigonos had both recognized, and there was no reason to dismiss the idea of super-satraps as regional coordinators. The whole scheme of course did require that there be a king overall, a matter that would increasingly bother the participants over the next five years.

The suggested redistribution was, of course, instantly rejected by Antigonos, who responded, perhaps very angrily, at what he would conceive as an insult, with a declaration of war. (This reaction was a clear indication that Antigonos' ambitions knew no limits, and the rest should have been warned.) It is difficult to know what either side in this meeting seriously expected. It must have been obvious that Antigonos would never accept any such serious destruction of his new-found power; at the same time, Antigonos cannot seriously have expected his 'allies' to accept that such an overwhelming power should remain with him. One must suppose that it was all a matter of public posturing, at least by the four allies, designed to demonstrate Antigonos' ambition and arrogance. In this, of course, it was successful, but scarcely relevant. If that is what was intended, we have good evidence that both sides were very conscious of what can only be called 'public opinion', though this is a difficult concept to define. At least they were convinced that their actions should appear reasonable and wanted to demonstrate the unreasonableness of their opponent or opponents. This suggests that these claims would appear reasonable to others.

The allies stood for a united empire divided among satraps, ratified by conferences, of which the meeting of Antigonos with their envoys might count as one, and eventually ruled by a king. Antigonos, while paying obeisance in some way to Alexander IV, was aiming in the first instance for a regency with himself as regent controlling all the empire through satraps whom he had appointed. The difference between the two sides was essentially Antigonos' personal position, which he still claimed as '*strategos* over Asia', and which the others rejected as having been extinguished by the removal of Eumenes.

Kassander's campaign in the Peloponnese had been interrupted by the need to deal with the threat now posed by Antigonos. He had made clear his belief that the suggested new divisions of the empire between the five contenders was viable by sending the expedition to Amisos on the Pontic coast of the Black Sea. The city was laid under siege, and Kassander's forces had penetrated into Kappadokia. This was territory which had been originally allocated to several successive satraps, but had never been governed by them. Perdikkas had probably conquered it, but the subsequent civil warfare seems to have meant a loss of control. Kassander was therefore operating to extend the empire in the same way as Lysimachos in Thrace and Ptolemy in Cyrenaica, and surely still operating as Antigonos' ally. When he rejected the allies' plan Antigonos necessarily had to reply by attempting to put his own overall plan into effect. His first move was to do so in Kappadokia. This was the first overt move in the new war he had declared. He also made preparations to resist an attack, which he apparently expected to come from Kassander across the Hellespont.

Antigonos was not only preparing his defences but was able to strike at his opponents' vulnerable regions. For Kassander this was Greece. It was in fact not easy for the allies to attack Antigonos in any serious way. He held the central position, and the allies were all marginal. In theory Antigonos could have tackled them one at a time. He had sufficient forces to defend against Ptolemy while attacking Kassander and Lysimachos, or vice versa, and he sent his nephew Polemaios to drive Asklepiodoros from Amisos and then to stand guard at the Hellespont.[32] In the event Antigonos was prevented from making other moves by a series of interruptions.

He sent out a series of envoys to contact the Greek states who were either neutral or were under threat from the allies, to Cyprus, aimed at Ptolemy, and to Rhodes, to persuade the island to assist him at sea. In addition, Aristodemos of Miletos, one of Antigonos' most effective agents, was sent to the Peloponnese with a variety of tasks to accomplish. With a treasure of 1,000 talents, he was to recruit a mercenary army. He did this by negotiating an agreement with the Spartan government to recruit at the Cape Tainaron mercenary camp, and fairly rapidly gathered an army of 8,000 men. He was also to contact any cities that could be persuaded to join Antigonos, and to negotiate with Polyperchon in Aitolia and Alexander son of Polyperchon in Corinth.[33] He was assisted in these endeavours by the production by Antigonos of his declaration of 'the freedom of the Greeks'.

Antigonos was besieging Tyre, which was held by a small force of Ptolemy's. The siege dragged on for more than a year, and meanwhile the other exploits of Antigonos' commanders and agents had only moderate success: he conquered southern Syria from Ptolemy – Ptolemy removed all the warships from the ports as he retreated – and he drove Kassander's forces out of Kappadokia; but he was unsuccessful in attempts to seize control of Cyprus in the face of Ptolemy's power at sea, where Seleukos was in command. Antigonos' reply to this rebuff was to order the production of a great new navy in the ports and dockyards of Phoenicia and Kilikia, which he controlled.[34]

Antigonos may well have had his next propaganda move in mind for some time, but it did depend on the success of Aristodemos in negotiations with Polyperchon and Alexander. Polyperchon now had little power or authority, but he was still officially the regent of the empire, appointed by Antipater. Aristodemos persuaded him to formally surrender the regency to Antigonos, presumably by appointing him his successor and simultaneously resigning the post. Acting for Antigonos, Aristodemos then appointed Polyperchon as Antigonos' *strategos* in the Peloponnese, and Alexander went off to visit Antigonos at Tyre to confirm all this.[35]

Antigonos could now proclaim the policy of the 'freedom of the Greeks', which he had inherited from Polyperchon along with the regency. At an army assembly at Tyre – the army consisted of his own troops – he made a speech in which he denounced Kassander as a usurper, the murderer of Olympias, forcing marriage on Thessalonike, and being the jailer of Alexander IV and Roxanne, complaining of the restoration of Thebes, and of founding a city with his own name; he then declared that he favoured the policy of 'the freedom of the Greeks', that is, the autonomy of all Greek cities. The declaration made some clear distortions of events; the 'freedom' proclamation had taken much from Polyperchon's original, but because of Antigonos' greater power and because he made serious attempts to implement it – except when it was inconvenient, of course – it had a much greater effect. He formally put it to the vote by his army's assembly, and then sent copies of the decree in all directions.[36]

In the Peloponnese, it was clear that Kassander's authority was extremely fragile. At Argos, which he had forced to join his alliance earlier, the brief absence on a raid into Arkadia of Kassander's commander in the city, Apollonides, brought a quick reaction, when 500 men of the city seized control and sent to Alexander for help. Apollonides returned more quickly than expected, before Alexander could react. Catching the 500 gathered in the *prytaneion* of the city he solved his immediate problem by burning them alive. He then purged the city of other opponents, killing or exiling them.[37] Such actions were obvious manna to Antigonos' 'freedom' propaganda.

Kassander, faced by Artemidoros' successful recruiting and diplomacy, attempted to persuade Polyperchon onto his side, but, given their mutual history of animosity, he was unsurprisingly not successful. He therefore marched south again to combat the growing Antigonid tide directly. He also sent an appeal for assistance to Seleukos in Cyprus; a fleet of fifty ships set out for Karia under the command of Polykleitos, with the further intention of intervening in the Peloponnese.[38] It got as far as Kenkreai, Corinth's port, but then turned back; on his way back towards Cyprus Polykleitos successfully ambushed a fleet of Antigonos' ships.[39]

Kassander paused at Thebes on his march south, and briefly assisted the Thebans in building their walls, no doubt with a view to making the city defensible against Antigonid attack, emphasizing his restoration of the city as a reply to Antigonos' propaganda, and discovering the situation in the Peloponnese. He attacked Alexander in his fortress in Corinth, avoiding a siege of the city, but capturing Kenchreai and ravaging the city's territory. He captured 'two forts' that Alexander had garrisoned, then seized the city of Orchomenos where, as at Argos, the victorious party in the city then carried through a nasty purge. Kassander did not intervene. He went again into Messenia, where Polyperchon, who was now Antigonos' commander in the Peloponnese, controlled Messene city; refusing to get tangled up in a siege at the farthest point from his lands, Kassander left Polyperchon alone and recrossed the peninsula to Megalopolis, where Damis, the defender of the city against Polyperchon earlier, was appointed 'governor' of the city (or perhaps just commander of the garrison). Kassander went on to Argos to preside at the Nemean Games in August.[40] The journey emphasized the lack of control of the area by his enemies.

By this time Alexander had returned from his visit to Antigonos at Tyre, and was perhaps both impressed and demoralized by Kassander's successes, and possibly less than reassured by Antigonos. The idea of Greek freedom was perhaps less than appealing to a commander whose command was effectively limited to several Greek cities – if they became truly 'free', he would be left with nothing. He and Kassander had tussled with each other over control of parts of the Peloponnese for several years now, with no obvious result for either side, and Polyperchon was now of little help. The prospect of fighting over the same old ground yet again was hardly appealing. Kassander, apparently sensing disillusion, sent an envoy of his own, Prepelaos, to see Alexander. He was persuaded to desert both Antigonos and his father and was then made the commander of Kassander's forces in the Peloponnese, which is what in fact he had been fighting to achieve for the past several years. Alexander thus in effect became Kassander's viceroy for the Peloponnese, just as his father was Antigonos' viceroy.[41]

Aristodemos replied to this setback by securing an alliance with the Aitolians, then crossed the Gulf of Corinth with his mercenaries to campaign along the Gulf's south coast in Achaia, fighting at Aigion and Dyme, where the usual massacres took place. Alexander was murdered at Sikyon, presumably as a result of his defection, for the leader of the assassins, Alexion, was said to have been one of Alexander's friends.[42] Alexander's widow Kratesipolis, kept a grip on the city, and presumably on Corinth as well, perpetrating the usual massacre and crucifying thirty of her most prominent enemies, to do so.[43] All Aristodemos had accomplished was to transfer the destructive campaigns to another part of the Peloponnese.

Kassander's reply was to march an army into Akarnania, where, as usual, a minor war with the Aitolians was going on, quite possibly one of the results of the alliance the Aitolians had made with Antigonos through Aristodemos. Kassander took his army into Aitolian territory, made camp, and from there he organized the synoecism of several of the Akarnanian small towns into much greater cities, notably Stratos and Agrinion, which were developed on either side of the Akheloos River. (Some of the Oiniadians were moved to a new site as well.)[44] But when he marched off to deal with a problem in Epeiros, the Aitolians replied by attacking Agrinion; they gained the city after a brief siege, but they do not seem to have then crossed the Akheloos to attack Stratos, so possibly Agrinion was seen by them as an invasion of their territory.[45] The failure to move against Stratos suggests that the Aitolians were much more wary of the Akarnanians now that they had Macedonian support. Kassander left Lykiskos in command in Akarnania but he was apparently unable to assist the Agrinians. It looks as though the fighting for the new city was over quickly, and then Kassander accepted that new situation.

The arrival of Lykiskos in Akarnania as Kassander's commander shows that his earlier position as his viceroy in Epeiros had ended. The king chosen by the Epeirotes to replace the expelled Aiakides, Neoptolemos II, had attained his majority during 315 and it seems that Lykiskos had handed over power to him peacefully and had then withdrawn. It may thus have been the new situation in Epeiros, with a new king, which brought Kassander to campaign in the area in support of Neoptolemos. The accession of a new king was always a moment of weakness, and the withdrawal of the capable Lykiskos will have made it worse.

Epeirote enemies gathered. Three cities, Kerkyra (the island of Corfu), Epidamnos and Apollonia, were allied with King Glaukias of the Illyrian Taulantii. Kassander from Akarnania first seized the island city of Leukas, off the Akarnanian coast, presumably to prevent it being used by his new enemies against his Akarnanian allies, then he is found attacking Apollonia.[46] He was presumably moving by sea, and in sufficient naval strength to evade or overawe the powerful fleet maintained by Kerkyra. Apollonia was quickly captured, Glaukias was defeated and induced to make peace, and the Epidamnian army was tempted away from the city, defeated, and its city occupied.[47] This campaign in Akarnania and Illyria displays Kassander's military capability at its best, organizing a defence, moving by sea, delivering swift and decisive attacks, together with an effective diplomacy.

The techniques of attacking these allies separately was exactly what Antigonos was attempting to do, using, like Kassander, diplomacy in addition to force. He had attempted already to make a separate peace with Ptolemy after the capture of his fleet off southern Asia Minor, but had failed when both sides pitched their demands too high.[48]

The crucial year of the war was 313. The Illyrian settlement imposed by Kassander in the previous year broke down; Aiakides of Epeiros reappeared out of Aitolia to reclaim the kingship; in Thrace Lysimachos came under attack from an alliance of Thracians, a detachment of Antigonos' forces, the Greek cities of the Pontic coast, and King Seuthes; Antigonos sent an expedition to Greece to land among the most vulnerable of Kassander's Greek allies, the Boiotians. All this was in addition to Kassander's sending an expedition to Karia, where the satrap Asandros had defected from Antigonos' alliance.

The Karian expedition consisted of 8,000 soldiers, escorted, or carried, by 36 ships from Pydna.[49] Meanwhile a squadron of twenty Athenian ships, commanded by Aristoteles, sailed to recover the Athenian island of Lemnos, which had been taken by Antigonos' fleet during a leisurely cruise around the Aegean gathering allies.[50] All these forces were lost, at least temporarily: the soldiers were defeated and captured, the Pydnaian ships encountered Antigonos' vastly greater fleet and were captured; the Athenian ships similarly.

The revival of Aiakides was very threatening. He moved into Epeiros and deposed Neoptolemos, then succeeded in gathering a substantial army from his own supporters, with which force he aimed to join with the Aitolians, a combination that would have been formidable.[51] The junction however did not take place; Aiakides' army was intercepted by a Macedonian army, which was apparently already in Akarnania, probably sent there for the very purpose of fighting Aiakides. It was commanded by Philip, Kassander's brother, who defeated the Epeirote forces. Fifty prominent followers of Aiakides were captured and sent to Kassander in chains; Aiakides and the remnant of his army retreated into Aitolia, possibly assuming that this was safe territory, on the analogy of the Aitolians' refusal to move across the Akheloos River earlier. Before he could recover, however, Philip followed him and defeated him again; this time Aiakides died in the fight. Philip's invasion was so formidable that many Aitolians fled for refuge into the hills; memories of Krateros' invasion were clearly ever-present.[52]

This had been a major threat that was averted by quick reaction and by Philip's evident military capability. At much the same time, and perhaps in concert with Aiakides, Glaukias of the Taulantii resumed his war by attacking Apollonia, which was held by a Macedonian garrison. Kerkyra sent help to the city, and to Epidamnos also. Both cities were freed of their Macedonian occupiers.[53]

The Aitolians had not taken a large part in affairs so far, but they were always intensely suspicious of Macedonian activities; Kassander's work in Akarnania seemed to them to be hostile, and the defeat of Aiakides was even worse. The alliance with the Epeirote king having failed, they looked elsewhere. The Boiotians were unhappy at the revival of Thebes, and they joined with the Aitolians to send a joint embassy to Antigonos, while he was operating in Karia, asking for help.[54]

Antigonos' general in Karia, his nephew Polemaios, had succeeded quickly in the face of the intrusion of the army sent by Kassander, commanded by Eupolemos. He hoped to take advantage of Polemaios' forces being in winter quarters, and that Polemaios was attending to his father's funeral, but Polemaios was too quick for him. In a night attack on Eupolemos' camp, he captured the general, and compelled the surrender of his whole force.[55]

This brought Antigonos personally from Syria with his main army to attend to the issue of Karia. In a masterly campaign he finally extinguished Asandros' pretensions.[56] It was just at this point, commanding a victorious army and with a substantial fleet in the south-east Aegean, that Antigonos received the appeal from the Aitolians and the Boiotians. This was the first time he had the serious prospect of being able to secure control of a major part of Greece, and he responded.

Kassander clearly knew what was intended, at least in outline, and moved to block Antigonos' approach to Boiotia. The city of Oreus in northern Euboia was apparently an ally of Antigonos and would provide him with a very useful base close to Kassander's territory of Thessaly; seizing it would also supplement Kassander's control of the area where he already held Attika and Chalkis in Euboia (and Thebes). He laid Oreus under siege but was foiled by the arrival of two forces from Antigonos, a small fleet detached from an expedition sent into the Peloponnese, and a much larger one from Asia; together they broke his blockade of the city. A squadron came up from Athens to assist Kassander's forces, and this allowed him to break out, taking the enemy by surprise.[57]

The smaller fleet that had foiled Kassander's attack was commanded by Telesphoros, another of Antigonos' nephews, who had sailed from Karia to the Peloponnese, and had swept up all Kassander's forces except those under

Kratesipolis at Corinth and Sikyon.[58] The second, larger, fleet from Asia was commanded by Medeios, where it had been taking part in Antigonos' campaign of conquest of Karia. Medeios had 100 ships, but he returned to Asia at once after the crisis at Oreus ended. There he collected more warships and troops and transported the army to be landed at Aulis in Boiotia. In other words, Kassander's attack on Oreus had significantly disrupted Antigonos' campaign by forcing him to react to support his ally. This army was then joined by the army of the Boiotian League, and they all camped outside Salganeus in order to attack Kassander's fortress of Chalkis, just across the Euripos Strait. Kassander left the siege of Oreus to take command at Chalkis.[59]

But Antigonos' wider view of events now became a liability. In the Peloponnese Telephoros, annoyed to find Antigonos' other nephew Polemaios preferred to him, seized power in Elis and set himself up as an independent tyrant; immediately Antigonos' position in the peninsula was weakened, as it was seen that the 'freedom' he promised was unlikely to be implemented by his subordinates.[60] In Thrace Lysimachos had been fighting vigorously and successfully against the long series of his enemies, including an expedition sent by Antigonos along the Thracian Black Sea coast.[61] Antigonos apparently spotted a new opportunity, with Kassander occupied in Euboia and Lysimachos fully occupied in Thrace, to launch an invasion of Europe in the north. He recalled Medeios' fleet and marched off to the Bosporos, hoping to persuade Byzantion into his alliance to give him a safe landing place in Thrace. The arrival of the victorious Lysimachos foiled this plan, leaving Antigonos miles away from the real centre of the action, which was Boiotia.[62]

In the absence of Medeios' main force, Kassander came out of Chalkis, leaving his brother Pleistarchos in command there, and campaigned through Boiotia. He captured Oropos, reinforced Thebes and made an alliance with the city, then neutralized by the Boiotian League, at least for the moment, by a truce. Then he returned to Macedon, since the apparent intention of Antigonos going to the north would be to invade that country.[63] (It may have been at this point that the two men met at the Hellespont and failed to agree on peace terms; the date of the meeting is extremely vague.[64])

Antigonos' exploits had therefore largely failed in the Peloponnese, at Byzantion, and in Boiotia, but he still had the resources to return to the attack, if he would only settle on, and carry through, a consistent plan. Kassander, on the other hand, was making war with very limited manpower.

Further, while Antigonos could choose between several possible areas where he could attack his enemies, Kassander was surrounded by active foes: in the Peloponnese, in central Greece, in Asia, in Epeiros and in the north. And yet Kassander's strategic situation was strong. Like Antigonos, but on a much smaller scale, he occupied a central strategic position from which he could strike in several directions; Antigonos on a continental scale occupied the same sort of position, but was clearly hampered, as the next year would show, by the sheer distances involved in reaching any site of conflict, and this meant that he could only respond to a distant threat by using up much time in marching. Lysimachos' victories in Thrace had been a welcome relief in that area, but the Boiotian truce was a fragile thing, and Polemaios was still in occupation at Salganeus.

Antigonos' several efforts in 313 might have often been failures, but Kassander had come under great pressure, and in the next year he had to concentrate on affairs in Epeiros and Illyria. The choice had been either there or Boiotia, and from the point of view of Macedon, Epeiros was the more important. The growth of Glaukias' power in alliance with Kerkyra was a clear threat, and when the Epeirotes chose a new king, Alketas, who was known to be hostile to Macedon, it was clearly necessary to deal with that threat first.[65] Kassander put Eupolemos, who had been freed by Polemaios, in charge in Boiotia, and used his own main army in the north-west.[66]

Since both of the chief men had to watch in several directions at once, most of the fighting that year was done by forces under subordinate generals. From Akarnania Lykiskos invaded Epeiros when Alketas came to power, accompanied by at least some of Kassander's men stationed in Leukas under the command of Athenian Lysander. From Salganeus Polemaios went out to regain control of Oropos, by a siege, took control of the cities in Euboia – Chalkis, Karystos and Eretria (to add to Oreus) – and then invaded Attika. Kassander's man there, Demetrios of Phaleron, was compelled by the Athenians to make a truce with the invader, and to send envoys to discuss an alliance with Antigonos, an initiative that apparently went nowhere, no doubt because Demetrios was only trying to gain time.[67] Polemaios had to turn off to reach into the Peloponnese to suppress Telesphoros in Elis and restore the treasure he had taken from Olympia to pay his mercenaries.[68]

Such a diversion was unhelpful to Polemaios' progress in central Greece. The neutralization of Athens could only be temporary, and it was slow work to conquer Boiotia city by city, even in alliance with the league. He had to take Thebes before moving north into Phokis, and then into Lokris, where he laid siege to Opous.[69] From Kassander's viewpoint this was exactly why he had planted garrisons and secured allies throughout central Greece, for while Polemaios was slowly conquering in that area Kassander was able to supervise events in Epeiros.

Lykiskos' invasion was enough to persuade many of Alketas' men to desert him – he was widely detested. Alketas took refuge in the city of Eurymenai, where he was reinforced by troops brought up by his son Alexander. A battle resulted in a marginal victory for Alketas, but then Lykiskos was reinforced by troops brought from Macedon by Deinias. Kassander himself also marched with more reinforcements from Macedon, but before he could reach the fighting a second battle had ended with the defeat of Alketas' forces. Alketas fled to another stronghold; Lykiskos captured Eurymenai and sacked it.

Kassander's arrival convinced Alketas to accept a peace, and Kassander then went on northwards to attempt to recover Apollonia. He had apparently only a small force with him, and the Apollonians resisted his attack successfully until Kassander withdrew to spend the winter in Macedon. This brought the general collapse of Kassander's supremacy in the area. The Kerkyrans took advantage of his weakness to drive his occupying force from Leukas. (Lysander had been killed in the fighting.[70])

By the end of 312, therefore, Antigonos' forces had secured some control over everything in Greece south of Thermopylai, with the exception of Athens, where Kassander's garrison still held the Munychia fort, while the city itself was neutralized by a truce, and Kratesipolis' cities of Corinth and Sikyon. Kassander had lost control of all central Greece, and much of the Peloponnese, and his Epeirote campaign had also been unsuccessful. He retained the alliance of Kratesipolis in Corinth, of Demetrios in Athens, and of the Akarnanians, and Alkestas in Epeiros was now preoccupied by internal affairs. Aitolia was hostile, as usual. It must have been clear to Kassander that next year he would be subject to a major assault on his home territory, where Thessaly was not wholly reliable.

Pressure on Antigonos brought the break. This came in Syria, where Antigonos' son Demetrios was defeated by Ptolemy in battle at Gaza.[71] Ptolemy then advanced into southern and central Syria while Seleukos rode off with a small force to (successfully) recover his Babylonian satrapy;

only a little later he was able to gain control of Iran as well, and during all this his armed forces expanded from 1,000 men to over 20,000, when he recruited the soldiers of the defeated armies. At a stroke Antigonos' empire was reduced geographically in size by two thirds, and large numbers of his soldiers were recruited by Seleukos and by Ptolemy. He had therefore now to retain a large part of his forces in southern Syria, send an army against Seleukos, and use another large force to face Lysimachos in Hellespontine Phrygia; he could spare nothing extra for Polemaios in Greece. In such circumstances Polemaios might not be able to stand against the full power of the Macedonian army under Kassander's command, especially as Kassander had seen off other dangers. Antigonos had fought himself to a temporary exhaustion. Both he and Kassander had reached the stage where they finally appreciated that it was necessary to make peace.

The initiative came from Kassander, or so at least Antigonos claimed afterwards. Kassander contacted Polemaios, who sent Artemidoros to Antigonos along with Prepelaos, who represented both Kassander and Lysimachos. No doubt the two envoys had long discussions on the journey to meet Antigonos, who was in Syria, recovering the territories briefly taken by Ptolemy after the battle. They had perhaps hammered out the basic terms between them before the meeting. Antigonos was quickly able to agree. Some of his aspirations – the 'freedom of the Greeks' especially – were incorporated in the official agreement, but his claim to the regency of the empire was ignored. The western part of the empire was divided between the three principals, with Kassander as '*strategos* in Europe', Antigonos as the '*strategos* in Asia', and Lysimachos to rule Thrace, but apparently without such a grandiose title.

Thus, Kassander and Lysimachos abandoned their allies. But Ptolemy quickly asked to be included and made a separate treaty with Antigonos soon after – it rather looks as though he knew what Kassander had planned. It must have taken some time to make all the arrangements in Greece, with discussions between Kassander and Lysimachos, with Polemaios and Aristodemos, before undertaking the long journey to Syria, so it was surely likely that Kassander had notified Ptolemy of what was happening. Seleukos and Polyperchon were not included, by implication being left for Antigonos and Kassander to deal with.[72]

Chapter 10

King Kassander

T he peace treaties agreed in 311 did not hold for very long. Seleukos, who had not been included in the peace process, was subjected to a new attack once Antigonos and his son Demetrios were free of war in Asia and against Ptolemy, though he held his own without too much difficulty; Ptolemy resumed the fighting in 310, in part to help Seleukos, but largely on his own account. Indeed, given that two of the contenders – Seleukos and Polyperchon – had been left out of the treaties, it could hardly be said that peace had ever resulted.

Nevertheless, given that Antigonos was more or less fully occupied in the east, against Seleukos and then against Ptolemy, the western arena was left in approximate peace for a time. Kassander faced several issues, however, and all of them involved him in violence. (Similarly, Lysimachos continued his intermittent warfare in Thrace – the 'peace' in the west was one between the greater commanders, not a general condition.) Kassander's problems included the issue of King Alexander and his mother, the problem of the northern frontier, and Polyperchon.

The northern frontier of Macedon had been the constant concern of every ruler who had held authority in the kingdom – indeed the kingdom may have originated from the need of the several constituent peoples to defend themselves against northern incursions. Philip II had expanded his control well over the frontier regions, pushing the Macedonian reach as far as the Danube, and later on Alexander had made military demonstrations as far as that river, but Alexander's diversion to the east had clearly let Macedonian control slip. Kassander had had to cope with the restless activity of King Glaukias of the Taulantii, who lived near the Adriatic coast, north of Epeiros. It may have been the warfare in Epeiros between Kassander and Aiakides that unsettled the rest of the region, but there was also constant fighting in Thrace, which must have been disturbing, and further off, there were tribal movements north of the Danube that would impact seriously on Macedon later; Alexander had already encountered Celts on the Danube.

In 312–310 the problem was the Autariatai, a people who had moved out of their more northern homeland in Dalmatia, possibly under pressure from other migrants, and were threatening to move into Macedon. Kassander met them with his army as he withdrew from Apollonia in 312, though it seems they did not fight; they made an agreement that the Autariatai could settle on the border of Thrace.[1] The trouble with such movements and settlements is that every other people in the area would automatically be upset. Within two years the Autariatai were fighting the Paionians of the Axios Valley, who were by this time a traditional Macedonian ally. Kassander assisted the Paionian King Audoleon in his fighting, and presumably defeated the Autariatai.[2] Their settlement, in a mountainous region called Orbelos, was confirmed, and perhaps their defeat was enough to convince them to stay put. They were soon visited by recruiting officers from Lysimachos,[3] and perhaps from Kassander; a restless tribe was always a useful source of recruits, and recruiting the young men left it less capable of causing trouble.

The problem of the young King Alexander IV was more difficult than that of fighting many tribesmen, since it was a new type of issue for everyone, and one that directly affected Kassander's relations with every other Macedonian warlord, and with his own Macedonian people as well. The treaty with Antigonos had assigned the protection of the king to Kassander; since he already held him in custody at Amphipolis, this was hardly a new development. But the treaty specified that this should only last until Alexander came of age, which would be when he was 18 years old – in 305.[4] But there was an earlier deadline, since at 14 he would need to begin his military training; this was the age at which adolescent Macedonian boys of good family became royal pages, and Alexander would be expected to join his age cohort for that experience.[5] These boys would become his friends and companions for the rest of his life. Kassander had already insisted that the king should not be attended by his own royal pages, and must be given the education of an ordinary child, not one suited to his royal or noble status,[6] and had secluded him and his mother in the Amphipolis citadel, but it would be very difficult to keep the king immured in Amphipolis in the face of the expectations of the Macedonians.[7] So the effective deadline for a decision on the king's future was not 305, but 309; as he reached 14 he would need to become visible.

Kassander's attitude personally to the king is not known, and all his actions clearly originated from political considerations, and indeed it is not known if he ever met or spoke with the king, but his political problem was clearly difficult. He had a number of alternatives. He could allow the king to grow, be educated, and then proclaim him of age and as the ruling king in 305. This, of course, would set up a new and even more difficult situation for him personally, and for every other Macedonian warlord, and would probably ignite a new round of warfare. Alternatively, he could keep him locked up, continuing to govern Macedon in his name – coins were minted in Alexander's name until 305 – though this would be even more destabilizing internally in the kingdom. Or he could use his control of the king to threaten his warlord contemporaries, maybe by issuing provocative proclamations in the king's name, which would destabilize their territories. No doubt he had thought of all these possibilities, and more.

Internally Kassander faced an equal or greater difficulty. There were elements among the Macedonians who wished to see Alexander as the ruling king.[8] There were other elements who were keen to return to being subjects of the Argead dynasty – any Argead would do. Kassander's marriage to Thessalonike was in effect his recognition of his need to conciliate these groups, who were already accusing him of wanting to be king, but the status of a husband of an Argead princess could hardly compete with the prospect of an adult Argead king. And there were other members of that royal family still alive who could substitute for Alexander should the king be removed – Kleopatra, the Epeirote royal family, and still more, of increasingly distant relationships.

The international peace arrangements began to break down in 310, if they could ever have been said to have really been implemented. Ptolemy announced that Antigonos was garrisoning and oppressing some Greek cities, thereby neatly turning Antigonos' main propaganda weapon against him, especially as the accusation was perfectly true.[9] That he and every other warlord maintained garrisons in Greek cities was a fact of political life, using a variety of excuses of which 'security' was the blanket choice, and Kassander was perhaps more guilty of the practice than most – though he did not subscribe to the others' genuflection towards 'freedom' and 'autonomy'. No doubt most warlords assumed that since all were guilty none of the rest would rock the boat as Ptolemy did. He followed up his accusation with raids into Kilikia, then into Lykia and Karia and Pamphylia, and on into the Aegean. As he approached Greece with his fleet his presence began to unsettle the situation there.

At the peace Kassander had accepted the position of '*strategos* over Europe', but this meant little unless he could enforce it, and in Greece his options were at first limited. Polyperchon was still in the Peloponnese, though exactly where is not clear; he had been in power in Messene earlier, and this may have still been the case. There was also Kratesipolis, who had maintained her control over Corinth and Sikyon, and perhaps Patrai, and so had control at the Isthmus. Neither of these were capable of serious expansion on their own, though Polyperchon was Kratesipolis' father-in-law, and they may well have been allied in some way, at least against a common enemy.[10] Kassander's man, Demetrios of Phaleron, maintained a relatively loose grip on Athens.

Boiotia, Lokris and Euboia, together with parts of the Peloponnese, had been left in the hands of Polemaios at the peace. He was technically Antigonos' viceroy, and had also established some authority in Elis by rescuing that city (and Olympia) from Telesphoros' occupation. He was also Antigonos' nephew, the son of his brother Philippos, but it seems that his loyalty was wearing thin. Telesphoros had struck out on his own in Elis because Polemaios seemed to have been favoured over him; Polemaios, who had been Antigonos' main commander for five years, began to feel that he was being superseded in Antigonos' favour. The new favourite was Antigonos' own son, Demetrios.[11] Polemaios might well feel annoyed at this, given that his own military record was one of repeated victories – Kappadokia, Karia, central Greece – whereas Demetrios had suffered major defeats – Gaza, Babylon – until he conducted a successful removal of Ptolemy's small garrisons in Kilikia.

It is clear that Antigonos was not good at managing his relatives; two of his nephews thus rejected him, yet he indulged his son far too much. (He was also liable to lose control of squads of soldiers, who frequently left his employ when given the chance of enlisting with a more sympathetic employer – Seleukos had collected 20,000 of Antigonos' men in a short time in this way. The practice of enlisting defeated enemy armies was widespread, but more than once Antigonos found that prisoners he had collected refused to follow this custom.) Polemaios began considering either joining another warlord, or perhaps striking out for independence. This latter option was rather closed off by his practice of respecting the policy of the 'freedom of the Greeks' and not imposing garrisons on his Greek cities, which policy had of course been forced on him by Antigonos, though he did keep a garrison in his capital, Chalkis. All this, of course, left him considerably weakened.

There was clearly enough material in Greece for diplomacy to have some effect. Kassander might complain that Polemaios' position in Greece was a contradiction of his own European command, and Polyperchon might still be reckoned one of Antigonos' allies. At some point in 310 Kassander and Polemaios contacted each other. Who took the initiative is not known, but Kassander, always prepared to exploit diplomacy rather than fight, seems the more likely. The two men had already had diplomatic relations in the preliminary peace negotiations, so Kassander probably knew of Polemaios' personal problem. The result of the contacts was that Polemaios defected from his uncle's authority, in effect declaring his independence, and at once made an alliance with Kassander.[12] He carried along with him a friend of his, Phoinix, a former officer of Eumenes who had been made satrap of Hellespontine Phrygia by Antigonos.[13]

This happened at the same time that Kassander had to campaign in the northern territories against the Autariatai in support of Audoleon. Antigonos was thus given time to deal with Phoinix. He sent his younger son Philip against him, apparently with success. This lack of support from Kassander may have sufficiently annoyed Polemaios to compel him to look elsewhere. In 309 Ptolemy and his fleet came into the Aegean and captured some cities in Karia, and then occupied the island of Kos.[14] To Polemaios this major force clearly looked like a more useful protector than Kassander, perhaps because Ptolemy's fleet might enable him to bring assistance to Phoinix. Also Kassander and Ptolemy may well have still been considered to be friends and allies. From Chalkis Polemaios took a force of his soldiers to meet Ptolemy at Kos (where the future Ptolemy II was born about this time to Ptolemy's second wife Berenike, Kassander's cousin).

Ptolemy was at first welcoming, but soon became disillusioned, perhaps experiencing Polemaios' arrogance. When he was found to be tampering with the loyalty of Ptolemy's own soldiers – was he hoping to bring assistance to Phoinix? or was this a later item of propaganda for Ptolemy's action? – he was jailed and then induced to drink the fatal hemlock cup. His soldiers enlisted with Ptolemy, being carefully distributed among several of Ptolemy's regiments.[15]

This in theory should have opened up central Greece for Kassander, who might have been able to take over Polemaios' position, acting as his ally. But, after dealing with Polemaios and the Autariatai during 310, he found that next year he was under attack by Polyperchon.[16]

Polyperchon was no doubt fully aware of his isolated position after the peace treaties, but he was still, like Polemaios, technically an ally of Antigonos, which should have been some protection. He was also of a similar age with Antigonos, in his seventies, and was perhaps desperate to attempt to revive his position as ruler of Macedon in one last endeavour. With the ending of the general fighting, and with Kassander's preoccupation with the northern frontier and with Polemaios, he seems to have quietly made contacts inside Macedon, made, or revived, his contacts with the Aitolians, and conjured up an Argead pretender to the Macedonian throne; he also clearly had substantial funds.

The pretender was Herakles, Alexander the Great's son by the Persian lady Barsine, who had been the wife of Memnon, Dareios III's commander.[17] He and his mother had been held at Pergamon, and so under Antigonos' guardianship, having evaded both Olympias and Kassander in Macedon, and no doubt Antigonos considered them, or at least Herakles, as useful pawns in the diplomatic and royal intrigues apparently going on. Diodoros says that Polyperchon 'summoned' Herakles and Barsine from Pergamon to join him, but they could hardly have left Pergamon and made the journey to Greece without Antigonos' permission and approval and assistance.[18] We may therefore assume that the attack, which Polyperchon launched in 309 on Kassander, was one of Antigonos' schemes, though it well might have originated with Polyperchon. Antigonos was perhaps annoyed that Kassander was involved in Polemaios' defection in 310; backing Polyperchon against Kassander next year would be a suitable reply and revenge. But he was always ambitious to gain control of Macedon, and the great obstacle he found was always Kassander; destabilizing Kassander's regime was necessary if Antigonos was to make progress there. We may assume that Polyperchon, even if he was apparently in charge of the expedition, was effectively Antigonos' tool.

Polyperchon certainly had funds, the most obvious source of which must be Antigonos. He recruited an army of 20,000 infantry and 1,000 cavalry mercenaries, and with this army, and reinforced by an Aitolian force, he was suddenly a major threat.[19] The man could hardly have done this on his own resources; again it would seem that Antigonos was the source. Polyperchon had contacts inside Macedon who were sympathetic towards his promotion of Herakles as an Argead king, which may be interpreted as a code for opposition to Kassander. Beyond that Polyperchon himself was a Macedonian grandee, being a member of the ruling family of Tymphaia, an upland region to the west of Thessaly, which had been incorporated into Macedon by Philip II; his ancestral estate there had been seized by Kassander, but he could certainly count on some support there; it was also helpfully close to Aitolia.

This was a major threat to Kassander's control of Macedon, but it was also involved in the much wider crisis over the aspirations of the last Argeads. Antigonos also had control over Alexander the Great's sister Kleopatra, who was living under guard and under restriction at Sardis. If Antigonos could loose Herakles and Barsine on Kassander, he might do the same with Kleopatra. She in turn had been courted – if that is not too romantic a term for a process that was mainly a grasp for power – by most of the warlords at one time or another, ever since Perdikkas. If Herakles could gain support in Macedon, as was certainly apparent to Kassander in this crisis, so could Kleopatra, and so how much more dangerous was Alexander IV to him.

Polyperchon marched through Aitolia, then possibly through Thessaly, and camped just inside Tymphaia. There he was blocked by Kassander with the Macedonian army. Diodoros claims that Kassander was worried that some or all of his men might desert because of the presence in Polyperchon's camp of Herakles, but it may also be that Polyperchon feared the same reaction among some of his own men at the prospect of fighting fellow Macedonians.[20] Macedonian armies had a record of refusing to fight each other, or of suddenly changing sides, especially in civil wars. But this situation was also exactly the moment for diplomacy, and this was something at which Kassander excelled, probably more so than any other contemporary.

Kassander took the initiative, contacting Polyperchon through an embassy. The argument he is said to have put forward was that if Herakles was made king, he would then listen to others rather than just Polyperchon; the implication was that one of the decisions the new king would be influenced to take would be to get rid of Polyperchon. Alternatively, Kassander offered to make Polyperchon his man in the Peloponnese with a Macedonian army to command, and in effect to act as Kassander's partner rather than Antigonos' stooge; he also offered to return Polyperchon's Macedonian estates, which he had apparently confiscated. The price would be the murder of Herakles and his mother.

Polyperchon fell for it, killed Herakles and Barsine, and received his reward; command of an army of 4,000 Macedonian infantry and 500 Thessalian cavalry, and his lands.[21] But the command in the Peloponnese eluded him; he found so much opposition on his march south, mounted by 'Boiotians and Peloponnesians' that he got no further than Lokris.[22] What motivated his opponents is not known, though the Peloponnesians had known him for some years, and probably found the prospect of his continued presence with enhanced power in the Peloponnese less than welcome. The Boiotians had been allies of Antigonos when Polemaios was present, but he had now left that connection. The prospect of yet another Macedonian army marching through their territory was presumably quite enough to provoke their opposition, and Polyperchon's force was small enough to be stopped; it is also quite possible that Kassander, who had interests in both regions, had instigated Polyperchon's opponents; as a result Polyperchon had to remain immobile throughout the winter of 309/308, and he may have returned to Thessaly or Macedon. (One can't help feeling that even the callous Greeks might have been alienated by his despicable conduct.)

Polyperchon was thus powerless amidst the two other major developments of 309/308. One almost immediate result, even as Polyperchon was moving south, was probably that Kassander gave instructions to Glaukias, his commander in Amphipolis, to kill Alexander and Roxanne. The experience of being threatened by a bastard half-Iranian son of Alexander the Great, when his hold on the Macedonians had shifted and become infirm, had been disturbing; the existence of a legitimate half-Iranian son of Alexander and his imminent entry into public life as he reached the age of 14 years and linked up with his age cohort was too much of a threat.

The death of Herakles is linked by several ancient historians with that of Alexander IV,[23] though it is not clear which boy died first; Kassander may have killed off Alexander before meeting Polyperchon, which may have been the trigger for Antigonus' promotion of the expedition – but if so, it is surprising that neither man publicly denounced Kassander; similarly Polyperchon may have promoted Herakles because he knew that Alexander was dead. Kassander may have resorted to killing Alexander because he had seen how dangerous the sons of Alexander the Great were to him, or having ordered it when Polyperchon's threat became clear. The link between the murders is obvious, however, even if the precise sequence is not known, and now can never be known. The threat to Kassander's control of Macedon had been very evident, and it was this which brought him to the point of ordering the killing.

Ptolemy at Kos contacted the one surviving member of the Temenid dynasty (apart from Kassander's wife Thessalonike), Kleopatra. She was living under the usual guard at Sardis. He promised marriage, or some political advancement – even aiming to use her in a campaign against Kassander. But when she attempted to leave the city she was stopped. Antigonos, having let Herakles out of his grasp and no doubt fully informed by now of the deaths of the two boys, ordered Kleopatra to be killed, which was done by a group of women. He then ordered that several of these women be tried for treason, and some of them were executed. He thus pretended he was not responsible and put on an elaborate funeral.[24] This display of murderous hypocrisy fooled no one, and it certainly brought Antigonos down to an equivalent low moral level with Polyperchon and Kassander; at least Kassander did not kill the actual murderer, but merely kept the killing secret. It may, however, have been of some satisfaction to Kassander that his wife was the only Argead left, and that his sons were thus half Argead. Any Argead loyalists left could only look to his family now.

In Greece, Polyperchon's failure to advance beyond Lokris left all but Attika uncontrolled by any of the warlords. Ptolemy determined to chance his hand. He took his fleet to the Isthmus where, perhaps by prearrangement, he took over Corinth and Sikyon from Kratesipolis, and quite possibly thought he might propose marriage: she was famously a beautiful woman.[25] His slogan was that he was bringing freedom to the cities. He secured promises of help from other Peloponnesian cities, but nothing was actually forthcoming[26] – the slogan did not work anymore, especially in that area that was all too familiar with warlords' promises; these had been announced repeatedly in the past years all to no effect, and especially in view of Ptolemy's garrisons being maintained in Corinth and Sikyon, not to mention Cyrene and in Syria. The failure to attract support and the almost simultaneous failure to join up with Kleopatra certainly discouraged him, and trouble in Cyrenaica required attention. After making an agreement with Kassander that they should respect each other's holdings, Ptolemy pulled back and returned to Egypt.[27]

The weakness of all these attempts to control Greece was evident after these general failures – Ptolemy rebuffed, Kassander reduced to Athens, Antigonos having lost his general Polemaios, Polyperchon both weakened and discredited and stuck in Lokris or Macedon. But in 308 Antigonos finally gave up his attempt to recover Babylon and the east from Seleukos, and this freed his army for other actions. Ptolemy returned to Egypt, thereby removing the threat to Antigonos' territories in southern Asia Minor and the Aegean. Polemaios' defection had ended in his death, and the rebellion of Phoinix had probably been suppressed. Antigonos, with his forces now available and with several problems cleared away, now spotted another opportunity, once again in Greece.

He gave 5,000 talents, a fleet and an army to his son Demetrios, and sent him to Greece. The target was Athens, where Kassander's garrison was small, and the lengthy control by Demetrios of Phaleron on Kassander's behalf had become increasingly resented by the Athenians. The disappearance of any obvious enemies had perhaps also removed the main reason for submitting to Kassander – and, of course, the population of Athens was always ready to return to a democratic political regime. They actually expected Ptolemy to return in 307 – his soldiers still controlled Corinth and Sikyon – presumably because some Athenians had made contact with him the previous year, so when Demetrios' ships appeared off the coast they were assumed to be Ptolemy's; but then they suddenly ran into the harbour at Peiraios. Demetrios landed troops, drove the garrison into the Munychia fort, seized the town, and sent a herald to proclaim 'freedom'. The military reaction by the garrison and by the Athenian commanders was ineffectual.[28]

The Peiraians rose to welcome him. Kassander's garrison withdrew to, or was driven into, the fort and Demetrios of Phaleron escaped into the city, from where next day, given a safe conduct pass by Demetrios, he left for Thebes.[29] Demetrios finished his task by attacking the fort, which fell to his combined artillery bombardment and overwhelming numbers in a few days.

Having captured the fort, Demetrios razed its fortifications in a symbolic gesture to 'freedom'.[30] In Athens the democratic regime was restored and celebrations to honour the 'liberator' were held, while Demetrios ordered supplies.[31] The regime of Kassander and Demetrios of Phaleron had proved extremely fragile. Demetrios moved out to besiege and capture Megara, which had been held by another of Kassander's garrisons.[32] All Greece south of Thessaly was now clear of Kassander's forces, and Greece was wide open to Antigonos if he chose to seize it.

Kassander had therefore suffered a series of serious defeats. The death of Herakles was blamed in part on him, quite justly. He had ordered the killing of Alexander, and though he kept it secret, it seems clear that rumours were spreading, for the boy had certainly disappeared; Antigonos' and Polyperchon's actions imply that they knew he was dead. He had lost control of Athens and Megara, and his ally Kratesipolis had retired from her cities. He had made peace, and perhaps an alliance, with Ptolemy, but Ptolemy had gone back to Egypt, his Aegean adventure abandoned, though he held on to Corinth and Sikyon, and might well return given favourable circumstances; he had allied with Polyperchon, who could apparently do nothing. And, also in 307, King Glaukias of the Taulantii invaded Epeiros to expel King Alketas, to the pleasure of the Epeirotes, and put forward Aiakides' son Pyrrhos as their new king. The boy was only 12 years old at the time, and had guardians to rule for him; his sister Deidameia had been betrothed to Alexander, and this might cause trouble later; similarly, Kassander had made several attempts to buy Pyrrhos from Glaukias, a clear indication of hostility. Pyrrhos' accession, therefore, might have appeared dangerous, but there was plenty of internal confusion, and opposition to the change, to keep the Epeirotes busy at home; nevertheless, Epeiros now seemed to be hostile to Macedon and Kassander, whereas earlier it had been neutral.[33]

Despite the defeats and threats, however, Kassander had carefully avoided risking his military strength and his soldiers' lives in the past few years. He had deflected Polyperchon by diplomacy, and the possible threat from Ptolemy had also been neutralized by diplomacy. The defeats in Attika and Megara had not cost him very much. He had therefore survived the immediate problems and upheavals of 307, and no doubt was further relieved when Antigonos called Demetrios and his forces back to fight Ptolemy for Cyprus, then to attack Egypt and fail, and finally to become involved in the long siege of Rhodes. All this took three years, and meanwhile Kassander staged a recovery in Greece.

Antigonos took advantage of an ephemeral victory at Salamis and Demetrios' conquest of Cyprus to have himself proclaimed as king, and he appointed Demetrios as king also. This was in 306, so it is probable that the death of Alexander IV was now public; the Babylonian Chronicle shifts its count of years at this point also. Kassander conducted a funeral for him – the second Macedonian king for whom he had done so.[34] He did not, however, lay much emphasis on his own new status. He was certainly 'King of the Macedonians', which was not a title the other new kings were able to use, though Seleukos did call himself both 'king' and 'the Macedonian', but this was rather on the pattern of the Persian kings than the Macedonian usage.[35]

Why Kassander seems to have been reluctant to insist too much on his royal title is odd but may be connected with his guardianship of King Alexander – he appears to have maintained the fiction of the boy king still being alive as long as possible, and if he did that he could not assume the Macedonian kingship. It may also be that, since he had in fact enjoyed royal power in practice since 317, and had acted as king since 316 with his performance of the funeral rites for Philip III, it was not anything new, except the actual title. Possibly he knew that this would be an unpopular move and so simply did not announce it in any formal sense. It is unlikely to be a case of modesty, for there is nothing in his life that suggested he was anything less than arrogant and ambitious, with a powerful dash of strong self-confidence.

These royal titles made no real difference in the political struggles these men were waging. After failing to capture Rhodes (though the city eventually accepted terms identical to those that were offered by Antigonos before the siege began, and so technically Demetrios was victorious) Antigonos sent his son back to Greece.

Kassander had used the time while Demetrios was fighting elsewhere to attempt to recover his position in Greece. It was obvious that whether Demetrios won or lost in his various adventures, he and his father would still be powerful, and one of the results would be yet another attempt by Antigonos' army to secure control of Greece, and Demetrios had a very convenient base in Athens from which to commence such a conquest. Athens meanwhile had rearmed, using money and arms contributed by Antigonos and Demetrios, had built itself a new navy, and had refortified the city. Antigonos had encouraged this, since he in fact could have the use of the ships;[36] he had returned to Athenian control the islands of Lemnos and Imbros, taken from the city several years before, but Ptolemy kept control of Andros.[37] An alliance was made with the Aitolians, and so when Kassander invaded Attika in 306, he found himself facing a much stronger defence than he had perhaps expected. His attack failed, and he retreated back to Phokis, and even there he was compelled to abandon the siege of Elateia and pull further back into Thessaly.[38]

Athens secured an alliance with the Boiotian League to add to that with the Aitolians, but even their joint forces could not hope to make any progress in an attack on Macedon itself. Antigonos' forces were needed. But Demetrios was trying to conquer Rhodes, and the hypocrisy of 'freedom' propaganda being proclaimed by kings who had made themselves kings and were attacking one of the free Greek states was disheartening. The Boiotians pulled out of the alliance; the Aitolians intervened to help bring the Rhodian siege to an end. And the unpopularity spread from the kings to their allies. The Boiotians joined Kassander when he came south again in 304; he had meanwhile built a new fleet. The Aitolians were also no help, now that Boiotia was hostile. Kassander captured Attika's border forts and besieged the city; the new Athenian fleet was defeated by the new Macedonian fleet, and Kassander captured Salamis. Athens appealed to Demetrios for help. Meanwhile Kassander's march south had brought with him Polyperchon and his little army, and at last he was able to act in the Peloponnese. Corinth was taken and put in the command of Prepelaos; Polyperchon secured control of a number of Peloponnesian cities.[39]

It was at this point that Demetrios arrived. He landed, as had Polemaios, at Aulis in Boiotia, and at once Kassander's hold on this land collapsed. The Boiotians surrendered at once, and Demetrios took over Chalkis. Kassander retreated northwards, though Polyperchon continued operating in the Peloponnese. Demetrios' great fleet of 330 ships was far too much for Kassander's. Demetrios followed up Kassander's retreat as far as Thermopylai, where Kassander stood to fight and was defeated; 6,000 of his men deserted to Demetrios – or perhaps were captured and were then enlisted in Demetrios' forces.[40]

Demetrios cleared out Kassander's garrisons, but largely refrained from putting in his own. He came back to Attika to do the same and went on as far as Kenchreai on the Isthmus, which he captured.[41] But then he stopped. The Athenians rendered him more honours, and he relapsed into dissipation and idleness, entertaining courtesans in the temple of Athena. Just as the attack on Rhodes had disillusioned the Greek cities who were seeking 'freedom', so did Demetrios' behaviour in the winter of 304/303 disillusion many Athenians. He compounded the offence by displays of arrogance and petulance.[42]

The excuse for his idleness was that his troops were in winter quarters. In the spring of 303 he moved into the Peloponnese. Possibly this was to avoid having to fight Kassander, and the Peloponnese might have held out the prospect of easy victories. The propaganda, of course, of 'freedom' required that he liberate cities that were garrisoned by his opponent and this may have been the rationale for moving into the Peloponnese, where many of Kassander's garrisons controlled the region. This did, however, ignore the fact that the main enemy was Kassander and his army, and even if he won in the Peloponnese Demetrios would still have to go and face the Macedonian army and Kassander in the end.

Demetrios certainly gained victories, capturing Sikyon from Ptolemy's men, and Corinth from Prepelaos, and Orchomenos from Polyperchon's; he overran Achaia but, with the job again only half-done, he turned away. A marriage – another marriage – was concluded with Deidameia the daughter of Aiakides of Epeiros, and one with Kratesipolis avoided, and the liberated Greek cities were organized into a new League of Corinth.[43] These measures were clearly preparatory to a campaign against Macedon. He was thus gathering support from Greece – he now controlled, or was allied with, virtually every Greek state (except Sparta, as usual) south of Thermopylai – and perhaps, through Deidameia, from Epeiros.

As before, Demetrios' particular concerns, which were usually, but not always, dictated by his father from Syria, gave Kassander time in which to prepare for what was coming. By haring off after fruitless campaigns against Ptolemy and Rhodes between 306 and 304, Demetrios had allowed Kassander to return to central and southern Greece, and Demetrios had then spent a year and a half recovering and extending his control in Boiotia and the Peloponnese. Now Kassander resorted to diplomacy, often his first and most effective recourse, and asked Antigonos for terms. It is unlikely he was surprised at the answer – 'Kassander [is to] surrender whatever he possessed', Antigonos demanded.[44]

Apart from the pointlessness of asking a man in command of a major kingdom and a substantial army for instant unconditional surrender, Antigonos had also once again handed his opponent clear evidence that his ambitions were limitless. Whereas in 315 it was Seleukos who sounded the warning, now it was Kassander who was able to report to his contemporary rulers that Antigonos was a threat not just to him but to all of them. Demetrios' activities in the Peloponnese, therefore, gave Kassander plenty of time to inform his contemporaries Lysimachos, Ptolemy and Seleukos.[45] This clearly took some time since, though Lysimachos was next door in Thrace and Ptolemy could be fairly quickly contacted in Egypt by sea, Seleukos had been fighting in eastern Iran and India for the last two or three years; it would take several months to reach him, and for his reply to arrive – and Seleukos' input was essential. It would not, of course, take much to convince any of these men of the truth of Kassander's evidence; they had all been Antigonos' victims more than once in the recent past.

If a plan was agreed among the coalition members it was only basic – they would fight in Asia Minor, and until they could gather their armies there, they would attack Antigonos where they could. Clearly this put the main work on Kassander to face Demetrios, and meanwhile Lysimachos would, with reinforcement from Kassander's forces, invade Asia Minor; both men had to be extremely careful to avoid being defeated and destroyed before the others could join in. Seleukos and Ptolemy would invade as they could, no doubt with the aim of joining Lysimachos; in order for an army to be collected that was large enough to face Antigonos, every ally would need to play a slow game, holding off counter-attacks. And this meant, above all, Kassander facing and stalling Demetrios.

Demetrios played his part and did not hurry. Lysimachos moved into Asia Minor in the early summer of 302, and campaigned with some success among the Greek cities in Hellespontine Phrygia and Lydia, while Antigonos' supporters in the region, such as Dokimos, wavered in their loyalty or began to desert him. Demetrios gathered his own forces at Chalkis in Euboia and set out to campaign into Thessaly. This move began later than Lysimachos' crossing. Kassander sent some forces to join with Lysimachos' army in Asia, commanded by Prepelaos; the numbers he took with him are not stated, but he was sent by Lysimachos on a march along the Aegean coastlands with 6,000 infantry and 1,000 cavalry, and this may well be the Macedonian contingent.[46]

Demetrios' force gathered at Chalkis consisted of 8,000 'Macedonian' infantry – that is, men trained in Macedonian methods and tactics, not necessarily originally from Macedon – 15,000 mercenaries, 25,000 Greeks contributed by the new League of Corinth members, 8,000 light infantry, and 1,500 cavalry. The heterogeneous nature of the army proved to be a liability eventually, but for the present it was almost double that of Kassander. He had 29,000 infantry and 2,000 cavalry, and the relative smallness of his army dictated his tactics.[47]

Kassander occupied the passes leading into Thessaly, so says Diodoros, presumably meaning Thermopylai and its neighbours and alternatives by land. Demetrios, accustomed to the sea, simply loaded his men on his ships and landed them at 'the port of Larissa Chremaste', from where he campaigned to capture two nearby towns. (Kassander had done the same fifteen years before, so he cannot have been surprised at Demetrios' manoeuvre.) But Demetrios' new situation was not necessarily a great improvement over being blocked at the passes, since he was still separated from the main part of Thessaly by the range of awkward hills of Phthiotis, through which even now there are no roads to speak of. His great superiority in numbers was thus of little use, for he had to fight on a narrow front. He therefore advanced only slowly, moving along the coast of the Gulf of Pagasai, though the details are not easy to discern. There was a contest for control of the city of Phthiotic Thebes, and then for the city of Pherai, which surrendered to him. But Demetrios' advance was very slow and gradual.[48] It slowed to nothing when he discovered Kassander's army in a fortified camp that was too strong to be attacked; Demetrios made camp as well; he did manage to secure Pherai but could not dislodge Kassander's army from its position.[49]

Antigonos reacted to Lysimachos' invasion of his original satrapy as expected. Gathering his forces in Syria he marched west. The disaffected and disloyal men along his route were brought back under his control, and he confronted Lysimachos' army in western Asia Minor. Neither felt strong enough to risk a battle, so both appealed for reinforcements from across the Aegean, Antigonos demanding a reinforcement from Demetrios, Lysimachos asking for help from Kassander.

It was up to Demetrios to make the first move, since Kassander could hardly afford, or be expected, to weaken himself further. At the same time,

Kassander was perfectly willing to agree a truce to allow Demetrios to leave, which he could do through the ports he controlled in the Gulf. The terms were clearly restricted to this movement alone, and Demetrios soon embarked part of his force and transported it across to Ephesos (which he had to retake from Prepelaos' forces). Exactly which forces he took with him is not clear, but it seems that many of the Greek allies were left behind, though we know that some Athenians fought on Antigonos' side in the final battle. He will have been able to take his Macedonians, his mercenaries and his cavalry (unless some of them were Greek) and his light infantry; but he reached Asia with perhaps only half of his original force. The Greek troops were probably expected to remain in Thessaly and to defend his conquests against Kassander.

Kassander waited until Demetrios had left – none of these warlords trusted each other – and then sent 12,000 infantry and 500 cavalry under the command of his brother Pleistarchos to join Lysimachos. This left him with less than 20,000 men. Part of the reinforcing force was captured, and another section suffered shipwreck in the crossing of the Black Sea, but perhaps half of the force reached Asia. Lysimachos had gathered all his forces together in the face of Antigonos' greater numbers and put them into a great fortified camp. Antigonos and Demetrios established their own camps, Demetrios in Hellespontine Phrygia, Antigonos some distance to the south. But crucially Lysimachos had secured control of the port-city of Herakleia Pontike, by the device of marrying its ruler, Amastris (the long-ago brief Persian wife of Krateros). His camp was nearby, well to the east of those of Demetrios and Antigonos, but positioned so that he could be joined by the armies of Seleukos and Ptolemy, who would be coming from even further east.[50] Everyone waited for the winter to pass.

Kassander in Thessaly had no difficulty in recovering the territory Demetrios had taken; presumably the Greek forces, and any others left by Demetrios, were too weak, or too uninterested and uninvolved, to make a fight of it.[51] There is no hint of any actual conflict in Greece once Demetrios had left; the decisive fight would take place in Asia and everyone knew it. The arrival of Seleukos from the east into winter quarters in eastern Anatolia provided the forces the allies needed to meet Antigonos and Demetrios on equal terms; and Seleukos' squadron of 400 elephants proved to be the decisive contingent; Ptolemy could not get past Antigonos' garrisons and army in Syria. After some manoeuvres during the campaigning season of 301, the final battle took place at Ipsos in Phrygia. Antigonos was defeated and killed; his surviving army surrendered; Demetrios escaped with a small army.[52]

Kassander had not been idle; apart from recovering full control of Thessaly, he had been busy at his diplomatic work. A notice in Diodoros reports that he was actively persuading the lord of Kios in Mysia, Mithradates, in the midst of the Antigonid armies' camps, to defect from Antigonos, though the plot was discovered and Mithradates was killed.[53] The apparent alliance which Demetrios had made with Pyrrhos of Epeiros by his marriage with Deidameia was unproductive, since Pyrrhos stayed out of the fighting, possibly because of Kassander's pressure or intrigues; Kassander and Demetrios had also both contacted the Syracusan warlord Agathokles, but he was far too wary to become involved.[54] One may note, however, that Kassander had survived the war having done very little actual fighting. He had preserved his forces largely complete, except for those drowned, and those killed at Ipsos; he had, characteristically, actively involved himself in the diplomacy surrounding the war, far more so it seems than any of the others.

The war, however, did not end with the battle and the subsequent agreement to divide up Antigonos' territories. Antigonos was dead, but Demetrios had survived, taking with him a small army, and he still controlled a large fleet. He took refuge first of all in Ephesos and was able to continue to control several of the Asian cities. Athens, however, seceded, sending Deidameia to Megara (which he therefore presumably still controlled) and handing over at least some of his ships to him when he demanded them. He also controlled Cyprus and the Phoenician cities of Tyre and Sidon, and his fleet dominated the eastern Mediterranean. Demetrios therefore was still not finished. In the division of territory Kassander gained none for himself, but Pleistarchos was given, probably by Lysimachos' intervention, Kilikia, thus placing him between Seleukos' new lands in Syria and those of Lysimachos in Asia Minor, perhaps as a useful buffer. In terms of power, the man who gained most had been Lysimachos.[55]

Kassander's career had been nail-bitingly precarious if one stood at, say, Athens; from the viewpoint of a Macedonian, however, it had been outstandingly successful. Since Olympias' debacle there had been no fighting within the kingdom. Polyperchon had marched through but had been deflected by diplomacy; Demetrios' invasion in 302 had been slowed to nothing by Kassander's tactics and had been confined to southern Thessaly. The northern and Thracian frontiers had been safeguarded. In all this Kassander followed his father's example: he could use his Macedonian forces outside the kingdom, but above all his aim had been to defer and deflect and defeat possible attacks. If he refrained for a time from using the royal title, by the time the danger from Antigonos and Demetrios had been removed, his position as effective king of Macedon was clear and firmly founded. But it lasted only seven more years.

Chapter 11

A Ruling Dynasty's End

After over thirty years of rule by father and son, with only a brief intermission in 319–317, the dynasty of Antipater should have been firmly established as kings of Macedon. And yet, after the battle of Ipsos, within seven years of that apparently decisive victory, the dynasty had failed, amidst a grotesque series of murders and betrayals.

It has to be admitted, however, that instability was the one common characteristic of all the new kings and kingdoms, for they were all essentially usurpers. None of them proved able to survive for long without repeated crises and challenges, some of which resulted in the overthrow of the dynasty. The fact that the Seleukids and Ptolemies developed established dynasties, which lasted for well over two centuries, and the Antigonids revived to rule Macedon for a century, should not hide the fact that Antipatros' and Lysimachos' dynasties failed, as did that of Pyrrhos in Epeiros, that the Seleukids only just survived a collapse when Seleukos I died, and that the Ptolemies resorted to much mutual murder within the family to prevent collapses. The odds were against a dynasty's survival beyond the first generation.

The perception among his contemporaries that Antigonos had been aiming to revive the united Macedonian Empire of Alexander was something others could understand and could try to emulate. Antigonos' son Demetrios was certainly one such adventurer, and Seleukos was another. Ptolemy had made his attempt on Greece in the decade before Ipsos, and the family was not yet purged of that ambition. And ambition had stirred in Lysimachos and brought him to empire in Asia Minor – and he also was not yet finished.

Kassander has been given the reputation of being concerned with Macedon alone, and that he had the ambition of ruling only there. But he had aimed for Kappadokia and Lykia in 315, had sent an army into Karia, and had repeatedly campaigned to control Greece, so it may be that his ambitions were stirred like everybody else's in the new conditions after Ipsos. But he was, like Seleukos, of a cautious and careful bent, and it is probable that he was more conscious than the others of the limitations imposed by the lack of Macedonian manpower. The theory that Alexander had drained the kingdom of its military resources has been exaggerated, and Antipater had been able to build an army of 40,000 men in 331, but Kassander could never top that figure, nor even reach it, and could therefore not afford to become too deeply involved in warfare. Even in the great crisis of 302–301 his was one of the smaller forces in the field. So his ambition may have not been extinguished, but he did tailor it to his military capabilities.

It is certain that after 300 he displayed no interest in the wider eastern Mediterranean, though he did look to revive his old policy in Epeiros and on the Adriatic coast. The other kings played a complex set of games of alliances and betrayals, marriages and intrigues, for a time, though this had no real result other than to confirm their positions and solidify their kingdoms as settled after Ipsos – a balance of power of a sort. They were all at odds with all the rest, which fluid situation allowed evanescent alliances to be lightly agreed, and as lightly broken.

One of the victims of this complex competition was Pleistarchos, Kassander's brother, whose minor kingdom (though he was never king) of Kilikia fell to Demetrios almost as soon as the latter could get there, in 299.[1] But Pleistarchos also ruled in Karia, either placed there along with Kilikia, or given that territory as compensation after he had lost his first lands.[2] No one helped him when Demetrios stole Kilikia, not Lysimachos, who had been his military colleague for a year before Ipsos, not Seleukos, to whom he appealed in person, and not even his brother Kassander; Demetrios, briefly reunited with his senior wife Phila for the moment, sent her to see Kassander in order to dissuade him from any interference; she was either successful, or Kassander had no intention of interfering in the first place, probably the latter.[3] It is noticeable, however, that Pleistarchos' new territory was an area in which Macedonian kings in the past and the future and Kassander too, displayed an interest. So perhaps Kassander did not help Pleistarchos because he was satisfied to see a member of the family in control in Karia. He had been well enough established to be the recipient of a book dedication from Diokles of Karystos, a doctor living in Athens, though this may have been earlier than his rule in Asia Minor.[4]

On the other hand, Kassander was watching events to his west with care and attention. His main enemies in previous conflicts in the west had been Glaukias of the Taulantii and the city of Kerkyra. Between them they had repelled Kassander's earlier invasions, and he had remained on the defensive on that front ever since, though he maintained an alliance with the Akarnanians and appears to have controlled the city of Ambrakia, since Pyrrhos demanded it as part of his price for helping King Alexander V in 294.[5] It is likely that Glaukias was now (in 298/297) dead, but even if he still lived he appears nowhere in the events of this crisis. But Kerkyra had gone through considerable tribulation. It had been seized by Kleonymos, the Spartan prince who campaigned in South Italy for a time. He had constructed a considerable, but brief, empire around the Ionian Sea and into the Adriatic – one of his achievements had been to rescue Apollonia from Kassander. But he then vanished. Probably the Kerkyrans drove his forces out, an event that would cut the heart from his little empire.

Kerkyra reverted to independence, but the island city was obviously weakened by the experience. It had earlier held a sort of coastal empire along the west Greek coast, though perhaps it is better described as an alliance. It included at various times Leukas, Apollonia and Epidamnos, all of which had been Kassander's targets in the past, and as a group they had defied his attempts at conquest – though he had never struck directly at Kerkyra. Given the ease with which it fell to Kleonymos, perhaps that had been a serious omission, but the enemy at the time had been Glaukias.

In this conflict the real prize would have been Epeiros, which repeatedly fell into internal crisis between 310 and 295. Epeiros was a coalition of tribal states, of which that of the Molossi was the most important, and it was the Molossian royal family that provided the kings for the federal state. But there were constant disputes between rival branches over who should be king, and in the 290s two men fought for the post: Neoptolemos II, who had been king for a time in the 330s, and Pyrrhos, the son of Aiakides. Pyrrhos, king from 307, had been driven out in 302 and had then returned, sponsored by Ptolemy, in 297.[6] The two rivals shared power for a couple of years, but the conflict had reduced Epeiros to powerlessness while it continued, and the division of power did not hold. This provided opportunities for the kingdom's neighbours, including Kassander.

Kassander's ambition in the west had not died. In 298 (probably) he took a seaborne expedition round into the Ionian Sea with the aim of seizing Kerkyra, from which Kleonymos had recently been expelled.[7] This would destroy whatever was left of the island's little empire, if any of it remained; the fragments could then be collected at leisure, and with the cities in his hands – Ambrakia, Kerkyra, Apollonia, Epidamnos – Kassander would have a stranglehold on Epeiros. The presence of Pyrrhos in Epeiros, married to a stepdaughter of Ptolemy, was also a clear threat to Kassander's power, and Pyrrhos had the same restlessness as Demetrios. Kassander also can hardly have forgotten the sudden lunge that the Egyptian king had made into the Aegean only ten years before. That is, the attempt of Kassander on Kerkyra was one more of those apparently minor moves in the overall international conflict, whose ultimate aim was to expand the power of the aggressor.

It was foiled in part by the resistance of the Kerkyrans, whose city Kassander had to besiege. But unexpectedly there came an intrusion by the Syracusan King Agathokles, who was invited in to rescue them by the Kerkyrans. Agathokles had secured control of most of Sicily and was building an empire in southern Italy and the Adriatic, emulating a series of Epeirote and Spartan earlier adventurers. The addition of Kerkyra would be a very useful element in his empire, and repelling Kassander would reduce the threat he would have mounted, for Kerkyra in the hands of a great Greek power was an essential base for operations further west – Athens and Kleonymos had shown this, and Pyrrhos would do so later. For a western power such as Agathokles, Kerkyra was an essential part of a defensive system, as the Romans quickly appreciated a few decades later.

But there was more than a distant defensive post for Sicily involved. Agathokles, like Pyrrhos, was also a son-in-law of Ptolemy, whose step-daughter Theoxene he had married. It seems highly unlikely that this concatenation was therefore in no way accidental, nor was it merely a matter of rescuing the Kerkyrans. The crisis was resolved by a complex fight between Kassander's Macedonians and Agathokles' Sicilian Greeks. The assault was a defeat for Kassander, part of whose fleet was burnt, and whose Macedonian soldiers were defeated by the Siceliotes, much to the latter's glee at defeating the troops who had conquered the world.[8]

It was evident that Kassander, in stretching out to extend his power west of the Pindos Mountains, was making a grasp too far. In all his attempts in the west for over twenty years he had either been repelled, or, when successful, he had been aiming to disrupt some local arrangement rather than conquer territory, as when he had disputed with Aiakides. Defeated again, he now returned to Macedon.

He was at this point about 60 years old, a good age for a man of the time, though many of his elders and contemporaries managed another twenty years more.[9] He had three children, all boys, Philip, Antipater and Alexander, whose genetic inheritance included not only Kassander and his father Antipater, but also Philip II and his Argead ancestors, through their mother Thessalonike. Genealogically he, and perhaps the Macedonians, should have felt well satisfied.

Yet it was clearly not so. Kassander himself died in May 297.[10] His death was ascribed to various causes, but it is likely that he had been intermittently ill for some time.[11] Clearly the illness, whatever it was (tuberculosis has been suggested), was not sufficiently disabling to prevent him from campaigning in Kerkyra in his last year, or in intriguing in Greece and elsewhere, but his death does not actually seem to have come as a surprise.

The evidence for this conjecture is in the marriages he arranged for his sons and for the arrangements made for the disposition of the kingdom.[12] When he died his sons were all under 20 years of age. The eldest, Philip, the son of a marriage made in 315, cannot have been more than 17 years old, and the others were younger than that – Antipater appears to have reached his majority (at the age of 18) early in 294. And yet, the two youngest were already married before Kassander's death. The age of marriage for Macedonian men was normally in their late twenties or thirties. Kassander himself had not been married until he was 40, and his father probably the same. Of course, this was a royal family, and the marriage practices of the royal families of the time ranged from the bizarre to the multiple to the incestuous; marriage for teenage boys, however, was one of the more unlikely developments.

Philip, the eldest, did not marry, at least as far as we know. He had a reign of only four months, so it may be reasonably assumed that he was already ill before his father died, and that his reign was essentially spent waiting for him to die.[13] Again, he was not inactive, and was on campaign and camped at Elateia in Phokis when he died, so the illness was not disabling, and it may be that in this case his death was not anticipated. The two younger boys were already married to daughters of other kings: Antipater to Eurydike, the daughter of Lysimachos, and Alexander to Lysandra, the daughter of Ptolemy; the boys were no more than 15 and 14 at the time. (All four of those married were in fact cousins, for the wives were the daughters of sisters of Kassander.)

The only intelligible reason for this highly unusual marriage procedure is that Philip's expected early death was to be countered by the assumed fertility of his brothers' marriages, so therefore to ensure the continuation of the dynasty. Of course, it is possible that these marriages were actually arranged by either Philip – but a reign of only four months is rather short for the negotiations and envoy-travel that were required – or by the king's mother, Thessalonike. But it seems more than likely that Kassander made the arrangements before he died. The disruption in the royal house brought about by the deaths of two kings in succession in such a short time was likely to prevent serious negotiations during Philip's reign and for a time afterwards; it is best to credit Kassander with the arrangements, perhaps in the last year of his life. He did have a record of successful diplomacy, and he could hint that both Ptolemy and Lysimachos would gain an interest in the success of the dynasty and the kingdom. (And, in fact, both of them did later exploit the connection that the marriages provided.)

This might thus be counted as a foreign policy success for Kassander, though he is much more likely to have been concerned with the effect of a minority succession on internal Macedonian affairs in arranging the marriages. Royal marriages took place at times when the rulers on either side were allies or at least friends, but they did not denote a political friendship that lasted much beyond the moment of the ceremony. For a start polygamy was the normal royal practice ever since Philip II, if not before, so to see any marriages as marks of alliances would be to assume that all the kings were allied to each other all the time. Any alliances were equally a matter for the moment, and were rarely in any way permanent. As it happens, Kassander and Lysimachos seem to have maintained a relationship approaching a long-standing alliance all through the wars, but this may be attributed to their joint concern for their northern frontier, and to the long threat posed to them jointly by Antigonos, and now by Demetrios. At no point was an alliance between Kassander and Ptolemy to be discerned, except on the occasions of their wars against Antigonos. In between these conflicts they were quite liable to be in conflict with each other.

So the marriages of the two boys did not have any permanent political significance, but were as much marriages of convenience as any others contracted by kings at the time; they were, in other words, marriages between families who now considered that only women of royal rank were suitable wives for their sons. Kassander's purpose was to provide for the continuation of the dynasty, establish a clear succession to himself and Philip, and to develop in some way an international defence against foreign interference in the process of the succession. He arranged the marriages himself presumably because he could not see anyone else in Macedon with the requisite diplomatic skills to do so, and with the necessary political weight to persuade Lysimachos and Ptolemy to surrender a daughter each. Lysimachos and Ptolemy were expected to refrain from acting against the Antipatrid power in Macedon in the interests of their sons-in-law. Whether they would do this was perhaps no more than a hope but, as it happens, they did refrain from interfering, though perhaps not for any altruistic reasons.

Kassander was therefore fully active in international affairs in the years after the victory at Ipsos, in the marriage negotiations, in the campaign against Kerkyra, and probably in affairs in Greece. He had to be on his guard, like everyone else, against the rage for revenge by Demetrios. His son Philip was at Elateia in 297, which city had probably been taken by Kassander some time after Ipsos. He had attempted to capture the city earlier, and had been prevented by an Athenian–Aitolian alliance.[14] But the fall of Antigonos, and Demetrios' subsequent weakness, had brought about internal conflict and therefore political weakness in Athens, and Kassander had exploited the result to return to the attack at Elateia, which he had thus eventually captured, as Philip's presence there indicates. The Aitolians reacted to this by reviving their alliance with the Boiotians, who were equally fearful of a Macedonian return, and they also took over control, or perhaps only protection, of the rest of Lokris.

As ever, however, the main target was Athens, the largest city state in Greece, the richest, the most populous. The expulsion of Demetrios from the city in the aftermath of Ipsos was done in such a way as not to allow any other of the kings to enter. Indeed, the formal expulsion of Demetrios was, at least in Athenian eyes, accomplished by a decree of the city's assembly by which it was forbidden for any king to be admitted to the city.[15] Of course, no king would actually pay heed to any such insulting prohibition (and Demetrios was the least likely of the kings to do so) but for the moment it reflected political reality. But there were other ways for the kings to ensure that they had influence in the city, as Kassander had long shown. In the midst of these conflicts at least one Athenian embassy went to Kassander, and another to Lysimachos. Lysimachos sent a gift of grain to the city, and then another for the weaving of the new *peplos* for Athene. An earlier embassy had gone to Lysimachos to secure the return of Athenian soldiers who had fought for Demetrios at Ipsos and who were either hostages or prisoners of war, and who were held in Asia.[16] But the embassy to Kassander is quite obscure in its purposes or results, being recorded only in a much later inscription celebrating the life of the embassy's leader.[17] Neither of these contacts seem to have had any serious political context, though they do show that Athens was still diplomatically active, even in its neutrality.

All Kassander had to do in order to revive his influence in the city was to watch for a moment in Athenian political life when the city was vulnerable. In this the city cooperated with continuing internal strife and instability. There was a dispute between two of the commanders, Lachares the commander of the mercenaries, and Charias the cavalry commander. Charias camped on the Museion Hill, was driven off, and then returned to seize control of the Acropolis. Lachares' forces took the hill and then he enforced the legal execution of the enemy survivors.[18] This became the basis for the Lachares' tyranny, in which he was supported in some way by Kassander, perhaps by providing supplies, possibly by more mercenaries – the details are vague.[19] But Lachares was an ineffective agent. His opponents occupied Peiraios, which effectively seceded from the city's control, and a low-level civil war was the result. It was a situation Demetrios felt he could exploit. He attempted to return in 295 but failed to gain any foothold, though this was due to a storm, which damaged his fleet, rather than to Athenian resistance.[20]

By then Kassander and Philip were both dead (which may be another reason why Demetrios made his attempt when he did). Philip IV died in September 297, and was succeeded by both his brothers, Antipater and Alexander, who became joint kings. This appears to have been a scheme devised by Thessalonike, who became their regent or guardian since neither boy was yet of full age to act, or so it is assumed; she certainly had strong influence over them, even if she was not voted or appointed the official regent.[21] The elder boy was Antipater, the younger Alexander, who was, it appears, favoured by his mother, though this may simply have been protecting the younger boy in a difficult situation. (All the ancient historians were male, and tended to ascribe personal motives such as favouritism of this sort to women – men, of course, had much higher motives for their favourites!)

There is little recorded of Macedonian events in the two years after Philip's death, perhaps because of the paralysis in the royal family. The elder boy became of age (18) in 295 or early 294, while Alexander was still perhaps a year or so younger. This was, for both Thessalonike and Alexander, a dangerous moment, for Antipater was now free to take decisions and give orders. The earlier murders by Kassander – Alexander IV, Roxanne, Olympias – and by Olympias – Eurydike, Philip III, Nikanor – though not all were carried out by the instigators, were no doubt in the minds of all participants. And, sure enough, Antipater followed the family tradition and murdered his mother.[22]

Thessalonike appears to have been responsible for the joint kingship; it may also be that she arranged a geographical division of the kingdom between her two sons, but this is perhaps unlikely; if she was acting as regent she would not need to. But she did operate to protect Alexander from Antipater's enmity, which amounted to a favouring of the younger boy. But once Antipater was of age he had the responsibility and it was up to him to act as protector. He did so by murdering his mother and turning against Alexander with the obvious same intent.

Killing Thessalonike must have raised all the old memories among the Macedonians. It also removed the last member of the Argead family by direct descent, and it is quite likely that Thessalonike had been seen as the one block preventing a civil war between the two kings. Alexander had escaped from whatever fate Antipater envisaged for him, and was apparently not actually hunted down – one source claimed he was in exile, and so presumably he was no longer in the kingdom. Certainly, he was able to send out appeals to active nearby kings, Pyrrhos and Demetrios.[23]

These were curious choices. One would have expected that Alexander would have appealed to his father-in-law Ptolemy, but probably Ptolemy was too far away and too busy for his help to arrive quickly. And, as it happened, Demetrios was also distant and busy. He had returned once more to Greece, and had seized control of Athens, driving out Lachares, and was, when Alexander's appeal reached him, campaigning in the Peloponnese, where he invaded Sparta, having earlier also attacked Messenia; once again, invading the Peloponnese brought him difficult entanglements and distractions.[24]

Pyrrhos, on the other hand, was available and delighted to help. His price was the cession of large areas of western Macedon and its satellites – Tymphaia, Parauaia, Ambrakia and Akarnania, and perhaps other regions. Alexander had no alternative but to accept, no doubt with the mental proviso that he would use Pyrrhos for the moment, then take back his lost provinces later.[25]

As it happened, none of the other possible interveners were available, so Pyrrhos could act alone. Demetrios had become inextricably involved in southern Greece, and meanwhile his allies and enemies and competitors and marriage relations – Seleukos, Ptolemy (who also briefly intervened at Athens) and Lysimachos – seized the opportunity of his preoccupation with Greece to finish off the remnants of the Antigonid empire elsewhere. Ptolemy seized Cyprus and perhaps Tyre and Sidon (though these may have fallen to him later); Seleukos took over Kilikia and repudiated his second wife Stratonike, Demetrios' daughter, but handed her on to his son Antiochos, whom propaganda claimed was in love with her; Lysimachos mopped up the Asian cities that Demetrios still controlled. Demetrios, locked in his campaign in the Peloponnese, could do nothing to prevent all these losses, and it looks very much as though the three kings had coordinated their plundering efforts just to make it impossible for Demetrios to react.[26]

These losses no doubt stimulated Demetrios to attempt to stage a recovery, and the appeal of Alexander V for help was just what he needed. He arrived, however, to find that the issue had apparently been settled by Pyrrhos' own intervention. But meantime Lysimachos had intervened on behalf of Antipater, his son-in-law, and had brokered a treaty involving the two brothers and himself, presumably mainly to restore the joint rule that had existed before Thessalonike's murder. Pyrrhos was not a party to this treaty, but he effectively acquiesced by not protesting, and kept his gains.[27] When Demetrios turned up, therefore, he had to be even more unscrupulous than Pyrrhos. He met King Alexander at Dion, where Alexander at first tried to persuade him to withdraw peacefully; Demetrios invented a plot aimed at subverting his own forces, accused Alexander of responsibility, and had the boy murdered.[28]

Demetrios met Alexander's troops and persuaded them to accept him as ruler of Macedon, possibly at first simply in place of Alexander; a meeting of the whole army assembly was then held and repeated this acceptance, thus repudiating Antipater, and validating the recent treaty.[29] Antipater fled the scene to take refuge with his father-in-law Lysimachos. Lysimachos himself was by then busy in Thrace, and could not help him, at least not immediately. But he had given refuge to Antipater and to Alexander's widow Lysandra (Ptolemy's daughter), keeping the former as a card to be played later, and arranging for the latter to be married to his own son Agathokles.[30]

There were still descendants of the first Antipater alive, but this debacle in effect marked the end of the dynasty as a family of Macedonian rulers, with the exception of some minor efforts later. It seems likely that it was about the same time, 294, when Alexander was killed, Thessalonike murdered and Antipater driven into exile, that Kassander's brother Pleistarchos, ruler in Karia, died. It may only be a coincidence of dates, but it is certainly a curious coincidence; Pleistarchos could lay claim to the succession if Antipater and Alexander died, or to the regency with the death of Thessalonike, and Lysimachos was campaigning in that region to take over Demetrios' cities – coincidence may not be an adequate explanation. Of Antipater's sons, therefore, none appear to have survived by this time; at least none was foolhardy enough to stand up to make a claim to the rule of Macedon in the face of Demetrios' new control and Lysimachos' frowning discouragement. There were, of course, his daughters, three of whom were still alive and had living children. Antipater's progeny were still active, therefore.

Part III

The Later Family

Chapter 12

Three Grandsons

The family of Antipater ceased to produce rulers in 294, but there were large numbers of members still alive and active in various ways. Two of them actually did achieve a sort of rulership, if only briefly, and less than successfully. These people can be considered, for the sake of convenience, in three groups: three grandsons of Antipater, his three surviving daughters and their children, and the longer family tail in Greece, culminating in the brief kingship (possibly) of Alexander of Corinth, son of Krateros, son of Phila. They will be considered in three separate chapters, though it will be helpful to recall that they were all contemporaries.

For the record: so far, of the children of Antipater, Kassander (and his wife and sons), Iolaos and Nikanor, were certainly dead, as probably was the anonymous daughter; Phila's first and second husbands, Balakros and Krateros, were dead, as was Nikaia's first husband, Perdikkas. Probably dead was another of Antipater's sons, Philip, who is not heard of after 313. Alexarchos (of the City of the Sun) and Perilaos are not heard of at any point after 316 or so, though they may have lived on as long as Kassander. The next generation, Antipater's grandsons, will be considered in this chapter; his three remaining daughters deserve a chapter to themselves (Chapter 13).

The section of the family of Antipater that had been ruling Macedon died out in the messy failure of 294, but there were collateral branches that were more able to continue, though at a lower social level. There were three of Antipater's daughters still alive and all of them had children, as had the anonymous other daughter, probably now dead as well. The sons of old Antipater were less prolific, but two of them, besides King Kassander, had sons. Further, there was the progeny of the elder Antipater's brother, the elder Kassander, also to be considered.

This makes a considerable list of people, all of whom, given their ancestry, were automatically prominent in the life of Macedon. Given the difficulty of the sources for the third century BC, however, their lives are too often badly recorded, or not at all. Two of the male descendants did briefly become kings of a sort, and the descendants of all three surviving women were either ruling kings or royal women, often of a formidable type. Since these families also tended towards intermarriage, it is difficult to describe their lives without entering into a wholesale history of the first half of the third century, and to do that would be to obscure the purpose of this book.

Arrhabaios, son of Alexander Lynkestis

It will be best, therefore, to consider first those of the descendants who are very little known, to clear the ground for the more complicated lives of the others. The anonymous daughter of Antipater who married Alexander Lynkestis had at least one child; they were perhaps not long enough married, or together long enough, to produce more children. The child was a boy, called Arrhabaios, named after Alexander's brother, or perhaps his great-grandfather, who had been a local king in Lynkos. He was born before 334, when his father was off on campaign with King Alexander, and was then locked up by the king from 333 onwards.

It may be assumed that the boy was brought up in the household of old Antipater, who could certainly shelter his deprived daughter and grandson, especially since her husband's family had been wiped out. Arrhabaios' name and ancestry would guarantee him a position in Lynkos, and no doubt he received the usual education in literacy and warfare of any Macedonian male child. It may also be presumed that Antipater saw to it that his ancestral estates in Lynkos descended to him – whatever King Alexander had decided.

His father and his uncles had been killed by Alexander, but he still could have claimed a hereditary social and political position in Lynkos, and therefore in Macedon as a whole. He appears in an inscription from Nesos, an island city off the Asian coast, which honoured a local man called Thersippos who had been generous to his native city and who had campaigned with Alexander in Asia.[1] Arrhabaios is mentioned in the inscription in a similar way with Polyperchon and Kleitos, who are also named on the inscription. This was before 317,[2] and so Arrhabaios, though still young – in his later twenties – was sufficiently prominent to be ranked high. It has to be admitted that part of this is conjectural, and to some extent disputed.[3] Nevertheless the name is unusual, the man was clearly important, and the context is Macedon. It is difficult to see who else he could have been.

Arrhabaios may thus be counted as a Macedonian aristocrat, becoming prominent in the last years of Antipater and then of Polyperchon, but he is not heard of later. The reference in Thersippos' decree is the last (and in fact, the only) reference to him that survives. This is hardly unusual for the third century BC, but there is one event that happened soon after his appearance in Thersippos' inscription that might suggest a context for an early end. In that very year, 317, Olympias emerged from Epeiros in a vengeful fury. She killed at least one of Antipater's sons, Nikanor, as well as King Philip III and his wife Eurydike, then set about murdering others, to the number, it is said, of 100 men.[4] Arrhabaios was another of Antipater's relatives, his grandson, and was associated with King Philip, and these factors might be considered to make him a possible candidate for the kingship. All these factors may have also put him at risk during Olympias' purge of Antipater's and Kassander's supporters that followed her arrival. As the son of a convicted traitor, and a member of the royal family, and the grandson of Antipater, he would surely be one of her prime targets. Conjecture again, of course, but the context fits very well.

However, it may also be, and it is more likely, that he survived. It is understood that he had a son, called Kassander, who is recorded as a *proxenos* at Epidauros in about 260 and described as a Macedonian.[5] This presupposes that Arrhabaios was married; he had been born about 335, so was only 18 at the time of Olympias' massacre. One must therefore assume that he had survived that episode and married later, perhaps in his twenties. He will have lived through Kassander's reign, and the fact that his own son was given Kassander's name aligns him quite certainly with the king.

Pleistarchos (and son?)

Kassander's brother Pleistarchos has been noted in the previous chapter. He is recorded in various ways in Karia, including renaming the city of Herakleia-by-Latmos as Pleistacheia, a change that did not last.[6] He had been a prominent general for his brother in Greece and in the Ipsos campaign, and it was his command at Ipsos that had earned him a slice of the territorial spoils when Antigonos' kingdom was carved up. He held Kilikia and Karia, probably in succession, receiving Karia when Demetrios seized Kilikia in 299. In Karia he is recorded in inscriptions from Sinuri, Hyllarima and Euromos.[7] By refounding Herakleia and naming it for himself, he was marking his territory well enough as an independent state under his rule. As noted earlier he seems to have ceased to rule by 294. There was a statue to him put up by a citizen of Tralleis.[8] He was the recipient of a dedication of a book by the doctor and medical writer Diokles of Karystos.

No children of his are known directly, but there is another inscription that may be relevant. At Olba in Kilikia an inscription mentions a 'Pleistarchos Pleistarchou'.[9] The date of the inscription is put at *c*.200 BC, which makes it far too late for the man to have been the son of Kassander's brother, even if the latter survived after 294. But the name is unusual, and Pleistarchos did have some Kilikian connections. After 281 both Karia and Kilikia were part of the Seleukid kingdom, and it was quite possible for a descendant of the first Pleistarchos to have recovered some influence and estates from Antiochos I. (Quite possibly the fact that Pleistarchos' appeal to Seleukos I for help when Demetrios seized Kilikia was rejected, may have played some part in this.[10]) Antiochos' early experience of unrest in his inherited kingdom could well have inclined him to be happy to implant a new loyal subject in Kilikia. Kilikians themselves could well have had pleasant memories of the residence there of Pleistarchos' sister Phila, during the time of Alexander the Great; her husband had been killed fighting the mountain barbarians, who were the ever-threatening enemies of the lowlanders. There is sufficient here to make the reasonable assumption that the second Pleistarchos may well have been a descendant of the first, probably a grandson, but again there is some conjecture in all this.

Antipater 'Etesias', son of Philip

Kassander and Pleistarchos' brother Philip had distinguished himself in 313 in defeating Aiakides of Epeiros, and in frightening the Aitolians to take refuge in their hill forts at the prospect of a Macedonian invasion.[11] We hear no more of Philip but he had a son, Antipater, who took refuge along with his cousin, the former King Antipater, at Lysimachos' court (and that of his sister Nikaia) when Demetrios seized Macedon in 294.[12] He apparently stayed there quietly while Demetrios made a mess of his Macedonian kingship.

When the Macedonians finally threw Demetrios out in 288, Lysimachos and Pyrrhos then divided the kingdom between them. Antipater the former king was not involved, other than to fall a victim of Lysimachos' policy and die.[13] Antipater the son of Philip once again survived the crisis and did so throughout Lysimachos' time as Macedonian king, which ended with the king's death in battle in 281.

The impression that the life of Antipater suggests, though little is really known about him, is therefore that he almost always showed little or no interest in seeking any sort of power. We may assume he had his place at the upper end of the social scale in Macedon under Kassander and his sons. He was, after all, a member of the royal family, and was able to persuade his brother-in-law King Lysimachos to give him shelter when Demetrios took over the kingdom in 294. On the other hand, Lysimachos also gave shelter to King Antipater for a time, but then killed him when he became too interested in recovering his former position. And yet Antipater son of Philip was left alone, which in the circumstances argues an obvious, serious, and long-standing refusal to be politically involved.

This changed in the chaos that descended on Macedon after 281. His protector Lysimachos died in battle in autumn 281 against Seleukos, who crossed the Hellespont and was preparing to return to his original home in Macedon as king, and then was also killed by Ptolemy Keraunos. Keraunos had been rejected as heir to the Egyptian throne by his father Ptolemy I, and had taken refuge with Seleukos in the same way as King Antipater had done with Lysimachos. The outcome of this protection was thus different: whereas Antipater was killed by his protector, Ptolemy the protectee killed his sponsor. Keraunos succeeded in then making himself king in Macedon in part by murdering two of the sons of Lysimachos, who had taken refuge at Kassandreia with their mother, his half-sister Arsinoe. He had married Arsinoe in pursuit of the Macedonian throne, and she then fled to Egypt, where she was protected by her full brother Ptolemy II.[14] They eventually, brother and sister, married.

Antipater therefore survived again, rather surprisingly – again Keraunos evidently saw no threat in him. Keraunos ruled for a year and five months, but his kingdom was then attacked by successive bands of Gauls from the north. The timing of their attack suggests strongly that it was the death of Lysimachos that had been the immediate trigger for their movements.

Lysimachos had gained an enviable reputation for successful conquest, not to mention devious and cunning generalship, in gaining full control of Thrace, in winning the battle of Ipsos, and, once he had taken over Macedon, in extending his territories northwards. His fall at the battle of Koroupedion, following his putting to death of his capable son Agathokles,[15] and the murder of his conqueror Seleukos had produced a brief power vacuum in Macedon and Asia Minor, which was followed by the arrival of Keraunos in Macedon. Keraunos' murderous progress, while not particularly unusual among the Hellenistic kings, inevitably caused annoyance among at least some of the Macedonians, and he no doubt had to work hard to secure full control of the kingdom, and very likely rarely received any real or sincere loyalty. A period of calmness for the kingdom was clearly requisite if he was to gain either, but he was not given enough time to plant his control thoroughly, other than by fear and violence.

He had also created any number of international enemies along his way to the kingship. These included: Antiochos, the son of the murdered Seleukos, who had resumed control of his father's kingdom by 280; Antigonos, the son of Demetrios, who was now the Antigonid claimant to Macedon; Pyrrhos of Epeiros, who had been pushed out of Macedon by Lysimachos, though for the moment he had now gone off to campaign in Italy and Sicily; Arsinoe, who influenced her brother Ptolemy II, bringing to him first-hand knowledge of the situation in the Aegean and in Macedon; and Ptolemy himself who in turn feared that Keraunos might use his Macedonian power to aim for the Egyptian throne. This was in addition to the usual Greek enemies of any Macedonian king, above all the Aitolians. He did show some diplomatic sense in putting off Pyrrhos by giving him some forces with which he could invade Italy,[16] and by writing to Ptolemy II disclaiming any intention of seeking the Egyptian kingdom.[17] But he was a treacherous murderer, and he could clearly not be trusted to keep his word. He was a typical Hellenistic king, in other words, if rather more personally murderous than most.

The suggestion that it was Lysimachos' death and the subsequent governmental confusion in Macedon that was the initial attraction for the Gallic invasion is supported by the fact that the first invasion, commanded by a Gallic king called Kambaules, invaded Thrace. This was Lysimachos' toughest conquest, and the area where his death would have caused the greatest joy among the conquered population and would probably promote the collapse of his kingdom. Kambaules no doubt expected to find friends among the Thracians, but he found himself facing a Greek army, and retired.[18]

This initial attack was followed by three separate and successive invasions of Macedon itself. An army commanded by Bolgios came south through Illyria. It was met by an army commanded by Ptolemy Keraunos. The account of the fighting presented by Justin and Diodoros cannot be accepted as in any way historical, except in the broadest sense, since it is presented as a classic case of arrogance leading to a fall. It is certain that Ptolemy was defeated, wounded, captured and then killed. He had a reign in Macedon of a year and five months, and died at the beginning (January/February) of 279.[19]

Keraunos' brother Meleagros was apparently present all this time, and the Macedonians now elected him as their king – or he made himself king – in place of his brother.[20] He was unsuccessful, hardly surprising in the circumstances, since by choosing him the Macedonians may well have been expecting help to come from abroad. But events in Macedon were moving too quickly, and Meleagros was judged not competent. He was deposed, and Antipater son of Philip was chosen as the new king.

Meleagros had lasted two months, and Antipater lasted only forty-five days, earning the nickname 'Etesias' from the length of his reign being about the same length of time as the hot summer, 'Etesian', winds. It was probably elected because of his ancestry. It is certain that Meleagros and Antipater came to have been chosen for that very reason. Antipater's long-standing reluctance to wield power was surely known, but perhaps it was expected he would rise to the occasion. Bolgios and his men, having killed Ptolemy and perhaps forced the end of Meleagros' kingship, had returned northwards, carrying their plunder, early in 279. It therefore seems likely that Antipater's reign was a moment of relative peace between invasions, for the second attack, commanded by Brennos, came only some time after Bolgios' retirement. Brennos had probably started out even before Bolgios got back to their homeland, which was probably in the Belgrade area and along the valley of the Morava River. He came by a different route, using the Axios Valley rather than by way of the more difficult Illyrian route.[21]

It is not to be expected that the reigns of these brief Macedonian kings followed one another immediately. The death of Keraunos and the choice of Meleagros will have been separated by a gap of at least several days, and perhaps up to a month. The deposition of Meleagros in March/April 279 was probably quickly followed by the elevation of Antipater, who was perhaps with the army at the time as part of the general mobilization in face of the invasions, but one must still allow a few days between these events. (A refusal to wield political power did not also mean a refusal to fight in defence of the kingdom; as a Macedonian gentleman he will have had military training.) Antipater's reign, therefore, probably did not begin until late May or even June, which was exactly in the period between the invasions. But the approach of Brennos along the familiar and well-travelled Axios route will soon have become known. He arrived in the late summer or early autumn, and the command incapacity of Antipater will have become clear – it was probably understood already – before he arrived. A commanding and capable soldier was clearly needed, and that was not Antipater's thing.

He did receive at least one embassy from abroad during his brief reign, from Athens, led by Demochares son of Laches, who was a nephew of the great Demosthenes, and one of the more staunch leaders of the democracy in the city.[22] He had returned from exile in 286, after King Demetrios finally left the city on his last adventure, and he had already been sent on embassies to Lysimachos and to Ptolemy, soliciting friendship and funds to fund the revival of the city and its democratic constitution. The friendship of the kings was to be a hopeful safeguard against the possible return of Demetrios (which was no longer possible from 285, for he had then become a prisoner of Seleukos). The funds were to refortify the city, including the walls of Peiraios. Demochares had already secured the return of Eleusis to the cities' authority; he was, that is, reconstituting the city state, and incidentally but perhaps not deliberately, demonstrating clearly that this could only be done with royal goodwill.

The third king that Demochares visited was Antipater. Both the date and the person are disputed. The deposed King Antipater, son of Kassander, can probably be ruled out since his friendship was no longer worth cultivating while he was a hostage/prisoner of Lysimachos, and it is unlikely that he would be able to provide the twenty talents that Demochares came away with; anyway, the embassies to Lysimachos would have made a separate contact with this Antipater not worthwhile. The same argument applies to most of the period during which Antipater son of Philip was a refugee with

Lysimachos, and also when he was living as a private gentleman in Macedon, that is until 279. His influence was unnecessary and pointless under such kings as Lysimachos and Ptolemy Keraunos, and attempting to exercise his own foreign policy would have brought down their wrath on him as well, probably with fatal consequences. Similarly, this applies to the time after his deposition as Macedonian king, when he was helpless in Macedon. So the only time when Demochares could visit Antipater and expect serious help and profit was while he ruled in Macedon, and this was in the lull between the invasions of Bolgios and Brennos. From Athens it may well have seemed that the initial invasion was the only one to be expected, and that the Macedonians had then repented of their addiction to the unpleasant Ptolemies, and had reverted once again to the dynasty of Antipater, men whom the Athenians themselves knew well, and the memory of whose domination may well have acquired a rosy tint after their experiences with Demetrios.

Demochares' embassy was well timed, therefore, and he came away with his twenty talents. But Antipater was not in the end acceptable as king in the emergency in Macedon, probably from lack of military ability and experience. He was deposed, as Meleagros had been, and a Macedonian soldier, Sosthenes, who may have been one of Lysimachos' officers, was chosen as *strategos* – he refused the title of king – he was clearly not of royal descent – but he was evidently a capable military officer.[23] He fought hard against the invaders when Brennos' band arrived, to such effect that Brennos and his men quickly moved on through the kingdom to attack Delphi. There they suffered a great defeat at Aitolian hands, and the survivors were harried northwards towards their homes by the Greeks of Aitolia, Malis, Thessaly and the Macedonians.[24]

Sosthenes may have been relatively successful, but the emergency continued. He had to control the Gallic bands, some of whom stayed on after Brennos retired, and had probably to fight roving Greek bands as well, and he had to face the competition for authority of at least three claimants to the kingship he had refused.[25] The surviving son of Lysimachos and Arsinoe, Ptolemy, was one of them, an otherwise unknown man called Arrhidaios was another,[26] and Antipater son of Philip continued to maintain his claim.[27] There may be others, and since at least two of these men survived the time of Sosthenes and the year or more of anarchy that followed, they were probably in control of useful military forces, and not subject to attacks by Sosthenes. Of course, the fact that Sosthenes refused the kingship left the field open for the claimants, and since Antipater was the last of the 'legitimate' kings, his claim may have been the more acceptable; indeed, Sosthenes might have been considered to be commanding in his name. The situation implied is one of local defence, organized by men who may or may not have supported Sosthenes. But once Sosthenes died, in June 277, none of his competitors was able to make good his claim.

The eventual winner was Demetrios' son Antigonos, who, on the basis of a successful destruction of one Gallic band at Lysimacheia in Thrace and a careful use of Greek mercenaries and enlisted Gauls, succeeded in driving out the invaders, and also in driving out his competitors.[28] He had done most of this by late 277, but it took another ten months to gain control of Kassandreia, which had been seized by a tyrant during the anarchic period.

Ptolemy son of Lysimachos and Antipater son of Philip fled for refuge to Egypt, though when this took place – during the anarchy, or in face of Antigonos' success – is not known. Ptolemy II give them shelter, no doubt regarding them as useful cards he might play in the continuing international competition. They turned out, as might have been expected from their origins, very differently useful. Ptolemy son of Lysimachos (and the son of Arsinoe II) was soon placed in a little principality of his own at Telmessos in Lykia.[29] This planted a son of Lysimachos on the borders of Seleukos' conquest, now under Antiochos I, and he clearly constituted a standing menace to Seleukid control. His principality was small, but it was isolated behind the mountains that protected it, and it was close to Karia, which had a long tendency to be detached from all imperial governments – recently under Pleistarchos and then under Eupolemos; later it was detached again under Olympichos; and, of course, earlier it had been Asandros' independent satrapy, and before that Mausollos' independent kingdom under the Persians.

Ptolemy's principality lasted almost a century under three generations of his descendants. Its last ruler was Berenike, who was also a priestess of Laodike, the wife of Antiochos III, so it seems that the family had succumbed to Seleukid charm.[30] She was probably deposed, or died, in the upheaval of Asia Minor in 188 after the Roman expulsion of Seleukid power.

Antipater's lack of ambition returned once he was safe in Egypt. He almost vanished from view. He is mentioned in a single source about twenty years after his flight from Macedon. He was living quietly in Egypt, and had developed, and was constantly indulging a passion for playing dice.[31]

Chapter 13

Three Daughters

ntipater had four daughters. One, whose name is not known, either died while her father still lived, or at least is not heard of after her marriage to Alexander Lynkestis. The other three had notable careers as wives of kings. All three were assertive and prolific in children, and ultimately two of them were rejected by their royal husbands or rejected them themselves. Rejection, however, did not stop their political activities, and all of them had a powerful influence on the political development of their times. To these three women we can add a fourth, not a daughter of Antipater, but a grand-niece, similarly active and prolific, and even more disruptive.

It is at marriage that the daughters emerge into the sources. One of them, Phila, had been married twice before finding a husband who survived. The second, Nikaia, also lost her first husband, but then married for life. The third, Eurydike, remained married to her first husband for thirty years, but was then displaced and eventually fled to seek refuge. All these ladies had to endure the polygamous habits of their husbands, and all three suffered from this apparent male instinct. And yet between them they produced numerous children, including kings. We may also note a number of stepchildren. Two of them were founders of dynasties.

The Anonymous Daughter (Table II)

This lady has been considered already in connection with the problem of her husband, Alexander Lynkestis, who was arrested and eventually murdered at King Alexander's orders. The lady is nearly invisible, except as the brief wife of the Lynkestian, but she had one child. She probably returned to her father's household when Lynkestis went off to war in 334, and presumably lived and died there. She is not heard of again, and presumably died as a member of Antipater or Kassander's court. Her son Arrhabaios will have grown up as Antipater's ward. He was politically important in that he was the last of the dominant family of Lynkos, a vital strategic area, and was in some way connected with the Argead royal family.

Nikaia (Table III)

The least assertive of the three women we know something about was Nikaia. She had been betrothed to Perdikkas, was at first rejected by him in favour of Kleopatra, King Alexander's sister, but then probably married him after all; Perdikkas' dithering was in a sense a tribute to her father, since he eventually chose Antipater's daughter over that of Philip II, but it is unlikely either Antipater or Nikaia saw it that way. The marriage lasted only a short time, for Perdikkas was soon murdered during his failed invasion of Egypt. Nikaia was then speedily married, along with her sisters, in the orgy of betrothals at the time of the Triparadeisos conference.[1] Her new husband was Lysimachos, the satrap of Thrace, who was a political ally of both Antipater and Kassander.

It is probable that this relationship protected Nikaia well, since neither her brother nor her husband could afford to break politically with the other. On the other hand, it is clear that Lysimachos did not confine his sexual or marital attentions to his well-born wife. He is said to have had fifteen children, and four wives have been identified (but only eight of the children). He appears to have fathered a son on an 'Odrysian woman', who may or may not have been one of his wives – he was called Alexander.[2] He married his third wife, Amastris, the Persian princess who had been Krateros' wife, and who had then been married to Dionysios the tyrant of Herakleia Pontike, whose tyranny she had effectively inherited. She brought that city to Lysimachos in the crisis of the war against Antigonos in 302, when it was especially useful for maintaining communications with Lysimachos' kingdom in Thrace.[3] His fourth wife was Arsinoe II, the daughter of Ptolemy, who was acquired in the great diplomatic shuffle of 299.[4] These women are known to have produced eight children between them – four by Nikaia, one by the 'Odrysian woman', and three by Arsinoe; Amastris produced none, probably being too old by the time of her marriage to do so – she did have children by Dionysios, and they inherited the Heraklian tyranny from her, and were therefore Lysimachos' stepsons. But Lysimachos dismissed her, when her political usefulness ended. Lysimachos' fifteen children suggests that he had a series of extramarital liaisons as well as his four wives, if indeed the 'Odrysian woman' was a wife.[5]

In all this Nikaia remains almost entirely invisible. It is not even certain that the four children credited to her were actually hers, though since they were apparently valued above most of the rest, at least until Arsinoe got to work on him, it seems highly unlikely that they were born of any other woman, who was clearly not his wife. The children included Agathokles, named for Lysimachos' father, and his presumed heir until 285 or so. There were also three daughters, Arsinoe I, who was married to Ptolemy I in the great wife exchange in 299, possibly a girl called Eurydike, and a daughter whose name is not known but who was married to a Thracian chieftain called Dromichaites.

Nikaia is also invisible in the messy court disputes that brought the reign to an end, and it is probable she was already dead. It has been suggested that because Lysimachos put away Amastris in order to marry Arsinoe II, he was a serial monogamist. But this had happened already to Amastris, when she was handed over to Dionysios so that Krateros could marry Phila; this therefore may have been at Amastris' insistence. The evidence of his many children does suggest that Lysimachos was by no means monogamous.

If Nikaia had died before Lysimachos' later recorded marriages she will have been spared the intrigues said to have been promoted by Arsinoe II to secure the succession for her own children, which included the execution of Nikaia's son Agathokles. It was this act that so reduced support for Lysimachos that his kingdom could be easily overthrown and extinguished by Seleukos in 281. In the event neither Nikaia's nor Arsinoe's children succeeded.

Eurydike and Berenike (Table IV)

There can be no doubt about the marriage practices of Ptolemy I. He was married four times, twice during Alexander's reign, and twice more while he ruled in Egypt. The first two wives were later divorced, dismissed, or ignored, though by one of them, Thais, a former Athenian courtesan, he had at least three children, none of whom were ever considered for the succession to the Egyptian rulership, or so it seems.[6] The second wife was

Artakama, one of the Persian aristocratic women forced on the Macedonians by Alexander at Susa in 324. There is no record of any children, and probably she was put aside as soon as Ptolemy could afford to, politically.[7]

The third and fourth wives were Eurydike, the daughter of Antipater, and her cousin Berenike, the granddaughter of Antipater's brother Kassander.[8] Despite the difference in generations, they were apparently roughly the same age, presumably as a result of Kassander being married much earlier than Antipater – possibly Kassander was the elder brother. Not only that but Berenike had been married before leaving Macedon, to a Macedonian called Philip, and she had three children by him.[9] It seems likely that she was some years older than Eurydike. Philip, who is otherwise unknown, is (therefore) often regarded as socially below the expected level – 'of lowly origin'[10] – but no reason other than that he is almost anonymous is ever produced; in fact, he was surely out of the same echelons of Macedonian society as his wife.

It did not take long for this situation to prove to be combustible. Eurydike was dispatched to Ptolemy as his wife as part of the Triparadeisos settlement in which two other of Antipater's daughters were married to prominent Macedonian commanders. Thus the marriage took place probably in 320;[11] but by 317 Ptolemy had also married Berenike.[12] He then maintained this *ménage à trois* for thirty years, with both wives regularly producing children. It was undoubtedly a skilful performance by Ptolemy, but the eventual result was that he was compelled to make a decision on the succession, and by choosing his son by Berenike (who became Ptolemy II) he decisively alienated Eurydike, who decamped, first to the court of Lysimachos, and then to that of Seleukos.

Eurydike had four, perhaps five, children by Ptolemy. Two sons are certain, Ptolemy Keraunos and Meleagros, who became the brief kings of Macedon during the Galatian invasions; a third son is only a possibility, Argaios, since the only source for his existence, Pausanias, is unclear on his parentage. But Pausanias does explain that Argaios was executed by Ptolemy II.[13] This would not be surprising, for the second Ptolemy was ruthless in eliminating rivals and enemies, and those who displeased him. Such an execution would no doubt be the result of, or in fear of, a conspiracy to usurp the throne. (He also systematically killed the offspring of his frequent extramarital affairs, though he set up the women in luxury.)

Ptolemy Keraunos understood his half-brother's fears, and one of his first acts on seizing the Macedonian kingship was to write to his half-brother in Egypt disclaiming any intention of attempting to gain power in Egypt.[14] Whether the Egyptian Ptolemy believed him we may doubt, but in the end Keraunos did not last long enough to be put to the test.

Eurydike also had at least two daughters. One, Lysandra, was old enough to be married to Lysimachos' son Agathokles in about 300, and she was thus born between 320 and, say, 315. The second daughter was Ptolemais, betrothed to Demetrios the son of Antigonos a few years later, perhaps in 296, but she had to wait ten years to be actually married, when Demetrios arrived in Ephesos, where she had been living.[15] She was then swiftly impregnated, and at once abandoned when Demetrios went off on his final disastrous campaign through Asia Minor, which ended with his capture by Seleukos. Ptolemais seems to have been taken into the household of Demetrios' son Antigonos Gonatas – as Antipater took in Lynkestis' widow. Her child, Demetrios, called 'the Fair', became the father of Antigonos III, the regent-king of Macedon between 229 and 219.

Berenike brought her three children by Philip to Egypt with her, and captured Ptolemy I in short order. Probably they became sexual partners within a year of his marriage to Eurydike, and she had then two or three more children. One became his father's heir, Ptolemy II. He was born at Kos in 309 during his father's unfortunate Greek campaign.[16] The other two were daughters, Arsinoe (II), who had a spectacular career of marriages and power. She was given in marriage to Lysimachos and some years later her half-sister Lysandra, newly widowed after the death of her Macedonian husband Alexander IV, married Lysimachos' son Agathokles.[17] As his wife Arsinoe produced three sons, with whom she fled from the collapse of Lysimachos' kingdom in 281. She took refuge in Kassandreia, and was persuaded to marry her half-brother Keraunos, who then promptly murdered the two youngest children (for they had better claims to the Macedonian throne than he did).[18] The eldest one avoided this fate, but both mother and son soon fled to Egypt. There she persuaded her full brother Ptolemy II to become her third husband.[19] Her son was presented with the little principality about Telmessos in Lykia, perhaps to remove him from the embarrassing new marital situation.[20] The marriage provoked a barrage of jokes in bad taste, and horror among the Greek population – but Arsinoe became revered in Egypt.[21]

As a contrast the other daughter of Berenike, Philotera, remained unmarried. Whether this was by her choice, or at her brother's insistence, is not known, but it later became Ptolemaic policy for them to avoid allowing the sisters and daughters of the kings to marry outside the family, since their husbands would then gain a claim to the throne.

Ptolemy I therefore used his daughters as marriage pawns in his political games, which was quite normal. In all this he also employed Berenike's earlier family. Her daughters Antigone and Theoxene were married off to King Pyrrhos of Epeirus, and King Agathokles of Syracuse respectively.[22] Antigone died early, but Theoxene had two children. She was put away by Agathokles – sent back to her stepfather – to avoid complicating the Syracusan succession and returned to Egypt with her children. (This was a mistake by King Agathokles, for the succession descended into a series of brutal familial murders very like those at Lysimachos' court, and ended with the elimination of the dynasty and the kingship.) The children, however, grew up in the Ptolemaic court, eventually producing a famous Minister of Ptolemy III and Ptolemy IV, called Agathokles (of course), whose policy was disastrous enough to bring that court into near collapse, and earn him an assassination by the Alexandrian mob.[23]

Berenike's other child, her son Magas, was used in a different way, and became Ptolemy I's viceroy in Cyrenaica, after several earlier experimental governors had failed; he succeeded in remaining in power in Cyrene by identifying with the Cyrenians, and eventually made himself an independent king. Upon marrying the daughter of Antiochos I in 274, he became extremely ambitious for such independence and promotion, and made himself king in Cyrenaica, where he ruled until 250; his daughter, another Berenike, married Ptolemy III.

Eurydike and Berenike clearly competed for Ptolemy I's favour, each by then having produced a son as his potential successor. Probably Ptolemy Keraunos, who was for a time the only son from these two women, was originally recognized as the likely successor, until Ptolemy (II as later known) was born in 309. Over the next two decades Berenike seems to have worked to convince Ptolemy I that her son was the better to succeed – and in this she may well have been right, since Ptolemy II was undoubtedly one of the greatest rulers of the third century. But Eurydike could not accept this, and removed herself and her children from the court in about 286, indicating that Ptolemy had made his decision in favour of Ptolemy II by then.[24] She ended by taking refuge with Seleukos, Ptolemy's most serious enemy. The alternative was Lysimachos' court, but there his wife Arsinoe II (Berenike's daughter) was intriguing in the same way as her mother Berenike in Alexandria. In moving to Seleukos, however, she found herself without serious influence, for Seleukos chose his enemies carefully. She was accompanied on this last move by Agathokles' widow Lysandra, her own daughter, seeking revenge on Lysimachos. Eurydike must surely have wished Seleukos to invade Egypt in order to put Keraunos on the throne there, but Seleukos was far too wary for that. The death of Ptolemy I in 283 had been preceded by two years during which he and his son Ptolemy II had ruled jointly;[25] when Ptolemy I finally died, therefore, Ptolemy II had a presumably firm grip on the kingship. Lysimachos' court, meanwhile, was collapsing by that time, as a result of the similar, even more ferocious and murderous succession dispute. Given the choice of attacking a disintegrating kingdom or one under a firm rule, Seleukos sensibly chose the former, and launched his armies into Asia Minor. And it was as he crossed into Europe that Ptolemy Keraunos stabbed him to death to make himself Macedonian king.[26] By that time Eurydike had vanished from our sources and was quite probably dead. (Born in the 330s, she will have been over 50 in 280, having given birth to several children on the way.)

All this is all too easily portrayed as a brutal family drama, with salacious elements and killings mixed in. It seems highly unlikely, however, that Ptolemy I was ever seriously swayed in his choice of successor by either of his wives. He had kept them both in his court for thirty years without succumbing to their pressures or their influence in any way which is visible to us. It may be, as Pyrrhos noted when he lived at the court, that Berenike was the most powerful of the women, but this was a view by an outsider, not necessarily reflecting the actual situation – it may only be that Berenike was louder.[27]

There were in fact only two possibilities for the succession, and it is clear that Ptolemy II was a much more stable and capable character than Ptolemy Keraunos. Berenike may have claimed to be victorious in the succession struggle, but it seems unlikely that an experienced ruler such as Ptolemy I took such a decision on the advice of his son's mother.

Eurydike may have seemed to have left Ptolemy I's court in high dudgeon because her son had been scorned; in reality, she probably left to save her and her children's lives. She must have known the temper of Ptolemy II, and will have seen just how dangerous it would be for a parallel family to attempt to exist in the Ptolemaic court after he had become sole king, or even once he had become the heir. She left and took her children away so as to avoid them being murdered. It is ironic that it was her son who committed the most spectacular murders both by killing Seleukos, and then murdering Arsinoe's children; Ptolemy II worked much more quietly, and through agents.

The net result of the life and marriages of Ptolemy I was that both of his two sons – and his stepson – became kings, and four of his daughters and stepdaughters became wives of kings, even if in some cases only briefly. He was the direct ancestor of all the Ptolemies and of some of the later Antigonids. And all of these were also descended from Antipater or his brother. Eurydike and Berenike between them tend to monopolize the accounts of the scandalous aspects of the court of Ptolemy I, but one may note that Eurydike maintained her position at court for thirty years, and even at the end was decisive enough to march away; this evidently marks a particular element in her character, which may well have originated with her father, though this had scarcely been evident in any other way during her lifetime. Berenike apparently did not have it all her own way. It is clear that even after thirty years of marriage to a dominating husband like Ptolemy I she retained an independence, something that was a mark of her sisters also.

Phila (Table V)

The most illustrious, and in a way the most tragic, of Antipater's daughters was Phila, possibly his eldest daughter, but more likely the second (after the anonymous wife of Alexander Lynkestis, who was certainly married first). She was the second to be married, and the only one to be married three times. Like her sisters she had children, and by all three of her husbands, four in all. But she was exceptional in that she attracted the admiration of men for her intelligence, and for this to have happened she must have lived a much more public life than Nikaia, immured in Lysimachos' secluded court, or Eurydike, or Berenike, stuck in Ptolemy's harem. Phila clearly became known outside her marriages, and this must have been her own decision. She is perhaps unique in the long work of Diodoros Sikulos in being given an extended encomium on her personal and political sense.[28] She was married, however, perhaps to the one man among her kingly contemporaries who failed to pay her due attention. If she was so sensible about public affairs, Demetrios should have profited from her presence. He clearly did not, or more likely did not listen.

One of the points made in Diodoros' short essay is that Antipater was willing to listen to Phila's advice on public affairs even before she was married; this would imply before *c*.336, when she was no more than 15, or perhaps he meant her third and most spectacular marriage to Demetrios when she was 30. It seems unlikely that a girl of 15 would command the attention of her father on public matters, and the story may legitimately be doubted. And yet her later life does indicate that she was alert, active and busy in many aspects, even if not too noticeably in politics. It implies that she – and this would apply also to her sisters – had received a well-rounded education, which included philosophy, music and mathematics, in the same way as her brothers.

Her first marriages, to Balakros and Krateros, have been noted already. When she was married a third time, to Demetrios, son of Antigonos in 320 or 319, she already had children by both earlier marriages, and three stepchildren of her first husband. She soon had two more children by Demetrios, and since he was hardly the type of man to run a court in the interests of anyone but himself, no doubt the care and education of all the children was left to her.

Phila did not wholly devote herself to her young husband. She maintained a communication, in a sense, with her second, Krateros, and probably stood as guardian to her first husband's family as well. Evidence for this in particular is the memorial that Krateros had commissioned to be displayed at Delphi launching his connection to Alexander the Great. This was a notable piece of sculpture showing Krateros combating a lion that had been menacing Alexander. It was to be sculpted by Lysippos and Leochares, two of the most prestigious artists of the day. But Krateros died soon after commissioning it, which he probably did while campaigning in Aitolia in the winter before he died, at which time Phila was pregnant with his child. The sculpture was dedicated when completed in the name of that boy, 'Krateros son of Krateros', who was still a child at the time.[29] It was obviously Phila who had pushed on the work, paid for it and presumably wrote the dedication. It may well be that this was a mark of her affection for her brief, generous, handsome and honourable husband. Balakros had been much older than her, and Demetrios was ludicrously disreputable; commemorating Krateros in his memorial can be seen as a riposte to Demetrios' philandering and erratic life, an emphasis on Krateros' character, no matter how sanitized, as compared with that of Demetrios.

Demetrios moved about a great deal, campaigning from Gaza to Macedon, and from the Hellespont to Babylon. Whether she accompanied him is perhaps unlikely, but where she lived is not clear, though perhaps Sardis (where her daughter Stratonike lived in retirement later) or north Syria, in the household of her father-in-law Antigonos, are possibilities. When Demetrios sailed east to rescue his mother from possible capture in Kilikia after the defeat at Ipsos, Phila was evidently with him, and when Demetrios suddenly allied with Seleukos, who married their daughter Stratonike, Phila was sent to explain matters to her brother Kassander. On the other hand, she was not with him in the siege of Rhodes, for she is recorded as sending him clothes and supplies from Ephesos. She was apparently with him at one of his stays in Athens, for the Athenians put up a temple to her in the guise of Aphrodite Phila. (Or was this a rebuke to her embarrassingly philandering husband, to emphasize the treasure he was ignoring in his own house?)[30]

She had to endure a series of joint wives, not to mention Demetrios' constant addiction to courtesans. Whether this bothered her is not known, though certainly in the case of Demetrios' marriage to Deidameia of Epeiros appears to have prompted him to make serious efforts to keep the two women apart. However, if Phila actually lived in Sardis for long periods, Demetrios' other marital and sexual affairs may only have impinged on her from a distance. (One of his courtesans, Lamia, gave birth to a child, and called her Phila: this was clearly an insult to Demetrios' senior wife, which she seems to have simply ignored.)[31]

It is also the case that these contemporary marriages, like the liaisons with the courtesans, were in fact brief. The marriages to Eurydike of Athens, Deidameia, and Lanassa of Syracuse, which all ran in parallel with that to Phila, were all concentrated in the years after 307, and ended in about 290. By 307 Phila was 43 years old, but Demetrios was still only 30, and clearly highly sexed. She was no longer capable of producing children, but if that was the aim of the other marriages, they all failed – until after Phila was dead.

In fact, of course, every one of Demetrios' marriages – and every one of Phila's – were dictated by political considerations. It is said that Antigonos had had to persuade Demetrios to undertake the marriage to Phila by emphasizing the political benefits (to himself, of course).[32] Eurydike was a symbol of his attachment to Athens, Deidameia was a symbol of his alliance with Pyrrhos – or perhaps a means of fending off Pyrrhos' aggressive abilities – and Lanassa, daughter of Agathokles of Syracuse, came with Kerkyra as her dowry; she was also the divorced wife of Pyrrhos, so this new marriage could well be construed as an insult to him. But all these marriages were only temporary. Only the marriage with Phila endured.

For Phila was far more important to Demetrios than any of the other wives, and the courtesans could be dismissed as expensive momentary indulgences of no importance. She was, rather as was Olympias for Philip II, the senior wife by reason of her ancestry and her family connections.[33] Her marriages had all been arranged by her father Antipater, and it was because she was Antipater's daughter that she was prized above the rest. The same was clearly also true of Nikaia and Eurydike, both of whose marriages were lengthy and productive: both kings were just about as polygamous as Demetrios, but none of them discarded their Antipatrid chief wives (though Eurydike did abandon Ptolemy in the end). And in the end Demetrios' time as king of Macedon between 294 and 288 was in part acceptable to the Macedonians because his queen was Antipater's daughter and Kassander's sister.[34] She was also the aunt of the sons of Kassander – the murder of one of these boys by her husband cannot have helped their relationship. Every king of Macedon between 317 (the death of Philip III) and 277 (the accession of Antigonos, Gonatas) was a descendant of Antipater; he was far more influential in this than Philip II or Alexander. (See Table VI.)

The repeated and lengthy separations of the two meant that Phila maintained her own court, with her own bodyguard. This was probably the case in Asia Minor while her father-in-law Antigonos ruled there. She could there dispense her own patronage and was involved in charitable works on behalf of, for example, the daughters of poor men who could be provided with dowries. She exercised an acceptable authority in the armed camp, ironing out disputes and quelling troublemakers, and administered justice, particularly by rooting out and dismissing false accusations. In all this, she set the pattern for her Hellenistic, and even Roman and later, queenly successors. She had acquired the new title of *basilissa*, effectively 'queen', again setting a pattern for later kings' wives; Demetrios' other wives did not have that title, though perhaps her sisters did, thus emphasizing Phila's pre-eminence. She was a loyal wife, in contrast to Demetrios who was scarcely a loyal husband, and always encouraged him in his military and political adventures, no matter what she might have thought of them – sending him clothing, for example, during the siege of Rhodes.[35]

But, above all, and in contrast all the other wives and mistresses, she was the mother of his legitimate children, a factor that gave her great prestige. Two were born in the early years of the marriage, Antigonos and Stratonike, and these two were as notable in their characters and ways as Phila, and rather more so than Demetrios. Antigonos was his father's heir, and achieved a rather greater success in becoming king in Macedon than his father, for he held on to that post for the rest of his life, and was the real founder of the Antigonid dynasty. Stratonike was married to Seleukos in the diplomatic revolution of 299, and then handed on to his son Antiochos in what was supposed to have been a love match – though it was as political as any other of these marriages. She was as notable a patroness as her mother, particularly in relation to several religious matters and temples; she was as conspicuously loyal to her (second) husband as was Phila to her third, and like her mother, she maintained her own court, at least after Antiochos' death. Her personality appears to have been such that men were sometimes overwhelmed by it, and she appears to have been something of a sex symbol.[36]

Stratonike had children by both of her marriages – Phila was Seleukos' child, while she had Antiochos, Seleukos and Apama from Antiochos I. This younger Phila married Antigonos Gonatas, her uncle; Seleukos proved to be too ambitious to succeed and was executed by his father; Antiochos (II) became the third Seleukid king; Apama married Magas of Cyrenaica, and so became, like Phila and Stratonike, the wife of a king; she was the mother of Berenike (II), who married Ptolemy III. Incest was close in all these marriages. Berenike II was another of these extremely assertive women, murdering her intended husband, Demetrios the Fair, when he stood in the way of her Ptolemaic marriage; she herself was also eventually murdered.[37]

When Demetrios' kingship in Macedon collapsed in 288 he faced yet another period of wandering, searching for a kingdom to rule or misrule. He found that Phila's patience had finally run out. In 287, the year after the collapse of his rule in Macedon, she committed suicide, apparently appalled at the prospect of yet another period of homelessness, or perhaps at the shame of her husband's failure, or even at the thought of having to take refuge with her son.[38] Demetrios, of course, had another marriage already arranged, with Ptolemy's daughter Ptolemais, a betrothal that by then was more than ten years in the past; from this marriage came Demetrios the Fair, later murdered by Berenike II in Cyrene. Phila's suicide may be seen as the final, and most decisive, display of her independence, an independence that had clearly been growing in her throughout her life. It was also another difficult model for later kings' wives. But it was also noticeable that the suicide of his chief wife and her severing from Demetrios was followed in less than two years by his final failure.

Conclusion

This is an extraordinary, gaudy, and astonishing parade of powerful and dangerous women, a complete contrast to the less than visible women of the previous centuries. Their power and display were clearly in large part a result of their own characters, though it must also have been a result of their social positions, and the complex and extremely interesting times in which they lived that provided them with unusual opportunities for their assertiveness. Because they were queens, or at least kings' wives, they were able to make choices: they could assert themselves, as Phila did; alternatively, like Nikaia, they could remain secluded in the court; or they could break out suddenly, as did Eurydike after apparent years of quiescence. But they also had a much wider choice of lifestyle than earlier women, or than those in lower social situations. They did, however, provide models of behaviour for their royal successors, and also provided a useful model for other women, should they choose to follow it. Their example was a notable part in the opening up of society that is a characteristic of the Hellenistic World.

Chapter 14

The Last of the Dynasty

The death of Kassander's sons marked the end of the brief dynasty of Antipater but, as was seen in the last chapter, there were plenty of descendants who made their mark on the times following this – both male and female. A look at another generation or two after the 290s will make it clear that members of the Antipatrid dynasty continued in power – and produced one more ruler, if not precisely actually a king.

Primarily, of course, the distribution and fertility of Antipater's daughters was the agency for the spread of his dynasty's influence and continuation. But beyond his daughters there were also Antipater's grandsons. Some of these have been located and discussed in earlier chapters – Arrhabaios son of Alexander Lynkestis, for example, and Antigonos Gonatas, son of Phila. Another son of Phila was Balakros' son Antipater, who made a dedication of a golden crown at Delos in the early third century, before 279.[1] This is the only record of his existence, but the fact of his ancestry and his ability to make an expensive gift to the temple implies his high social and economic position. He was, in other words, a prominent Macedonian, a man who had been born in the reign of Alexander the Great and was still alive and active years later.

He had two brothers, Thraseas and Balakros, who may be the sons of Phila's husband by his earlier marriage. However, one of these, Thraseas, was still active as late as 261, which makes it more likely that he was a son of Balakros and Phila, and so another grandson of Antipater. The third, Balakros, may have been the son of Phila or of her husband's earlier wife.[2] It is supposed that all these were in service with Demetrios I, their stepfather. All three were thus prominent Macedonians, and by the 270s were probably domiciled once more in that country.

The other sons of the elder Antipater have left only small traces, just like the younger Antipater. Iolaos was dead by 317, when his grave was disturbed by Olympias; she also killed Nikanor. Perilaos is described by Plutarch as acting as his brother's 'assistant' in Macedon, though this is undated, and is notably unspecific – it presumably must refer to an occasion when Kassander was out of Macedon, perhaps in Greece, for some time; he is also noted as commanding an army in Asia Minor on behalf of Antigonos in 315 only to be captured by Polykleitos and then released by Ptolemy.[3] After that we have no information, but there may be – very speculatively – a clue in Egypt. In 262/261 Aristonikos was priest of Alexander in Alexandria, the most senior and prestigious such appointment of the Ptolemaic government. He was identified as 'son of Perilaos'.[4] No further identification is made, but the name is very rare. His half-brother Antipater Etesias and Ptolemy the son of Lysimachos had been given refuge in Egypt by Ptolemy II. Possibly Perilaos had also fled from the Galatian invasion, or from Antigonus Gonatas' seizure of the kingdom; it would be fairly typical of Ptolemy II to receive a member of a rival dynasty, and then to hold him in part as a diplomatic threat or an insult. The date is perhaps significant – it was the date of the end of the war in the Aegean, the Kremoneidian War, in which Ptolemy II had been fighting Antigonos Gonatas.[5]

Social prominence and wealth, such as is displayed by these men, would be the normal status of any descendant of Antipater, if he was not actually a king, like Antigonos. Demetrios 'the Fair' must count as another such. The son of Demetrios I and his last and briefest wife, Ptolemais, he was fostered by Antigonos Gonatas, and was related to both Antigonos and the Ptolemies. He married a Thessalian woman, Olympias of Larissa, in the tradition of Macedonian-Thessalian alliances. He had a son who eventually became king of Macedon, Antigonos III. He was considered eligible for marrying Berenike, the heiress of Cyrene, and when she proved unwilling, he married her mother Apama, the daughter of Antiochos I and Stratonike and widow of Magas. Thereby he became king of Cyrene before being murdered, almost at once, by Berenike, the woman who had rejected him. One could hardly exist on a higher social plane than Demetrios without actually being a king.

Phila's stepson Nikanor, this time certainly the son of Balakros by an earlier wife, must have been of a similar social rank. He would be the equal of an Arrhabaios, for instance, and of Phila's other children. It is just possible that he was the man installed by Kassander in Peiraios as his viceroy, though he is never identified as anything but just 'Nikanor'. It was he who then returned from his naval victory in the Hellespont with delusions of self-importance, only to be soon executed by Kassander's orders. It would be very like Kassander to be employing a man related to him – he would be his nephew – just as he employed his brothers Philip and Pleistarchos as his commanders; he was also quite capable of ordering such an execution, despite the relationship.[6]

Firmer ground lies under the career of Phila's son by Krateros, also called Krateros. It was in his name that his father's celebratory sculpture was dedicated at Delphi, suggesting that Phila, and therefore probably the boy, retained a loyalty to his memory. He will have lived at Demetrios', or rather Phila's, court as a child. Born in 320, he had thus just reached adulthood when Demetrios crashed to ruin after Ipsos. The subsequent wanderings of Demetrios in the 290s may have brought Krateros into close association with him – his half-brothers, Antipater and so on, were part of Demetrios' entourage. However, the only real indication we have of his career is as a lieutenant of his half-brother Gonatas in southern Greece. This would suggest a long-term association between the two, who were close in age, at first at Phila's court, and perhaps as a commander in Antigonos' forces after Demetrios' capture in 285 and death in 283.

There are a few clear notices of Krateros in action, though they are no more than separate incidents. The earliest record of him is just in this period, while Antigonos was based in Athens after his father's death, in a papyrus recording a letter of Epikouros that may be dated around 280, perhaps reflecting Krateros' time in Athens.[7] In 272 a struggle for power was going on in Elis (the scene earlier of the usurpation of Telephoros) and one of the principals, Aristotimos, called for help to Krateros, who was able to reach Elis 'the next day' with a force with which he hoped to enable Aristotimos to prevail, though he actually arrived too late, for Aristotimos had been assassinated in the meantime.[8] This episode was, in fact, part of a much larger ongoing conflict between Macedon and the Aitolian League, the latter being in expansive mode, and Elis being one of the areas where it was busy. But the point here is that Krateros was nearby and in command of an army at the time – to reach Elis in a day he cannot have been more than twenty miles away when the message was sent. He was therefore operating in the Peloponnese as his half-brother's agent.

Krateros' position as his half-brother's agent in central and southern Greece could have started at almost any time after 285, but until the early

270s Antigonos himself was mainly based in Athens, so a viceroy would have been superfluous. By 277, however, Antigonos was on campaign, first in the Hellespont, and later in Macedon. It was presumably at this time that Krateros was appointed to safeguard Antigonid interests in the south. After the papyrus record connected with Epikouros *c*.280, the next reference to Krateros was that he was besieged in Troizen by a force commanded by Kleonymos. The besiegers succeeded in stirring up the Troizonians against the Macedonians, who were compelled to evacuate the city. (Kleonymos is identified either as an Athenian or as the Spartan king of that name.) This incident seems to have taken place in the early 270s, when Antigonos was preoccupied in Macedon.[9]

Krateros was clearly in authority in the area when Pyrrhos came through in 272 and died in his attack on Argos, since he was active in Elis in the same year. Antigonos himself was present in the Peloponnese to mop up the pieces after Pyrrhos' disaster, but this was an emergency, and Krateros may have had sufficient force to deal with Elis, but even Antigonos refused to face Pyrrhos directly. It would seem therefore that Krateros was his viceroy in the south from the early 270s (Troizen), though not in the 280s (according to the papyrus record), in 272 (Elis), and through to his death in the 250s.[10]

Krateros is also known to have made a collection of Athenian decrees, which he published, and which implies a reasonably long residence in the city.[11] It is not known when this period of residence was, though the reference connecting him with Epikouros would suggest that it was during the 280s, while Antigonos was present in the city as well. However, Athens was independent of Antigonos for most of the Kremoneidian War (268–262) so Krateros' presence must have been either in the first period of Antigonos' control (before 268) – which would therefore include the time he led the force at Troizen in 277, and that against Elis in 272 – or after 262. The decade following the surrender of the city in that latter year was one of the gradually lightening of Macedonian control, particularly with the withdrawal of several Macedonian garrisons in 255. If he was based in Athens before 268, he cannot have been present from then until 262, and it seems probable that he then moved to Corinth, where he was later based.

Krateros' sphere of action seems always to have extended beyond Athens and beyond Corinth, wherever were his headquarters. His centre later was certainly Corinth, with Chalkis in Euboia as a secondary base, no doubt under a subordinate commander. Antigonos laid siege to Athens all through the Kremoneidian War and Krateros in Corinth was in a suitable position to guard Antigonos' back. So it would seem – though it will be obvious that much of this is conjecture, and stretching the evidence very thin by linking up the several dots – Krateros had governing authority in central Greece for over twenty years, loyally supporting his half-brother all that time.

His exact position in these decades, when he appears to have been located in and about Athens and then Corinth, and in at least two operations in command of an armed force, is not precisely known. The possibility is that he was Antigonos' appointed viceroy, supervising the various posts, garrisons, allies and commanders in the southern part of Greece, though Athens and Attika, with their forts, seem to have been under a separate command, whose personnel gradually became exclusively Athenian. So Krateros' area of authority now included the cities of Chalkis in Euboia and Corinth, while in the Peloponnese tyrants such as Aristotimos in Elis (who did not actually last very long) and the dynasty of tyrants descended from Aristippos in Argos, were more like Macedonian allies than Antigonos' subjects.

This conglomeration of cities, garrisons, tyrants and allies required that a man who was to be Antigonos' viceroy would, above all, be a diplomat. This must have been obvious from the start. None of the cities that were subject to the Macedonians in various ways – within the Macedonian sphere of influence, might be the best formulation – could be considered fully and permanently 'loyal'; but a half-brother of the king, an educated man who was also capable of commanding an army, a man who was in the king's confidence, and a man interested in the history of Athens – and quite likely, in that of other cities as well – would be an ideal viceroy. And so this is probably the position, possibly even informal, which is likely to have been Krateros' between the 270s and the mid-250s.

As the Macedonian viceroy in central and southern Greece, Krateros was responsible for administering the system of supporting friendly city governments as well as supervising the Macedonian garrisons. It is unlikely that the Macedonians deliberately set out to use tyrants as their agents in these cities. There was no reason that they should, when a democracy or an oligarchy might be as supportive. But several tyrants have been located as the most conspicuous Macedonian agents. Apart from Aristotimos in Elis, who is said to have seized power with help from Antigonos, but who only retained it by excessive brutality, and only for a short time, there was the dynasty of five Argive tyrants, Aristodamos in Megalopolis and Abantidas at Sikyon. Such men did not gain power by using Macedonian help (though Aristippos at Argos was a very early ally) but once in place they could get Macedonian support by offering their alliance. Many of them looked to be fairly well-seated in power, though, of course, being tyrants they were actually anything but, and any tyranny could fall suddenly and quickly. Krateros' intervention in Elis therefore was not to install Aristotimos, but to support him – though in fact he failed, since the tyrant had been killed just before Krateros' forces arrived – a perfect example of tyrant-vulnerability.

The tyrants feared two enemies – their own people, and Sparta. With numerous tyrants in power Sparta could come forward as the champion of freedom with some conviction. Kleonymos at Troizen, supposing it was the Spartan king, succeeded by using the rhetoric of liberation successfully – but then left the garrison in the city, King Log replacing King Stork. But the closer to Sparta a city physically was, the less likely it was to fall for the Spartan line – Aristodamos of Megalopolis actually defeated a Spartan attack with the enthusiastic support of the citizens.[12] Both Antigonos and Krateros must have known that their tyrant-support policy was not likely to endure very long, but once embarked on it they had no way of getting off with any ease.

Krateros died some time in the 250s, probably after 255, but certainly before 251. He had reached the age of well over 60 (he was born in 320/319) and had an adult son called, after his great-grandfather, Alexander. Alexander was installed as, or was permitted to become, Krateros' successor in central Greece. But Alexander had less loyalty to Macedon or to King Antigonos than his father. He detached his cities from Antigonos' distant control, either with the assistance of Ptolemy II, or by accepting such assistance after he had made his decisive break.[13]

The tyrant system around him in the Peloponnese was already breaking down, and by striking for independence Alexander effectively encouraged the continuing collapse. In fact, it may be that he encouraged the removal of the tyrants himself. There had already been trouble in Sikyon, where Abantidas was assassinated in 252; his father Paseas seized power in his place, but he was then also killed by Nikokles, who made himself tyrant in his place.[14] Aristodamos at Megalopolis was also assassinated, by a pair of professional liberators, in about 250.[15] The Argos tyrant Aristomachos moved his policy away from support from Macedon, presumably in response to local opinion; but he had much local power and support and perhaps did not need much Macedonian support to stay in office. The speed with which the system of indirect control broke down after Krateros' death is a measure of the skill with which he had maintained it.

As the system crumbled around him, Alexander made attacks on the main enemy, his uncle Antigonos, by making raids from Corinth and Chalkis into Attika.[16] A new political alignment thus emerged and was made clear when Nikokles of Sikyon was assassinated by Aratos, the son of an earlier democratic leader. Aratos restored the city to democracy, and at the same time took it into a league of nearby small cities, which league – the Achaian – thereby suddenly achieved a greater importance.[17] Aratos also allied with Alexander of Corinth, who could now look to supporting the anti-Macedonian democracies; Antigonos retained the support of the tyrants, and of Athens.

Aratos, fertile in diplomatic expedients, cunning and unscrupulous, persuaded Ptolemy to subsidize his city to smooth the way for the restoration of the exiles who had been driven out by the tyrants.[18] So now Ptolemy and Antigonos were once again enemies, though open war was avoided for a time. In the end, however, probably in 246, the two royal fleets met in battle near Andros, meeting, it seems, accidentally, with the victory going to the Macedonians, rather surprisingly.[19] This allowed Antigonos to move more strongly and confidently against Alexander, but it was Alexander who had already brought about a partial peace, by offering a treaty to Aristomachos of Argos in exchange for cash; Aristomachos agreed, provided Athens was included; Alexander increased the price, and the peace was agreed. (Antigonos, formally Athens' suzerain, was apparently not consulted or involved, but he was adaptable enough to accept the situation.[20])

Alexander's realm – he does not seem to have called himself king, but he did rule a territory regarded in one source as a kingdom[21] – was essentially the cities of Corinth and Chalkis, plus much of Euboia, the area he had inherited from his father. But without the punch of Macedonian power behind him, his control over his neighbours in the Peloponnese was so much weakened that he had had to negotiate the peace treaty with Aristomachos, the tyrant of a single city, as an equal.

Ptolemaic interference became unlikely after the defeat at Andros in 246 or 245. (The death of Ptolemy II in the former year clearly derailed Ptolemaic policy for a time, and Ptolemy III soon became involved in war in Syria.) Antigonos was able therefore to move south once more, without exposing his kingdom to attack. Part of Euboia – notably Karystos – had remained loyal to him all along, and he had access to Athens, where his garrisons still held the forts.[22] An Antigonid attack on Corinth was clearly imminent.

At that point Alexander died. The timing was such that there were immediate accusations of poisoning by Antigonos, but all such accusations in the ancient world have to be disbelieved except where there is clear and explicit evidence.[23] How old Alexander was at his death is not known, but one must suppose he was in his forties. His widow was older than her next suitor, who was 40, so probably Alexander was older than she. His death was thus not too surprising.

There then followed a political comedy, or perhaps a farce. Alexander's widow, Nikaia, probably a well-born Macedonian, inherited his command. Antigonos proposed that she marry his son Demetrios, who was also his heir, much as the first Krateros' discarded Persian wife had married Lysimachos so that he could gain control of her city of Herakleia Pontike. This seemed to Nikaia a bargain: she would become a king's wife, he would acquire Corinth; and probably he would have assumed the same role in the Macedonian system as his cousin Krateros had done earlier. (Demetrios already had a wife, Stratonike, a Seleukid princess, but polygamy was a royal habit; she did decamp later, but for a different reason.) Nikaia accepted the proposal, and the wedding ceremony followed. During the celebrations Antigonos, aged 66, energetically climbed up Akrokorinth and demanded admission to the citadel; of course, he was admitted, and he took over control of the citadel and the city. Nikaia vanished, at least from our sources; she was certainly married to Demetrios, but was never queen, so far as we know.[24] (Antigonos, however, held the city for no more than a year; Aratos of Sikyon seized it in a clandestine attack in 243, and held it, bringing the city into the Achaian League.)

Alexander 'of Corinth' was the last of Antipater's dynasty to hold independent power, so long as one regards the Antigonids and Ptolemies, descended like Alexander from one of Antipater's daughters, as separate dynasties. What his overall aim had been in making a bid for independence is unclear; he may have aimed to displace Antigonos as king in Macedon, though he does not appear to have made any moves in that direction, or he may have simply aimed to construct a viable kingdom in central Greece. Whatever his aim, he failed; his death occurred just before he would have been overwhelmed by Antigonos' offensive.

Conclusion

A Brief but Effective Dynasty

The dynasty founded by Antipater lasted as a ruling entity only from 334 to 319 (as a regency) and from 317 to 294 (as royalty); to this may be added the brief five-year career (251–246) as ruler of Corinth by Alexander son of Krateros and his widow; his father's two decades as his predecessor might be added as well. This is not really a long time – between the extremes it is only ninety years, with gaps. It is not therefore comparable with the other Hellenistic dynasties: Antigonids, Ptolemies, Seleukids, even Attalids, who all lasted considerably longer.

And yet the Antipatrids had their own importance. Antipater's work in Macedon held Alexander the Great's base firm while he campaigned as far as India, maintained the control of Greece established by Philip II, and fed Alexander with reinforcements as the Asian task expanded in scope year by year. Kassander held Macedon as a kingdom for another generation and contributed powerfully to the defeat of the attempt by Antigonos I to reconstitute Alexander's empire. As it was, several descendants of Antipater – Ptolemy Keraunos, Meleagar, Antipater Etesias, Antigonos Gonatas – fought to revive the kingdom after its conquest by the Galatians, in the end successfully.

These men, of course, were descendants of Antipater through his daughters, a formidable, fascinating and admirable set of ladies. Since the male descendants after Kassander – his sons, and his grandsons – were either failures as kings, or existed only as Macedonian lords, it is through these ladies that Antipater's influence on events continued. All of them gave birth to notable individuals – Krateros, Antigonos Gonatas, Agathokles son of Lysimachos, even Ptolemy Keraunos, Alexander of Corinth – who had major effects on their times. But, above all, it was the independence of these women that was one of the main elements in the later social history of the Hellenistic period, providing models for their royal successors, and for women everywhere.

Finally, we may note that the two kings who dominated the last great Hellenistic generation, Philip V of Macedon, and the Seleukid Antiochos III, were both descendants of Phila, Antipater's daughter. The fight they made against Rome to retain the independence of the Hellenistic kingdoms would perhaps have been approved by both Antipater and Phila.

Abbreviations

AHB – Ancient History Bulletin

AM – Ancient Macedonia

Austin – MM Austin, *The Hellenistic World from Alexander to the Roman Conquest*, 2nd ed. (Cambridge, 2006).

Burstein – SM Burstein, *The Hellenistic Age from the Battle of Ipsus to the death of Cleopatra VII* (Cambridge, 1985).

Carney, *Women and Monarchy* – ED Carney, *Women and Monarchy in Macedonia* (Norman OK, 2000).

CP – Classical Philology

CQ – Classical Quarterly

CJ – Classical Journal

FGrH – Felix Jacoby – *Die Fragmente der Greichische Historiker.*

Habicht, *Athens* – Christian Habicht, *Athens from Alexander to Antony*, trans. DL Schneider (Cambridge, MA, 1997).

Harding – Philip Harding, *From the end of the Peloponnesian War to the Battle of Ipsus* (Cambridge, 1985).

Heckel, *Who's Who* – Waldemar Heckel, *Who's Who in the Age of Alexander the Great* (London, 2006).

HM – History of Macedonia, Vol. II by NGL Hammond and GT Griffith, Vol. III by Hammond and FM Walbank (Oxford, 1979 and 1988).

IG – Inscriptiones Graecae

JHS – Journal of Hellenic Studies

Macedonians in Athens – Olga Palagia and Stephen V Tracy, (eds.), *The Macedonians in Athens* (Oxford, 2003).

SEG – Supplementum Epigraphicum Graecum

SIG – W Dittenberger, *Sylloge Inscriptionum Graecarum*, 3rd ed. (Leipzig, 1915–1924).

Tod – MN Tod, *A Selection of Greek Historical Inscriptions*, Vol. II (Oxford, 1948).

ZPE – Zeitschrift fur Papyrologie und Epigraphik

Notes and References

Chapter 1

1. For Archelaos' reign, see *HM* 2.137–141, and RM Errington, *A History of Macedonia* (Berkeley and Los Angeles, California 1993) pp. 23–28.
2. Thucydides 1.62.2.
3. Heckel, *Who's Who*, s.v. Antipater.
4. *Suda*, s.v. Antipatros (aged 79).
5. Justin 12.16.6.
6. John Walsh, 'Antipater and Early Hellenistic Literature', *AHB* 24 (2012) pp. 149–162.
7. *Suda*, s.v. Antipatros.
8. George Cawkwell, *Philip II of Macedon* (London 1978) pp. 54–55.
9. Plutarch, *Moralia* 178; Philip is also said to have dismissed the judge when he heard he dyed his beard.
10. Plutarch, *Moralia* 180.
11. Athenaios 435d.
12. Plutarch, *Moralia* 179B.
13. *HM* 2.337.
14. Theopompos, *FGrH* 115, F 160.
15. Demosthenes 3.32
16. Isokrates, Epistle 4.
17. Demosthenes 19.69; Aischines 3.72; Deinarchos 1.28.
18. Plutarch, *Alexander* 9.
19. Theopompos, *FGrH* 115, F 217; an anecdote of Philip arranging for a letter to Antipater to fall into Athenian hands to deceive them (Frontinus, *Strategems* 1.4.13) does not show Antipater to be in Thrace at the time.
20. Athenaios 1.18a (from Hegesandros).
21. Takati, *Macedonians Abroad*, has suggested that an Archias, son of Antipater, noted by Arrian, *Successors of Alexander*, *FGrH* 156, F9 21, was the twelfth child; without further detail this is unproven.
22. Diodoros 17.16.2.
23. It may be that he was preceded by an earlier son; the custom was to name a son after his grandfather, so Antipater's first son should have been called Iolaos. His much later son of that name may thus have been named after the eldest son died; but this 'rule' is not by any means invariable.
24. Justin 11.7.1; Curtius 7.1.7; Alexander was one of those with a strong claim to the kingship if King Alexander died in the war; another indication of Antipater's prominence.
25. *IG* xi.2, 161b, 85; *IG* xi.2, 287b, 57.
26. Plutarch, *Demetrios* 14.

27. *IG* XI.2.287b and 161.85; W Heckel, 'A Grandson of Antipatros at Delos', *ZPE* 70 (1987) pp. 161–162; the marriage is noted by Photios, *Bibliotheca* 166, 111 a–b; Heckel, *Marshals* 260 seems to give Balakros two other sons, possibly from an earlier marriage, but the dating and identities he suggests seem inconsistent.
28. *HM* 2.180–189.
29. Plutarch, *Alexander* 3.
30. Philip's reign and work are of course dealt with in detail by the usual biographers, notably Griffith in *HM* 2; Cawkwell, *Philip of Macedon*; JR Ellis, *Philip II and Macedonian Imperialism* (London, 1976); Nicholas Hammond, *Philip of Macedon* (London, 1994); S Perlman (ed.), *Philip and Athens* (Cambridge, 1973).
31. Justin 9.4.5; Hypereides, *Against Demades*, frag. 77; *IG* II.239.

Chapter 2
1. Ephesos: Arrian, *Anabasis* 1.17.9–19; Eresos in Lesbos: *IG* XII.2.52b.
2. Tenedos: Arrian, *Anabasis* 2.2.2–3; Chios: Tod II, 192; Lesbos [Demosthenes] 17.7.
3. Ian Worthington, *Alexander, Man and God*, 2nd ed. (London, 2004) pp. 40–42.
4. Arrian, *Anabasis*, 1.25.1–2; the post seems to date from about 339: JR Ellis, *Philip II and Macedonian Imperialism* (London, 1976) p. 160 and note 60.
5. See Justin 9.8.2–21 for an interesting comparison of the two men, though a little forced.
6. Athenaios 13.557d (Satyros).
7. As Justin 9.7.7 suggests she was doing.
8. Diodoros 17.91.4.
9. Plutarch, *Alexander* 9.6; Justin 9.7.6.
10. The date of this marriage is not known, but the couple had a daughter of marriageable age by 320, so the marriage must have occurred by, say, 337, or a little earlier: Satyros *FHG* 3.161; Arrian, *Successors of Alexander* 22; Polyainos 8.60; Carney, *Women and Monarchy* pp. 69–70.
11. Hammond in *HM* 2.590, though the suggestion is confined to a queried note in the index; in the text he calls the group of ambassadors 'a group of backwoodsmen'.
12. Athenaios 560f; Polyainos 8.60; Arrian, *Successors of Alexander* pp. 22–23; Carney, *Women and Monarchy* pp. 57–58.
13. Arrian, *Anabasis* 1.25.2; Curtius 7.1.6–7; Justin 11.2.2.
14. This claim is frequent in modern accounts, usually prefaced by some such distancing term as 'undoubtedly' (W Heckel, *The Marshals of Alexander's Empire* (London, 1992) p. 40; however, it really is most likely that he was present, and in that case he will surely have encouraged Lynkestis forward.
15. Justin 11.2.1; the sequence is reversed in Diodoros 17.2.1; ignored by Plutarch, *Alexander*.
16. Diodoros 16.94.4; J Rufus Fears, 'Pausanias, the Assassin of Philip II', *Athenaeum* 53 (1975) pp. 111–135.
17. The responsibility for Philip's death is, of course, the subject of much discussion even now, and features in all the biographies of both Philip and Alexander, to no clear resolution.
18. Curtius 6.9.17 and 10.24.
19. JR Ellis, 'Amyntas Perdikka, Philip II, and Alexander the Great', *JHS* 91 (1971) pp. 15–24.
20. NGL Hammond, *Alexander the Great* (London, 1981) p. 39.

21. Justin 11.2.2.
22. Hammond in *HM* 3.24–16; this is not always accepted – e.g. by Heckel, *Marshals* – but it makes a good explanation for Alexander's paranoia about the family.
23. Diodoros 17.2.3–6 and 5.1–2; Curtius 8.1.42; Justin 12.6.14.
24. Diodoros 17.5.1; Curtius 7.1.3.
25. Justin 9.7.12.
26. Justin 9.7.3 and 11.2.3; Diodoros 17.2.3; see Griffith in *HM* 2.681; maybe the child has been invented to give someone else for Alexander to kill.
27. It is only noted in Justin 12.6.14, and he is referred to as 'a Macedonian chieftain'.
28. Polyainos 8.60; a planned marriage with the Agrianian King Langaros did not take place because the groom died before the ceremony: Arrian, *Anabasis* 1.5.4–5.
29. Arrian, *Anabasis* 1.17.9; Curtius 3.11.18 and 4.1.27; Ellis, 'Amyntas Perdikka'.
30. Arrian, *Anabasis* 1.25.3.
31. *HM* 2.176.
32. Plutarch, *Alexander* 11.4.
33. Diodoros 17.17.5.
34. Polyainos 5.44.4, though this round figure is clearly no more than approximate.
35. Hammond, *Alexander* pp. 42–45, for a summary account.
36. Deinarchos, *Against Demosthenes* 1.18.
37. See Hammond, *Alexander* pp. 57–58; he ignores Antipater's role.
38. Arrian, *Anabasis* 1.7.6.
39. Argos and Elis were also preparing to join in, according to Diodoros 17.8.5.
40. Polyainos 4.3.12.
41. Arrian, *Anabasis* 1.7.6.
42. Plutarch, *Alexander* 11.8; Diodoros 17.8.7.
43. Plutarch, *Alexander* 11.6–12.12: Arrian, *Anabasis* 1.7–8; Diodoros 17.8.2–14.1.
44. Arrian, *Anabasis* 1.9.10.
45. Justin 11.2.9; Hammond, *Alexander* p. 22.
46. Diodoros 17.16.1.
47. Diodoros 16.91.2.
48. Diodoros 17.16.2.
49. Diodoros 16.91.2 and 17.3–5; Arrian, *Anabasis* 1.11.3 and 6; Plutarch, *Alexander* 15.1.
50. Arrian, *Anabasis* 1.25.2.
51. Arrian, *Anabasis* 1.11.3; Diodoros 18.12.1; Curtius 4.1.39; Justin 11.7.1; all these notices are retrospective; none refer to Antipater's actual appointment.
52. E Badian, 'Agis III', *Hermes* 95 (1967) pp. 170–192.
53. Diodoros 17.15.2; Plutarch, *Demosthenes* 23.5.
54. EJ Baynham, 'Why didn't Alexander marry a nice Macedonian girl before leaving home? Observations on Factional Politics at Alexander's Court in 336–334 BC', in TW Hillard et al., *Ancient History at a Modern University*, Vol. I (Macquarie University Australia, 1988) pp. 148–155.
55. Arrian, *Anabasis* 1.19.8; 4.1.1–2.
56. Arrian, *Anabasis* 1.29.5–6; Curtius 3.1.9.
57. Arrian, *Anabasis* 2.1.3–5.
58. Arrian, *Anabasis* 2.2.3.
59. Arrian, *Anabasis* 1.20.1; Diodoros 17.2.5–23.3.
60. Curtius 3.1.19–20; Arrian, *Anabasis* 2.2.3.

61. Arrian, *Anabasis* 2.2.4–5.
62. Arrian, *Anabasis* 1.29.4.
63. JD Grainger, *Hellenistic and Roman Sea Wars, 336–31 BC* (Barnsley, 2011) Ch 1.
64. Diodoros 18.22.1.

Chapter 3
1. Curtius 4.1.37; Arrian, *Anabasis* 2.5.7.
2. Referred to in several speeches, e.g. Demosthenes 17.21.
3. A Moreno, *Feeding the Democracy, the Athenian Grain Supply in the Fifth and Fourth Centuries BC* (Oxford, 2007); Signe Isagen and Mogens Herman Hansen, *Aspects of Athenian Society in the Fourth Century BC* (Odense, 1975) pp. 200–213, a commentary on the speech *Against Dionysiodoros* LVI.
4. Arrian, *Anabasis* 3.6.4 and 7.
5. Arrian, *Anabasis* 1.24.2; Curtius 3.1.1; W Heckel, 'Q. Curtius Rufus and the date of Kleandros' Mission to the Peloponnese', *Hermes* 119 (1991) pp. 124–125.
6. Arrian, *Anabasis* 2.3.3; Curtius 3.1.19.
7. Supposedly 8,000 men (Diodoros 17.48.1; Curtius 4.1.39) but this was the total who escaped from the battle to Cyprus, and at least 4,000 of them went on to Egypt.
8. Arrian, *Anabasis* 3.6.4–7.
9. Arrian, *Anabasis* 2.20.5; Curtius 4.3.11; like Harpalos, Kleandros was at once promoted, in his case to commander of the Greek mercenaries.
10. Bonnie Kingsley, 'Harpalos in the Megarid (333–331 BC) and the Grain Shipments from Cyrene', *ZPE* 66 (1986) pp. 165–177, is the basis for this discussion. Earlier, less convincing, discussions include E Badian, 'The First Flight of Harpalos', *Historia* 9 (1960) pp. 245–246; W Heckel, 'The Flight of Harpalos and Tauriskos', *CP* 72 (1977) pp. 133–135; ED Carney, 'The First Flight of Harpalos Again', *CJ* 77 (1987) pp. 9–11; I Worthington, 'The First Flight of Harpalos Reconsidered', *Greece and Rome* 31 (1984) pp. 161–169.
11. Aristotle, *Oeconomicus* 1352 b 19; Demosthenes 42.20; see the discussion focused on the Athenian harvest of 329/328 (and so three years after Harpalos' activities) in Peter Garnsey, *Famine and Food Supply in the Graeco-Roman World, Responses to Risk and Crisis* (Cambridge, 1988) pp. 89–106, also pp. 150–164 with reference to the supply from Cyrene.
12. See the calculations by Donald W Engels, *Alexander the Great and the Logistics of the Macedonian Army* (California, 1978) appendix 1, 'Rations'.
13. Austin 116.
14. This is Kingsley's main point, reinforced by a map.
15. Arrian, *Anabasis* 1.1.5.
16. Assuming that Alexander Lynkestis replaced an earlier governor in 336.
17. Curtius 9.3.21; Diodoros 17.62.4–5.
18. Justin 12.2.16.
19. Justin 12.1.4: this is not a record of Zopyrion's death, as Badian ('Agis III: Revisions and Reflections' – see note 27) assumed, but of his warfare there; his death occurred some years later.
20. Heckel, *Marshals* pp. 352–353.
21. Diodoros 17.62.6.
22. Arrian, *Anabasis* 2.13.5–6.

23. Diodoros 17.49.1; Curtius 5.1.40–42.
24. Arrian, *Anabasis* 3.16.9; Curtius 5.1.43 says the money was 1,000 talents; Menes was to take it to Syria, take up the post of governor there, and send on 'whatever Antipater needed'; that is, it would only go to Macedon if the war was still on.
25. Aeschines 3.165; Agis (probably) set up a victory monument at Amyklai (one of the Spartan villages made up Sparta city: *SEG* 1.87; cf. Paul Parrolla, *A Prosopography of Lacedaemonians*, 2nd ed. by Alfred S Bradford (Chicago, 1985) 27a, p. 192.
26. Demosthenes 17.10; he was a wrestling victor at the Isthmian and Olympian games, and a student of Plato: Pausanias 7.27.7; Athenaios 11.509 b.
27. The main discussions are by E Badian, 'Agis III', *Hermes* 95 (1967) pp. 170–192, around which comments have swirled; also EN Borza, 'The end of Agis' Revolt', *CP* 66 (1971) pp. 230–235; GL Cawkwell, 'The Crowning of Demosthenes', *CQ*, NS 19 (1969) pp. 163–180; Paul Cartledge and Antony Spawforth, *Hellenistic and Roman Sparta, a Tale of Two Cities* (London, 1987) Ch. 2; Badian returned to the question in 'Agis III: Revisions and Reflections', in *Ventures into Greek History*, ed. I Worthington (Oxford, 1994) pp. 258–292.
28. Engels, *Logistics*, table 5 in appendix 5, calculates that Alexander's forces at Babylon, including the original force and the reinforcements already received, amounted to 65,000 men; these were almost entirely Greek or Macedonian at this point; Dareios still had several thousand Greeks in his own forces.
29. Curtius 6.1.20; Pausanias 7.27.7; Deinarchos 1.34; EL McQueen, 'Some Notes on the Anti-Macedonian Movement in the Peloponnese in 331 BC', *Historia* 27 (1973) pp. 40–64.
30. Diodoros 17.48.1; Deinarchos 1.34; Badian, 'Agis III'.
31. GEM de Ste Croix, *The Origins of the Peloponnesian War* (London, 1972) appendix 30, pp. 376–378.
32. Aeschines 3.165.
33. Arrian, *Anabasis* 3.6.3; Curtius 4.8.15; they disagree on Amphoteros' point of departure (Egypt or Tyre) but the ships were mainly Phoenician.
34. DS Potter, '*IG* II (2) 399: Evidence for Athenian Involvement in the War of Agis III', *Annual of the British School at Athens* 79 (1984) pp. 229–235, argues for Athenian involvement, but much of his argument was dismantled by Badian, 'History from Square Brackets', *ZPE* 79 (1989) pp. 59–70; on the other hand, it would not be at all surprising to find individual Athenians taking part in the fighting on the Spartan side, from pure hatred of Macedon.
35. This follows from the fact that Mantineia was not punished by the League afterwards.
36. Curtius 6.1.1–2; all ancient accounts are brief: Diodoros 17.62–63; Plutarch, *Agis* 3.2; Pausanias 1.13.6; Justin 12.1.4–11.
37. Curtius 6.1.16; Diodoros 17.63.3; Cartledge and Spawforth, *Sparta* pp. 23–24.
38. Diodoros 17.73.5; Curtius 6.1.17–20.
39. Justin 12.1.4; misinterpreted seriously by Badian, 'Agis III: Revisions and Reflections', p. 349.
40. Diodoros 17.18.2; Justin 12.14.1; Curtius 7.1.5–9.

Chapter 4

1. C Habicht, 'Zwei Angehorige der Lynkestische Konigshauses', *AM* II (Thessaloniki, 1977) pp. 511–516.

2. Heckel, *Marshals* pp. 260–261; id. *Who's Who* pp. 207–208 (Phila); pp. 68–69 (Balakros); Balakros is also recorded as Balagros.

3. Diodoros 18.22.1; WE Higgins, 'Aspects of Alexander's Imperial Administration: some Modern Methods and Views', *Athenaeum* 58 (1980) pp. 129–152.

4. RA Billows, *Antigonos the One-Eyed and the Creation of the Hellenistic State* (California, 1990) p. 44.

5. Arrian, *Anabasis* 2.4.2; Curtius 3.1.24.

6. 'Pontus' is said to have been part of Zopyrion's satrapy (Justin 12.1.16), but governing Thrace and Pontus is an impossible combination; it is assumed to be a mangled reference to his campaign which ended at Olbia on the Pontic coast.

7. Memnon of Herakleia, *FGrH* 434 F 12.4.

8. Heckel, *Marshals* pp. 327–328 (Philip); id, *Who's Who* pp. 211–212 (Philip – a much more definitive notice than in *Marshals*) p. 177 (Nikanor).

9. Arrian, *Anabasis* 1.4.5 and 1.14.2–3; Diodoros 17.57.3; Curtius 4.13.28.

10. Gary Reger, 'The Family of Balakros son of Nikanor, the Macedonian, on Delos', *ZPE* 89 (1991) pp. 147–154.

11. Justin 12.14.9; Plutarch, *Alexander* 7.4.2; Heckel, *Marshals* pp. 293– 294.

12. NGL Hammond, 'Royal Pages, Personal Pages, and Boys Trained in the Macedonian Manner during the Period of the Temenid Monarchy', *Historia* 39 (1990) pp 261–290.

13. Diodoros 17.17.4.

14. Arrian, *Successors* 1.21.

15. Diodoros 19.74.3–5.

16. Diodoros 19.77.6.

17. Sch. on Theokritos, *Idyll* 17.

18. W Heckel, *The Last Days and Testament of Alexander the Great, a Prosopographical Study*, *Historia Einszelschriften* 56 (Stuttgart, 1988) p. 10.

19. Carney, *Women and Monarchy* pp. 85–88.

20. E.g., Plutarch, *Alexander* 34.7.

21. Diodoros 18.49.4; Pausanias 1.11.3.

22. Christopher D Blackwell, *In the Absence of Alexander, Harpalus and the Failure of Macedonian Authority* (New York, 1999).

23. Alexander Lynkestis was condemned by a court of courtiers, Philotas by an army assembly, Parmenion by a private decision of the king alone.

24. Diodoros 18.8.6; Plutarch, *Alexander* 49.6.

25. Plutarch, *Alexander* 49.14–15.

26. Diodoros 17.22.5.

27. Demosthenes 17.20.

28. Arrian, *Anabasis* 1.16.6, 29.5, and 3.6.2.

29. Plutarch, *Moralia* 188f.

30. Blackwell, *Absence of Alexander*, discusses these contacts.

31. Lykourgos, *Leokrates*; Blackwell, *In the Absence of Alexander*; C Habicht, *Athens from Alexander to Anthony* (Cambridge MA, 1997) p. 27; L Tritle, 'Leocrates: Athenian Businessman and Macedonian Agent', *AM* Vol. I, (Thessaloniki, 1999) pp. 1227–1233.

32. Demosthenes 17.4, 7, 10, and 16; G Cawkwell, 'A Note of Ps. Demosthenes 17.20', *Phoenix* 15 (1961) pp. 74–78.

33. Arrian, *Anabasis* 3.19.5; Curtius 6.2.17; Diodoros 17.74.3–5.

34. Curtius 7.10.11–12.

35. This seems implied by Justin 12.1.4; other suggestions include 328 and 327/326; that is, we do not know.
36. Macrobius, *Saturnalia* 1.11.33.
37. Tod II 193.
38. Curtius 10.1.43; Justin 12.1.4; Curtius dates the news of the defeat reaching Alexander to his campaign in India.
39. Arrian, *Anabasis* 6.27.3–5; Curtius 10.1.1–8.
40. Diodoros 17.1 13.3–4; Justin 12.1–3; Arrian, *Anabasis* 7.19.1–2.
41. Harding 114; Heckel, *Who's Who* p. 127.
42. Harding 127.
43. Diodoros 18.8.8–5.
44. *SIG* (2), 312.
45. For examples of the complexity at the local level, see Harding 113, from Mitylene in Lesbos (= Tod II 201), and 122 from Tegea (= Tod II 202).
46. Habicht, *Athens* pp. 30–32.
47. Arrian, *Anabasis* 7.23.2.
48. At Babylon, Kassander is said to have been scornful of the importation of such Persian practices into the court as *proskynesis*; this practice was seen as a halfway stage towards demanding divine honours.
49. Plutarch, *Moralia* 213e (Damis); Hypereides, *In Demosthenam* 31 (quoting Demosthenes).
50. Diodoros 17.10 8.4–8; Curtius 10.2.1; Plutarch, *Demosthenes* 25.3; E Badian, 'Harpalos', *JHS* 81 (1961) pp. 16–43, for a detailed consideration; Heckel, *Marshals* pp. 213–221.
51. Pausanias 2.33.4–5; Hypereides 1.8; Plutarch, *Moralia* 531 a.
52. Arrian, *Anabasis*, 3.6.4; Plutarch, *Alexander* 21.1.
53. Diodoros 17.108.7.
54. Diodoros 17.108.8; Curtius 10.2.3; Pausanias 2.33.4–5.
55. Arrian, *Anabasis* 7.12.4; Justin 12.12.8–9.
56. Arrian, *Anabasis* 7.12.4.
57. NG Ashton, 'Craterus from 324 to 321 BC', *AM* V (Thessaloniki, 1991) pp. 125–131.
58. So Heckel, *Who's Who* p. 98.
59. GT Griffith, 'Alexander and Antipater in 323 BC', *Proceedings of the African Classical Association*, 8 (1965) pp. 12–17.
60. Athenaios 13.586c and 595d–e (Theopompos); Kleitarchos, *FGrH* 137 F30.

Chapter 5

1. Arrian, *Successors of Alexander*, 1.1–8; this is much argued over: see *HM* 3, Ch. 1, and AB Bosworth, *The Legacy of Alexander* (Oxford, 2002) Ch. 2; there are many other discussions.
2. In fact his complete absence in all accounts, factual and fictional, from Babylon at the time of Alexander's death, is notable, given that he is accused of providing the poison supposedly administered by Iolaos. He may well have left before the king's death: Bosworth, *Legacy* p. 32, note 17.
3. Diodoros 18.4.1–6.
4. Heckel, *Marshals* pp. 107–133, and 127–129.
5. Diodoros 18.3.1; Justin 30.4.12; Arrian, *Successors of Alexander* 1.5.
6. Harding 128, with references; Habicht, *Athens* pp. 33–34.

7. Pausanias 1.25.4 and 8.52.5 (claiming that he had 'rescued 50,000' mercenaries).
8. Diodoros 18.10.2.
9. Diodoros 17.1 11.3 and 18.9.4.
10. Plutarch, *Demosthenes* 27.
11. Diodoros 17.1 11.3.
12. Plutarch, *Demosthenes* 27 (quoting Phylarchos).
13. Curtius 10.10.2 and 4; Diodoros 18.3.1–2; Arrian, *Successors of Alexander* 1.6–7; Justin 13.4.16.
14. Diodoros 18.14.2–4; Arrian, *Successors of Alexander* 1.10.
15. E Will, *Histoire Politique du Monde Hellentistique*, Vol. I (Nancy, 1982) pp. 29–33, and Habicht, *Athens* pp. 36–27, for the list of allies, the sources for which are various and many.
16. *HM* 3.108 and 122; AB Bosworth, 'Why did Athens lose the Lamian War?' in *Macedonians in Athens* pp. 14–22, with references to other studies.
17. Diodoros 18.11.5; Hypereides 4.5.15–16.
18. Though it seems that at least one Thracian group joined the alliance: *IG* II(2) 249; Diodoros 18.11.1; no doubt Lysimachos' forces neutralized it as a threat to Macedon.
19. So assumed, reasonably, by *HM* 3.109; they refer to Antipater's 'deputy commander', as being in charge; various suggestions to emend 'Sippas' have included Sirrhas and Simmias (Heckel, *Who's Who* p. 249); but if 'Sippas' was in this command, where was Kassander?
20. Diodoros 18.12.2.
21. Diodoros 18.12.3.
22. Diodoros 18.12.1.
23. Polyainos 4.4.2; he claims that Lamia was on the Greek side, though Diodoros put it as Macedonian; no doubt it changed sides when Antipater took over.
24. Diodoros 18.12.4.
25. Plutarch, *Eumenes* 3.6–8; Diodoros 18.14.4.
26. Plutarch, *Eumenes* 3.8–10; Cornelius Nepos, *Eumenes* 2.4–5.
27. Arrian, *Successors of Alexander* F 19.
28. Diodoros 18.12.4–13.3.
29. Diodoros 18.15.8.
30. Diodoros 18.10.2, naming his colleagues; for Athenian ship numbers see NG Ashton, 'The Naumachia near Amorgos in 322 BC', *Annual of the British School at Athens*, 72 (1977) pp. 1–11.
31. Diodoros 18.13.4.
32. Ibid.
33. Diodoros 18.13.5.
34. Diodoros 18.14.5.
35. Diodoros 18.15.1–2.
36. Diodoros 18.15.3–7.
37. Diodoros 18.15.8–9.
38. Diodoros 19.67.4.
39. Plutarch, *Phokion* 25.1–4.
40. AB Bosworth, 'Why did Athens lose the Lamian War?', in *Macedonians in Athens* pp. 14–21, argues for the Akarnanian campaign; *HM* 3.113 and 122 prefers the Malian Gulf as the scene of fighting, though there are serious mistakes in geography in the discussion.

41. Marmor Parium (*FGrH* 239, 9 = Austin 1); Athenaios 12.55.
42. Diodoros 18.16.4–17.2.
43. Diodoros 18.17.7.
44. Diodoros 18.17.8; Plutarch, *Phokion* 26.
45. This was what Leochares had been tried for eight years before; neither Demosthenes not Hypereides seem to have been blamed; they did not live long enough to be tried.
46. Diodoros 18.18.1–3.
47. Diodoros 18.18.3–4; Plutarch, *Phokion* 26.
48. Plutarch, *Phokion* 28; see also the essays by Peter Green and Elizabeth Baynham in *Macedonians in Athens* pp. 1–7 and 23–29.
49. Plutarch, *Phokion* 28.
50. Diodoros 18.18.9.

Chapter 6

1. *Suda* Z 742; Zenobios VII 39; Theopompos *FGrH* 115 F 235; AB Bosworth, 'The Early Relations between Aitolia and Macedon', *American Journal of Ancient History*, 1 (1976) pp. 164–181.
2. HH Schmitt, *Die Staatsvertrage des Altertums* III, *Die Vertrage der greichisdhe-romischen Welt von 338 bis 200 v. Chr.* (Munich, 1969) no. 409.
3. Arrian, *Anabasis* 1.10.2.
4. I have discussed all this in *The League of the Aitolians* (Leiden, 1999) pp. 45–52.
5. Arrian, *Successors of Alexander* 1.11: Diodoros 18.16.1–3 and 22.1; Appian, *Mithradatic Wars* 8; Justin 13.6.1–3.
6. Strabo 4.3.10.
7. Memnon *FGrH* 434 F 1 4.4; Diodoros 18.18.7; Plutarch, *Demetrios* 14.2.
8. See JD Grainger, *Great Power Diplomacy in the Hellenistic World* (London, 2016), Chapter 2.
9. Arrian, *Successors of Alexander* 1.17; see John Whitehorne, *Cleopatras* (London, 1994) pp. 61–64.
10. Billows, *Antigonos* pp. 36–46.
11. Diodoros 18.23.3–4; Arrian, *Successors of Alexander* 1.20 and 24.
12. Polyainos 8.60.
13. Ibid; Arrian, *Successors of Alexander* 1.23: Carney, *Women and Monarchy* pp. 128–131.
14. The timing is not easy to work out, but the war lasted over one winter, which should be that of 322/321. In Asia Perdikkas was fighting in Kappadokia, Kynanne's journey and killing took place, and Antigonos arrived at Antipater's headquarters towards the end of the Aitolian War.
15. Diodoros 18.24.1–25.1.
16. Diodoros 18.25.2.
17. Diodoros 18.23.2–3; Justin 13.6.5–6.
18. Arrian, *Successors of Alexander* 1.24.
19. Arrian, *Successors of Alexander* 1.17; Diodoros 18.25.3–4.
20. Arrian, *Successors of Alexander* 1.16; Pausanias 1.6.3; Strabo 11.18; Diodoros 18.28.1–4.
21. Diodoros 18.25.5.
22. Diodoros 18.25.6.
23. Diodoros 18.29.1.
24. Arrian, *Successors of Alexander* 1.25.1.

25. Arrian, *Successors of Alexander* 1.24.3–5.
26. Justin 13.6.16; Arrian, *Successors of Alexander* 1.24.2; Billows, *Antigonos* pp. 382–393.
27. Arrian, *Successors of Alexander* 1.24.6.
28. Curtius 10.6.16; Arrian, *Successors of Alexander* 1.24.6; H Hauben, 'An Athenian Naval Victory in 321 BC', *ZPE* 13 (1974) pp. 61–64.
29. Curtius 10.6.16; Arrian, *Successors of Alexander* 1.24.6
30. Plutarch, *Eumenes* 5.3.
31. Arrian, *Successors of Alexander* 1.26; Plutarch, *Eumenes* 5.4.
32. Justin 30.6.16; Arrian, *Successors of Alexander* 1.26.
33. Plutarch, *Eumenes* 6.7, 7.5–13; Nepos, *Eumenes* 3.5–6, and 4.2–4; Arrian, *Successors of Alexander* 1.27; Diodoros 18.30.5–31.1; Justin 13.8.8.
34. Diodoros 18.30.5–33.5.
35. Diodoros 18.38.1–6.
36. Justin 13.8.10; Diodoros 18.36.5; Pausanias 1.6.3.
37. Diodoros 18.37.3–4.
38. Diodoros 18.39.6; Arrian, *Successors of Alexander* 1.34.
39. Diodoros 18.39.1–2.
40. Arrian, *Anabasis* 7.8.1; Arrian, *Successors of Alexander* 1.32; J Roisman, *Alexander's Veterans and the Early Wars of the Successors* (Austin TX, 2012) pp. 137–138; as Roisman suggests, the pay demand may well not have emerged until after Perdikkas' army contacted Krateros' men at the camp.
41. Arrian, *Successors of Alexander* 1.33; Diodoros 18.39.3–4; Polyainos 4.6.4. These are hardly compatible with each other and the temptation is always to constrain them into a straight story, but this can hardly be done, not least because people at the time probably did not understand much of what happened.
42. Arrian, *Successors of Alexander* 1.33; Polyainos 4.6.4.
43. Arrian, *Successors of Alexander* 1.33.
44. Diodoros 18.39.4: Carney, *Women and Monarchy* p. 133.

Chapter 7
1. Pausanias 1.6.8; Appian, *Syrian Wars* 62.
2. Plutarch, *Demetrios* 14.
3. J Seibert, *Historische Beitrage zu den dynastischen verbundingen in der Hellenisticshe Zeit, Historia Einszelschriften* 10 (Wiesbaden, 1987) suggests the spring of 321 for both marriages.
4. Strabo 12.565; Helen S Lund, *Lysimachos, a Study in Hellenistic Kingship* (London, 1992) p. 54; Seibert (previous note) puts this marriage only 'before 319', but 321 would suit it very well.
5. Arrian, *Successors of Alexander* 1.21.
6. Arrian, *FGrH* 154 F 9, 37–38 (= Austin 30).
7. Billows, *Antigonos* pp. 41–46.
8. Diodoros 18.39.7; Arrian, *Successors of Alexander* 1.38.
9. Arrian, *Successors of Alexander* 1.38; Diodoros 18.39.7 is not so explicit, but both link Antigonos' appointment to command the royal army with the intention to eliminate Eumenes; cf. Billows, *Antigonos* pp. 70–71.
10. Diodoros 18.3.3; Justin 13.4.23; Arrian, *Successors of Alexander* 1.24.3–5.
11. Curtius 5.2.16; Billows, *Antigonos* pp. 440–441; Heckel, *Who's Who* p. 272.

12. This is an assumption based on the movements of the regiment (and Antigenes) and the fact that there was a large treasure in Kilikia by 319
13. For the continued activity of the Macedonians, see Roisman, *Alexander's Veterans*.
14. That these names are also the names of two of Antipater's sons might cause momentary confusion; in fact Antipater's son Iolaos was dead before 317, and Philip is last heard of in 313.
15. SM Burstein, '*IG* II (2) 561 and the Court of Alexander IV', *ZPE* 24 (1977) pp. 223–225; W Heckel, '*IG* II (2) 561 and the Status of Alexander IV', *ZPE* 40 (1980) pp. 249–250; W Heckel, 'Honours for Philip and Iolaos (*IG* II (2) 561), *ZPE* 44 (1981) pp. 75–77, all summarized in Heckel, *Marshals* pp. 279–285; Billows, *Antigonos*, has other opinions on this.
16. Diodoros 18.44.1 and 46.1–2.
17. Arrian, *Successors of Alexander* 1.41.
18. Plutarch, *Eumenes* 8.5.
19. Justin 14.1.7–8; Arrian, *Successors of Alexander* 1.40; Plutarch, *Eumenes* 8.4. Diodoros 20.37.4 implies that Eumenes made her an offer of marriage.
20. Gothenburg Palimpsest of Arrian, *Successors of Alexander* 72r–73v; Roisman, *Alexander's Veterans* pp. 147–148.
21. Arrian, *Successors of Alexander* 1.41; Antipater's troops were annoyed that he did not attack.
22. Arrian, *Successors of Alexander* 1.40.
23. These numbers are a problem: 8,500 is likely to be the total, infantry and cavalry together: Roisman, *Veterans* pp. 152–155, with earlier references.
24. Arrian, *Successors of Alexander* 1.42–43; Billows, *Antigonos* pp. 72–73.
25. Arrian, *Successors of Alexander* 1.44–45.
26. See Lund's comments, *Lysimachos* p. 54.
27. Habicht, *Athens from Alexander to Anthony* pp. 32–33.
28. Harding 122 (Tegea); 113 (Mytilene); 128 (Samos).
29. Diodoros 18.8.6.
30. Many did not do so, of course, choosing to settle in the conquered eastern lands.
31. Discussed by Elizabeth Baynham, 'Antipater and Athens', in *Macedonians in Athens* pp. 23–29.
32. Diodoros 18.41.1–3; Plutarch, *Eumenes* 10.1.
33. Arrian, *Successors of Alexander* 1.41.
34. Polyainos 4.6.7; Diodoros 18.44–45; Billows, *Antigonos* pp. 77–79; Sir WM Ramsay, 'Military Operations on the North Front of Mount Taurus IV: the Campaigns of 320 and 319 BC', *JHS*, 43 (1923) pp. 1–10.
35. Diodoros 18.50.1–3.
36. Antigonos was given the news of Antipater's death as he marched north away from the battlefield: Diodoros 18.47.2; Billows, *Antigonos* p. 30.
37. Appian, *Syrian Wars* 52; Diodoros 18.43.2; Pausanias 1.6.4.

Chapter 8

1. Diodoros 18.48.2; Plutarch, *Phokion* 30, naming Antigonos as Demades' correspondent; Arrian, *Successors of Alexander* 1.14.
2. Arrian, *Successors of Alexander* 1.15; Diodoros 18.48.3; Plutarch, *Demosthenes* 31.

3. Plutarch, *Phokion* 1; diplomatic agreements usually expired on the death of one of the parties, and Kassander will have known this, as will Antipater; the trial of Demades may be seen as a precaution taken in advance of such a crisis.

4. Plutarch, *Demosthenes* 31.

5. Antipater: Diodoros 18.48.3; Kassander: Plutarch, *Phokion* 30 and *Demosthenes* 31; Arrian, *Successors of Alexander* 1.14.

6. Diodoros 18.49.1.

7. Diodoros 18.48.4–5.

8. Heckel, *Who's Who* pp. 226–231.

9. Diodoros 18.49.4 and 57.2.

10. Diodoros 18.49.2–3.

11. Diodoros 18.51.1–52.5, and 72.2.

12. Diodoros 18.50.4 and 53.5; Plutarch, *Eumenes* 12.1–3; Nepos, *Eumenes* 5.6–7.

13. Diodoros 18.52.1–4.

14. Several identifications with other Nikanors have been suggested, including the adopted son of Aristotle, the son of Balakros and stepson of Phila, or his brother, and the uninstalled satrap of Kappadokia; it will be seen that identification has failed.

15. Diodoros 18.54.3 and 68.1.

16. Diodoros 18.56.1–8.

17. Diodoros 18.58.1–2.

18. W Heckel, *The Last Days and Testament of Alexander the Great: a Prosopographical Study*, *Historia Einszelschriften* 56 (Wiesbaden, 1988).

19. Heckel, *Who's Who* pp. 140–141.

20. His grave was desecrated in 317 by Olympias.

21. Plutarch, *Alexander* 74, *Demetrios* 37, and *Moralia* 180f; Plutarch at times believes and at others ignores these stories and the poisoning theory.

22. Plutarch, *Moralia* 183f.

23. Not well sourced; it is in *The Last Days*, but otherwise only in Valerius Maximus (1.7 ext 2), who may have got it from *The Last Days*; even if he got it elsewhere, two unreliable sources do not add up to one good one.

24. Plutarch, *Alexander* 74.4.

25. Diodoros 18.65.3–66.1.

26. Plutarch, *Eumenes* 32–34; Diodoros 18.66.1–67.6. The defending speakers in the assembly were interrupted as much as they had been by Polyperchon; the condemnations appear to be illegal under Athenian law, not for the first time.

27. Diodoros 18.68.1.

28. Diodoros 18.68.2–3.

29. Diodoros 18.69.1–2.

30. Diodoros 18.69.3–4.

31. Diodoros 18.69.4–71.6.

32. Diodoros 18.72.2–4.

33. Diodoros 18.72.5–9; Polyainos 4.6.8; Marmor Parium B 13 (= Austin 1).

34. Polyainos 4.11.13; Pausanias 1.25.6; Robert Garland, *The Piraeus from the Fifth of the First century* BC (Ithaca NY, 1987) p. 48, adds the long walls, and WS Ferguson, *Hellenistic Athens* (London, 1911) adds 'the open country' to Kassander's conquests, but neither of these can be justified from Pausanias' words.

35. Diodoros 18.74.1–3; Ferguson, *Hellenistic Athens* pp. 36–37; Habicht, *Athens* pp. 53–53.

36. Diodoros 18.75.1; it is possible that the Nikanor was Phila's stepson, the son of Balakros' first marriage; it would be like Kassander to employ a relative, it would also be like him to have no compunction about killing him if he felt it necessary for his own power.
37. Justin 14.5.2–4; Diodoros 19.11.1.
38. Diodoros 19.35.7.
39. Justin 14.5.5–7; Diodoros 19.35.1–2; Cartledge and Spawforth, *Sparta* pp. 26–27.
40. Diodoros 19.11.2.
41. Justin 14.5.8; Diodoros 19.35.1–2.
42. Diodoros 19.11.1.
43. Diodoros 19.11.2–3; Justin 14.5.8–10.
44. Diodoros 19.11.4–7; Justin 14.5.10.
45. It is Olympias' action here which implies that the accusation of the involvement of Antipater and Iolaos in Alexander's death had now been published; otherwise there was no reason for her to behave in this way.
46. Diodoros 19.11.8.
47. Diodoros 19.35.3.
48. Diodoros 19.35.4–36.1.
49. Pausanias 1.11.4; Diodoros 19.36.2–5.
50. Diodoros 19.36.6.
51. Diodoros 19.50.7–8.
52. Diodoros 19.49.1–50.5.
53. Diodoros 19.50.6.
54. Diodoros 19.51.1–5; Justin 14.6.6–12; Pausanias 9.7.2; for Olympias, see ED Carney, *Olympias, Mother of Alexander the Great* (New York, 2006).
55. Diodoros 19.50.8–51.1.
56. Diodoros 19.52.4; Justin 14.6.13 and 15.1–3.

Chapter 9

1. Diodoros 19.52.5; Diyllos, *FGrH* 73, F1.
2. Diodoros 19.35.5.
3. Stephanos of Byzantion, 'Thessalonike'.
4. A brief notice of her life is in Carney, *Women and Monarchy* pp. 155–158.
5. Justin 14.6.13; Diodoros 19.52.1–2.
6. Billows, *Antigonos* pp. 103–106.
7. Diodoros 18.43.1–2.
8. Appian, *Syrian Wars* 53.
9. Diodoros 19.55.2–5.
10. Marmor Parium 16; Diodoros 19.52.2–3; Getzel M Cohen, *The Hellenistic Settlements in Europe, the Islands, and Asia Minor* (Berkeley and Los Angeles, 1995) pp. 95–99.
11. Strabo 7, F 21.
12. Cohen, *Hellenistic Settlements* pp. 101–105.
13. Diodoros 19.53–54; Pausanias 9.7.1 and 4: Cohen, *Hellenistic Settlements* pp. 119–120.
14. Polybios 5.10 8.2; Cohen, *Hellenistic Settlements* p. 76.
15. Pliny, *Natural History* 4.37; Athenaios 3.38d–f; Cohen, *Hellenistic Settlements* p. 121.
16. Athenaios 3.98.
17. Diodoros 19.53.14.
18. Marmor Parium 14; Diodoros 19.53.2, 54.1.

19. Diodoros 19.54.2–3; *IG* VII, 2419 (= Harding 131) is a fragmentary list of donors.
20. 'Herakleitos Kreticos' 13–15 (= Austin 101) emphasized the city's modern layout (in the third century BC) and its horse-breeding prowess, not its size or power.
21. Diodoros 19.54.3.
22. Diodoros 19.54.3–4.
23. Diodoros 18.39.6, 19.27.4.
24. Appian, *Syrian Wars* 53; Diodoros 19.55.6–7.
25. Diodoros 19.56.5–6.
26. Diodoros 19.56.1.
27. Diodoros 19.56.4.
28. Billows, *Antigonos* p. 109, calls it an 'extraordinary set of demands'.
29. Diodoros 19.57.1.
30. Diodoros 19.57.4.
31. Billows suggests it was 'an initial bargaining position', a representative reaction mirrored by other commentators; but the proposal at least needs to be considered seriously. The fact that Antigonos dismissed it does not mean it was unrealistic.
32. Diodoros 19.57.4.
33. Diodoros 19.57.4–5.
34. Diodoros 19.58.1–60.2.
35. Diodoros 19.60.1 and 61.1
36. Diodoros 19.61.1–4.
37. Diodoros 19.63.1–2.
38. Diodoros 19.64.4.
39. Diodoros 19.64.5–7.
40. Diodoros 19.63.3–64.1.
41. Diodoros 19.63.1–64.4 and 66.1.
42. Diodoros 19.67.1; Pascalis Paschides, *Between City and King, Prosopographical Studies on the Intermediaries between the Cities of the Greek Mainland and the Aegean and the Royal Courts in the Hellenistic Period (322–190 BC)*, Meletemata 59 (Athens, 2008), 'B10 Alexion', pp. 229–230, makes a good case for the connection between defection and assassination.
43. Diodoros 19.67.2.
44. Diodoros 19.67.3–5.
45. Diodoros 19.68.1.
46. Diodoros 19.67.5.
47. Diodoros 19.67.6–7.
48. Ptolemy at Ekregma: Diodoros 19.64.8.
49. Diodoros 19.69.3; H Hauben, 'The Ships of the Pydnaians, Remarks on Kassandros' Naval Situation in 314/313 BC', *Ancient Society* 9 (1978) pp. 47–54.
50. Diodoros 19.68.3–4.
51. Diodoros 19.74.3.
52. Diodoros 19.74.4–6.
53. Diodoros 19.78.1; Glaukias' alliance with Aiakides is suggested by the fact that he fostered Aiakides' son Pyrrhos.
54. Diodoros 19.75.6.
55. Diodoros 19.68.5–7.
56. Diodoros 19.75.1–5; see Billows, *Antigonos* pp. 120–121 and his map 1.

57. Diodoros 19.75.6–8.
58. Diodoros 19.74.1–2.
59. Diodoros 19.75.7–8.
60. Diodoros 19.87.1.
61. Diodoros 19.73.1–10.
62. Diodoros 19.77.5–6.
63. Diodoros 19.77.6.
64. *OGIS* 5, lines 5–9 (= Austin 38).
65. Diodoros 19.88.1.
66. Diodoros 19.77.6.
67. Diodoros 17.79.3–4.
68. Diodoros 19.87.1.
69. Diodoros 19.78.5.
70. Diodoros 19.88.2–89.3.
71. Diodoros 19.80.1–85.1; AM Devine, 'Diodoros' Account of the Battle of Gaza', *Acta Classica*, 27 (1984) pp. 31–40.
72. Diodoros 19.10 5.1; *OGIS* 5.

Chapter 10
1. Justin 15.2.1–2; the reason for their migration he gives is 'an infestation of mice and frogs', which might be their description of their enemies.
2. Diodoros 20.19.1.
3. Lysimachos and a contingent of 2,000 men from this people at Ipsos in 301: they deserted to Antigonos in a spectacular display of bad timing.
4. Diodoros 19.10 5.1.
5. See Hammond, 'Royal Pages'.
6. Diodoros 19.5.4.
7. Diodoros 19.10 5.2, detaching the comment on Macedonian expectations from the context of Diodoros account of his murder.
8. Ibid; King Alexander was already betrothed to Deidameia, an Epeirote princess who was another of the royal court captured at Pydna.
9. Diodoros 20.19.3–4.
10. Grace McCurdy, 'The Political Ambitions and the Name of Kratesipolis', *American Journal of Philology*, 50 (1929) pp. 273–278, included Patrai, but this is only where she lived after leaving Corinth and Sikyon; PV Wheatley, 'The Date of Polyperchon's Invasion of Macedonia and the Murder of Heracles', *Antichthon*, 32 (1998) pp. 12–23, assumes that Polyperchon spent the years 313–310 in Corinth, but Diodoros does not actually say so, only 'in the Peloponnese' (20.20.1).
11. Diodoros 20.19.2.
12. Diodoros 20.19.2.
13. Ibid; for Phoinix see Billows, *Antigonos* p. 424.
14. Diodoros 20.27.1–2.
15. Diodoros 20.27.3.
16. The date of this episode is unclear; Wheatley, 'Date of Polyperchon's Invasion', prefers 308; it is linked with the death of Alexander IV, which in turn is disputed – that is, unknown.

17. PA Brunt, 'Alexander, Barsine, and Heracles,' *Rivista di Filologia e Istruzione Classica*, 103 (1975) pp. 22–34, refuting the argument of WW Tarn, 'Heracles son of Barsine', *JHS*, 41 (1921) pp. 18–28; for Barsine, see Carney, *Women and Monarchy* pp. 101–105 and 140–150.

18. Diodoros 20.20.1.

19. Diodoros 20.20.3.

20. Diodoros 20.28.1–2.

21. Diodoros 20.28.2–3.

22. Diodoros 20.28.3–4.

23. Diodoros 19.10 5.2–4; Justin 15.2.5; Pausanias 9.7.2.

24. Diodoros 20.37.3–6; Carney, *Women and Monarchy* p. 127.

25. Polyainos 8.58; Diodoros 20.37.1; Macurdy, 'Political Ambition'.

26. Diodoros 20.37.2.

27. Ibid.

28. Diodoros 20.45.1–2; Plutarch, *Demetrios* 8.

29. Diodoros 20.45.3–4; Plutarch, *Demetrios* 9.

30. Diodoros 20.45.5–7; Plutarch, *Demetrios* 9–10.

31. Diodoros 20.46.1–3; Plutarch, *Demetrios* 10.

32. Diodoros 20.46.3; Plutarch, *Demetrios* 9–10; whose garrison held Megara is never stated; Billows, *Antigonos* p. 150, assumed it was Kassander's; Habicht, *Athens* pp. 65–66, implies it was Ptolemy's. It seems most likely to have been Kassander's.

33. Plutarch, *Pyrrhos* 6; Justin 17.3.18.

34. Diodoros 20.37.4; one of the tombs at Verghina is identified as Alexander's; cf. Errington, *History of Macedonia* p. 281, note 5: not all agree.

35. 'King of the Macedonians, Kassander son of Antipater' on a statue base from Dion, quoted in *HM* 3.174.

36. Thirty of these Athenian ships were in Demetrios' fleet at Salamis: Diodoros 20.50.3.

37. Diodoros 20.46.4–5.

38. Pausanias 1.26.3 and 10.34.3.

39. Diodoros 20.100.5–6; Plutarch, *Demetrios* 23.2; Polyainos 4.11.1; Pausanias 1.35.2.

40. Diodoros 20.100.5–6; Plutarch, *Demetrios* 23.1.

41. Plutarch, *Demetrios* 23.2.

42. Plutarch, *Demetrios* 23.4.

43. Diodoros 20.102.1–103.7; Plutarch, *Demetrios* 9 and 25; Schmitt, *Staatsvertrage* 445 (alliance with Sikyon) and 446 (fragmentary record of the constitution of the league).

44. Diodoros 20.106.1–2.

45. Diodoros 20.101.2–5.

46. Diodoros 20.107.1–5.

47. Diodoros 20.110.2–3.

48. Diodoros 20.107.2 and 110.2–3.

49. Diodoros 20.110.4–6.

50. Map 6 in Billows, *Antigonos* p. 464, for their approximate positions.

51. Diodoros 20.112.1.

52. Diodoros 20.113.4; Plutarch, *Demetrios* 28–29.

53. Diodoros 20.111.4.

54. Diodoros 20.105.1.

55. Plutarch, *Demetrios* 30.

Chapter 11

1. Plutarch, *Demetrios* 31.
2. The evidence for Karia is wholly from inscriptions, but Pleistarchos' name appears often enough to imply a principality; he was succeeded in the area by Eupolemos, a general who seems to have been Pleistarchos' subordinate, and possibly the earlier commander in the area for Kassander. Karia was always liable to be detached from the overall authority in the rest of Asia Minor; for Pleistarchos see RA Billows, *Kings and Colonists, Aspects of Macedonian Imperialism* (Leiden, 1995) pp. 92–94, with references there.
3. Plutarch, *Demetrios* 32.
4. Athenaios 7.320d.
5. Plutarch, *Pyrrhos* 6.
6. Plutarch, *Pyrrhos* 5.
7. Diodoros 21.2.1.
8. Diodoros 21.2.2–3.
9. Seleukos, Antipater, Antigonos, and Ptolemy all reached 80 or so; those who died at 60 or so included Demetrios, Pyrrhos, Antiochos I and Ptolemy II, as well as Kassander; it is noticeable that the second generation did not live as long as the first.
10. Porphyry, *FGrH* 260 F 3.64; also Phlegon, *FGrH* 257 a.
11. *HM* 2.208; attempts to diagnose the cause of death at this distance seem fruitless.
12. For the following section see Elizabeth Carney, 'The Curious Death of the Antipatrid Dynasty', *AM* VI (Thessaloniki, 1999) pp. 209–216.
13. Porphyry, *FGrH* 260 F 3; Justin 15.4.24; Pausanias 9.7.3.
14. Pausanias 10.8.6 and 34.2–3.
15. Plutarch, *Demetrios* 30.
16. *IG* II (2) 657; see the discussion in Paschidis, *Between City and King* pp. 116–122.
17. *IG* II (2) 641; Paschidis, *Between City and King* pp. 113–115.
18. Habicht, *Athens* pp. 82–83.
19. Ibid, 84–85; Pausanias 1.25.7 and 29.10; Garland, *Piraeus* p. 49.
20. Plutarch, *Demetrios* 33.
21. *HM* 3.210–211; Errington, *History of Macedonia* p. 148, slides over the issue, but had argued against a regency earlier in 'The Nature of the Macedonian State under the Monarchy', *Chiron*, 8 (1978) at note 124.
22. Plutarch, *Demetrios* 36.1, and *Pyrrhos* 6.3; Pausanias 9.7.3; Diodoros 21.7.
23. Plutarch, *Pyrrhos* 6.
24. Plutarch, *Demetrios* 33–34; Polyainos 3.7.1 and 4.7.5.
25. Plutarch, *Pyrrhos* 6.
26. Plutarch, *Demetrios* 35, 38.
27. Plutarch, *Pyrrhos* 6; Justin 10.1.8.
28. Plutarch, *Demetrios* 36–37.
29. Plutarch, *Demetrios* 37.
30. Justin 16.2.4.

Chapter 12

1. *I. Adramytteion* 34 (= *IG* XII, 2 645 = *OGIS* 4); Paschidis, *Between City and King* pp. 406–413; Curtius 4.1.14; Arrian, *Anabasis* 2.14.4.
2. Thersippos is referred to as a *philos* of both Philip III and Alexander IV; Philip was killed in 317.

3. C Habicht, 'Zwei Anzehorige die lynchestischen Konigshauses', *AM* II, pp. 511–616; Elisabetta Poddighe, 'Il decreto dell'isola di Nesos in onor di Tersippo: Ancora una nota sulla politica geriada Polipercote nel 319', *AHB* 15 (2001) pp. 95–101.
4. Justin 14.5.10; Diodoros 19.11.3–9.
5. *IG* IV, 1(2), 96.67; Tataki, *Macedonians Abroad* p. 202.
6. Stephanos of Byzantion, 'Pleistarcheia'.
7. L Robert, *Le Sanctuaire de Sinuri pres de Mylasa* (Paris, 1945) pp. 55–61; Billows, *Kings and Colonists* pp. 93–94.
8. R Merkelbach, 'Ein Zeugnis aus Tralleis uber Pleistarchos', *ZPE*, 16 (1975), at 165.
9. E Meyer, *Die Grenzen des Hellenistischen Staaten in Kleinasien* (Leipzig, 1925) p. 131.
10. Plutarch, *Demetrios* 31.
11. Diodoros 19.74.3–6.
12. Diodoros 21.7.
13. Justin 16.1.19.
14. This family horror story is related in all the books: *HM* 3.246–251; Errington, *History of Macedonia* pp. 156–159, are examples. For the chronology of the confused years after 281, see *HM* 3, appendix 2, pp. 580–583, though the interpretation is very rigid.
15. Another family horror story; see Lund, *Lysimachos*, Ch. 7, for the final family crisis.
16. Justin 17.2.13–14.
17. Justin 17.2.9.
18. Pausanias 10.19.4; the best modern treatment of these invasions is by G Nachtergael, *Les Galates en Grece et les Soteria de Delphes* (Brussels, 1977).
19. Justin 24.14.6–11; Diodoros 22.3.
20. For the succession of these brief kings see *HM* 3, appendix 2; the sources are there detailed and discussed.
21. Pausanias 10.19.6–7.
22. Plutarch, *Moralia* 851e; see the discussion in Paschidis, *Between City and King* pp. 153–159, with an extensive bibliography of discussions of the issue; I do not agree with his conclusion as to the date of Antipater's visit.
23. Justin 24.5.12–14.
24. Pausanias 10.23.13–14; Diodoros 22.9.
25. Some Thessalians and Ainianians had joined the invaders: Justin 34.7.2.
26. His name and its royal connections have provoked suggestions that he was a distant member of the Argead family–possible, but unlikely.
27. Justin 24.5.14; these names are only mentioned, without details, here and there.
28. WW Tarn, *Antigonos Gonatas* (Cambridge, 1913, reprinted 1969) Ch 7.
29. Burstein 100 = *OGIS* 55 = Austin 270.
30. Billows, *Kings and Colonists*.
31. P. *Cairo Zen* 1.59019, line 6; Porphyry, *FGrH* 260 F 3.10.

Chapter 13
1. See Chapter 7; Strabo 12.565; Stephanos of Byzantion, s.v. Nikaia.
2. Pausanias 1.10.4; Appian, *Syrian Wars* 64.
3. Diodoros 20.109.6; Memnon *FGrH* 434, F 4.9.
4. Plutarch, *Demetrios* 31.
5. For his children, not all of whom can be identified, see D Ogden, *Polygamy, Prostitutes and Death* (London, 1999).
6. Athenaios 13.576e; the children were Lagos, Leontiskos, and Eirene.

7. Arrian, *Anabasis* 7.4.6.
8. Ian Worthington, *Ptolemy I* (Oxford, 2017) pp. 113–114.
9. Pausanias 1.7.1.
10. Worthington, *Ptolemy* p. 113.
11. Pausanias 1.6.8; Appian, *Syrian Wars* 62.
12. Their first child was born in 315.
13. Pausanias 1.7.1; Worthington, *Ptolemy* p. 115.
14. Justin 17.2.9–10.
15. Plutarch, *Demetrios* 32.3 and 46.
16. Marmor Parium B 19 (= Austin 1).
17. Plutarch, *Demetrios* 37.
18. Polyainos 8.57; Justin 17.2.6–11 and 24.7.5–3.9; Carney, *Women and Monarchy* pp. 173–178.
19. Pausanias 1.7.1.
20. *OGIS* 55 (= Burstein 100).
21. The most notorious joke was by the poet Sotades; at court, Demetrios of Phaleron also intervened in the question of the succession; both men were murdered at Ptolemy II's orders.
22. Plutarch, *Pyrrhos* 4 (Antigone); Justin 23.2.6–8 (Theoxene).
23. Dee L Clayman, *Berenice II and the Golden Age of Ptolemaic Egypt* (Oxford, 2014) pp. 175–177; Polybios 16.32–33.
24. Memnon, *FGrH* 434 F 8.2.
25. Porphyry, *FGrH* 260, F 2.2.
26. Memnon, *FGrH* 434, F 11.8.
27. Plutarch, *Demetrios* 4.4.
28. Diodoros 19.59.4–5.
29. Plutarch, *Alexander* 40.4–5; *Fouilles de Delphes* 3.4.2 no. 137 for the dedication; Andrew Stewart, *Faces of Power, Alexander's Image and Hellenistic Politics* (Berkeley CA, 1993) pp. 46–47 and 390–391.
30. Athenaios 6.254a, 13.577c; Ogden, *Polygamy* pp. 232–233; Patrick Wheatley, 'Lamia and the Besieger: an Athenian hetaera and a Macedonian king', in *Macedonians in Athens* pp. 30–36.
31. Plutarch, *Demetrios* 31–32; Tarn, *Antigonos Gonatas* p. 19.
32. Plutarch, *Demetrios* 14.2–3, and *Comparison of Demetrius and Anthony* 1.3.
33. This point is well made by Carney, *Women and Monarchy*, in her short biography of Phila at pp. 165–169.
34. Plutarch, *Demetrios* 37.3.
35. Diodoros 20.93.4; Plutarch, *Demetrios* 23.1.
36. Amelie Kuhrt and Susan Sherwin-White, *From Samarkhand to Sardis* (Berkeley CA, 20/1993).
37. Clayman, *Berenice II*.
38. Plutarch, *Demetrios* 45.1.

Chapter 14
1. W Heckel, 'A Grandson of Antipater at Delos', *ZPE*, 70 (1987) pp. 161–162.
2. G Reger, 'The Family of Balakros son of Nikanor, the Macedonian, on Delos', *ZPE*, 89 (1991) pp. 151–154.

3. Plutarch, *Moralia* 486; Diodoros 19.64.5–6 and 8.
4. *P. Hibeh* 85; *Prosopographia Ptolemaica* VI 14897.
5. There is another Perilaos, who was an intermediary at Babylon in 323 and a commander for Antigonos captured by Ptolemy's fleet in 309; this cannot be the son of Antipater; see Billows, *Antigonos*, 416, though he could be the father of Andronikos.
6. B Bosworth, 'A New Macedonian Prince', *CQ*, 44 (1994) pp. 57–65.
7. Noted in Ferguson, *Hellenistic Athens* p. 169, note 3.
8. Plutarch, *Moralia* 253a.
9. Frontinus 3.6.7; Polyainos 2.29.1.
10. This is also the general conclusion of historians of Macedon: Errington, *History of Macedonia* p. 167, and *HM* 3.272, for example.
11. Ferguson, *Hellenistic Athens* p. 169.
12. Pausanias 8.27.11 and 30.7; Plutarch, *Agis* 3.7.
13. Trogus, *Prologue* 26. The date of Alexander's move is, like most dates in this century, disputed: 252–249 is the range. The death of Krateros is clearly required first, followed by Alexander laying his plans for independence – but we do not know the date of Krateros' death.
14. Plutarch, *Aratos* 6.2; *HM* 3.298.
15. Plutarch, *Philopoimen* 1; Polybios 10.22.2.
16. Largely based on evidence from Athenian inscriptions: *IG* II (2) 1225, honouring Herakleitas, commander in Peiraios; *ISE* 23 + *SEG* 29 (1988) p. 131; *ISE* 45; plus Plutarch, *Aratos* 25 and Agatharchides, *FGrH* 86 F 9; dating is, again, still under discussion.
17. Plutarch, *Aratos* 4–9; Polybios 2.43.3.
18. Assuming that 'the king' in Plutarch's account (*Aratos* 11.2) was Ptolemy.
19. Trogus, *Prologue* 27; *HM* 3.248–249; dating again is uncertain.
20. *ISE* 29 and 43; see discussion by Paschidis, *Between City and King* pp. 215–219.
21. *Suda*, s.v. Euphorion – the word used is *basileuontos*.
22. *HM* 3.301, note 3.
23. Plutarch, *Aratos* 17.2 – probably a rumour initiated by the unscrupulous Aratos.
24. Plutarch, *Aratos* 17.2–5; Polyainos 4.6.1; Carney, *Women and Monarchy* pp. 188–189.

Bibliography

Ashton, NG, 'Craterus from 324 to 321 BC, *AM*, V (Thessaloniki 1991) pp. 125–131.

Ashton, NG, 'The Naumachia near Amorgos in 322 BC', *Annual of the British School at Athens*, 72 (1977) pp. 1–11.

Badian, E, 'Agis III', *Hermes*, 95 (1967) pp. 170–192.

Badian, E, 'Agis III: Revisions and Reflections', in *Ventures into Greek History*, ed. I. Worthington (Oxford 1994) pp. 258–292.

Badian, E, 'Harpalos', *JHS*, 81 (1961) pp. 16–43.

Badian, E, 'History from Square Brackets', *ZPE*, 79 (1989) pp. 59–70.

Badian, E, 'The First Flight of Harpalos', *Historia*, 9 (1960) pp. 245–246.

Baynham, E, 'Antipater and Athens', in *Macedonians in Athens* pp. 23–29.

Baynham, EJ, 'Why didn't Alexander marry a nice Macedonian girl before leaving home? Observations on Factional Politics at Alexander's Court in 336–334 BC', in TW Hillard et al., *Ancient History at a Modern University*, Vol. I (Macquarie University Australia, 1988) pp. 148–155.

Billows, RA, *Antigonos the One-Eyed and the Creation of the Hellenistic State* (California, 1990).

Billows, RA, *Kings and Colonists, Aspects of Macedonian Imperialism* (Leiden, 1995).

Blackwell, Christopher D, *In the Absence of Alexander, Harpalus and the Failure of Macedonian Authority* (New York, 1999).

Borza, EN, 'The end of Agis' Revolt', *CP*, 66 (1971) pp. 230–235.

Bosworth, AB, *The Legacy of Alexander* (Oxford, 2002).

Bosworth, AB, 'The Early Relations between Aitolia and Macedon', *American Journal of Ancient History*, 1 (1976) pp. 164–181.

Bosworth, AB, 'Why did Athens lose the Lamian War?', in *Macedonians in Athens* pp. 14–22.

Bosworth, B, 'A New Macedonian Prince', *CQ*, 44 (1994) pp. 57–65.

Brunt, PA, 'Alexander, Barsine, and Heracles,' *Rivista di Filologia e Istruzione Classica*, 103 (1975) pp. 22–34.

Burstein, SM, '*IG* II (2) 561 and the Court of Alexander IV', *ZPE*, 24 (1977) pp. 223–225.

Carney, ED, *Olympias, Mother of Alexander the Great* (New York, 2006).

Carney, ED, *Women and Monarchy in Macedonia* (Norman OK, 2000).

Carney, ED, 'The Curious Death of the Antipatrid Dynasty', *AM*, VI (Thessaloniki, 1999) pp. 209–216.

Carney, ED, 'The First Flight of Harpalos Again', *CJ*, 77 (1987) pp. 9–11.

Cawkwell, GL, *Philip II of Macedon* (London, 1978).

Cawkwell, GL, 'A Note of Ps. Demosthenes 17.20', *Phoenix*, 15 (1961) pp. 74–78.

Cawkwell, GL, 'The Crowning of Demosthenes', *CQ*, NS 19 (1969) pp. 163–180.

Clayman, Dee L, *Berenice II and the Golden Age of Ptolemaic Egypt* (Oxford, 2014).

Cohen, Getzel, M, *The Hellenistic Settlements in Europe, the Islands, and Asia Minor* (Berkeley and Los Angeles, 1995).

Croix, GEM de Ste, *The Origins of the Peloponnesian War* (London, 1972).

Devine, AM, 'Diodoros' Account of the Battle of Gaza', *Acta Classica*, 27 (1984) pp. 31–40.

Ellis, JR, *Philip II and Macedonian Imperialism* (London, 1976).

Ellis, JR, 'Amyntas Perdikka, Philip II, and Alexander the Great', *JHS*, 91 (1971) pp. 15–24.

Engels, Donald W, *Alexander the Great and the Logistics of the Macedonian Army* (California, 1978).

Errington, RM, *A History of Macedonia* (Berkeley and Los Angeles, California, 1993).

Fears, Rufus J, 'Pausanias, the Assassin of Philip II', *Athenaeum*, 53 (1975) pp. 111–135.

Ferguson, WS, *Hellenistic Athens* (London, 1911).

Garland, R, *The Piraeus from the Fifth of the First Century BC* (Ithaca NY, 1987).

Garnsey, P, *Famine and Food Supply in the Graeco-Roman World, Responses to Risk and Crisis* (Cambridge, 1988).

Grainger, JD, *Great Power Diplomacy in the Hellenistic World* (London, 2016).

Grainger, JD, *Hellenistic and Roman Sea Wars, 336–31 BC*, (Barnsley, 2011).

Grainger, JD, *The League of the Aitolians* (Leiden, 1999).

Griffith, GT, 'Alexander and Antipater in 323 BC', *Proceedings of the African Classical Association*, 8 (1965) pp. 12–17.

Habicht, C, 'Zwei Angehorige der Lynkestische Konigshauses', *AM*, II (Thessaloniki, 1977) pp. 511–516.

Habicht, C, *Athens from Alexander to Anthony* (Cambridge, MA, 1997) p. 27.

Hammond, NGL, *Alexander the Great* (London, 1981).

Hammond, NGL, *Philip of Macedon* (London, 1994).

Hammond, NGL, and Griffith, GT, *A History of Macedonia*, Vol. II (Oxford, 1979).

Hammond, NGL, and Walbank, FM, *History of Macedonia*, Vol. III (Oxford, 1988).

Hammond, NGL, 'Royal Pages, Personal Pages, and Boys Trained in the Macedonian Manner during the Period of the Temenid Monarchy', *Historia*, 39 (1990) pp. 261–290.

Hansen, Signe Isagen and Mogens Herman, *Aspects of Athenian Society in the Fourth Century BC* (Odense, 1975).

Hauben, H, 'An Athenian Naval Victory in 321 BC', *ZPE*, 13 (1974) pp. 61–64.

Hauben, H, 'The Ships of the Pydnaians, Remarks on Kassandros' Naval Situation in 314/313 BC', *Ancient Society*, 9 (1978) pp. 47–54.

Heckel, W, '*IG* II (2) 561 and the Status of Alexander IV', *ZPE*, 40 (1980) pp. 249–250.

Heckel, W, 'A Grandson of Antipatros at Delos', *ZPE*, 70 (1987) pp. 161–162.

Heckel, W, *The Last Days and Testament of Alexander the Great, a Prosopographical Study, Historia Einszelschriften*, 56 (Stuttgart, 1988).

Heckel, W, *Who's Who in the Age of Alexander the Great, a Prosopographical Study* (London, 2006).

Heckel, W, 'Honours for Philip and Iolaos *IG* II (2) 561), *ZPE*, 44 (1981) pp. 75–77, all.

Heckel, W, 'Q. Curtius Rufus and the date of Kleandros' Mission to the Peloponnese', *Hermes*, 119 (1991) pp. 124–125.

Heckel, W, 'The Flight of Harpalos and Tauriskos', *CP*, 72 (1977) pp. 133–135.

Higgins, WE, 'Aspects of Alexander's Imperial Administration: some Modern Methods and Views', *Athenaeum*, 58 (1980) pp. 129–152.

Kingsley, Bonnie, 'Harpalos in the Megarid (333–331 BC) and the Grain Shipments from Cyrene', *ZPE*, 66 (1986) pp. 165–177.

Kuhrt, Amelie, and Sherwin-White, Susan, *From Samarkhand to Sardis* (Berkeley, CA, 1993).

Lund, Helen S, *Lysimachos, a Study in Hellenistic Kingship* (London, 1992).

McCurdy, Grace, 'The Political Ambitions and the Name of Kratesipolis', *American Journal of Philology*, 50 (1929) pp. 273–278.

McQueen, EL, 'Some Notes on the Anti-Macedonian Movement in the Peloponnese in 331 BC', *Historia*, 27 (1973) pp. 40–64.

Merkelbach, R, 'Ein Zeugnis aus Tralleis uber Pleistarchos', *ZPE*, 16 (1975).

Meyer, E, *Die Grenzen des Hellenistischen Staaten in Kleinasien* (Leipzig, 1925).

Moreno, A, *Feeding the Democracy, the Athenian Grain Supply in the Fifth and Fourth Centuries BC* (Oxford, 2007).

Nachtergael, G, *Les Galates en Grece et les Soteria de Delphes* (Brussels, 1977).

Ogden, D, *Polygamy, Prostitutes and Death* (London, 1999).

Palagia, Olga, and Tracy, Stephen V, *The Macedonians in Athens* (Oxford, 2004).

Parrolla, Paul, *A Prosopography of Lacedaemonians*, 2nd ed. by Alfred S Bradford (Chicago, 1985).

Paschides, Pascalis, *Between City and King, Prosopographical Studies on the Intermediaries between the Cities of the Greek Mainland and the Aegean and the Royal Courts in the Hellenistic Period (322–190 BC)*, Meletemata, 59 (Athens, 2008).

Perlman, S, (ed.), *Philip and Athens* (Cambridge, 1973).

Poddighe, Elisabetta, 'Il decreto dell'isola di Nesos in onor di Tersippo: Ancora una nota sulla politica geriada Polipercote nel 319', *AHB*, 15 (2001) pp. 95–101.

Potter, DS, '*IG* II (2) 399: Evidence for Athenian Involvement in the War of Agis III', *Annual of the British School at Athens*, 79 (1984) pp. 229–235.

Ramsay, Sir WM, 'Military Operations on the North Front of Mount Taurus IV: the Campaigns of 320 and 319 BC', *JHS*, 43 (1923) pp. 1–10.

Reger, G, 'The Family of Balakros son of Nikanor, the Macedonian, on Delos', *ZPE*, 89 (1991) pp. 147–154.

Robert, L, *Le Sanctuaire de Sinuri pres de Mylasa* (Paris, 1945).

Roisman, J, *Alexander's Veterans and the Early Wars of the Successors* (Austin, TX, 2012).

Schmitt, HH, *Die Staatsvertrage des Altertums III, Die Vertrage der greichisdhe-romischen Welt von 338 bis 200 V. Chr.* (Munich, 1969).

Seibert, J, *Historische Beitrage zu den dynastischen verbundingen in der Hellenistische Zeit, Historia Einszelschriften*, 10 (Wiesbaden, 1987).

Spawforth, Paul Cartledge and Antony, *Hellenistic and Roman Sparta, a Tale of Two Cities* (London, 1987).

Stewart, Andrew, *Faces of Power, Alexander's Image and Hellenistic Politics* (Berkeley, CA, 1993).

Tarn, WW, *Antigonos Gonatas* (Cambridge, 1913).

Tarn, WW, 'Heracles son of Barsine', *JHS*, 41 (1921) pp. 18–28.

Tataki, Argyro B, *Macedonians Abroad, a Contribution to the Prosopography of Ancient Macedonia, Meletemata*, 26 (Athens, 1998).

Tritle, L, 'Leocrates: Athenian Businessman and Macedonian Agent', *AM*, V1 (Thessaloniki, 1999) pp. 1227–1233.

Walsh, John, 'Antipater and Early Hellenistic Literature', *AHB*, 24 (2012) pp. 149–162.

Wheatley, PV, 'Lamia and the Besieger: an Athenian hetaera and a Macedonian king', in *Macedonians in Athens* pp. 30–36.

Wheatley, PV, 'The Date of Polyperchon's Invasion of Macedonia and the Murder of Heracles', Antichthon, 32 (1998) pp. 12–23.

Whitehorn, J, *Cleopatras* (London, 1994).

Will, E, *Histoire Politique du Monde Hellentistique*, Vol. I (Nancy, 1982).

Worthington, I, *Alexander, Man and God*, 2nd ed. (London, 2004).

Worthington, I, *Ptolemy I* (Oxford, 2017).

Worthington, I, 'The First Flight of Harpalos Reconsidered', *Greece and Rome*, 31 (1984) pp. 161–169.

Index